T0324796

Parsing Schemata for Practical Text Analysis

Mathematics, Computing, Language, and Life: Frontiers in Mathematical Linguistics and Language Theory

Series Editor: Carlos Martin-Vide
Rovira I Virgili University, Tarragona, Spain

Vol. 1   Parsing Schemata for Practical Text Analysis
by Carlos Gómez-Rodríguez

Mathematics, Computing, Language, and Life:
Frontiers in Mathematical Linguistics and Language Theory

Vol. 1

Parsing Schemata for Practical Text Analysis

Carlos Gómez-Rodríguez

University of A Coruña, Spain

Imperial College Press

Published by

Imperial College Press
57 Shelton Street
Covent Garden
London WC2H 9HE

Distributed by

World Scientific Publishing Co. Pte. Ltd.
5 Toh Tuck Link, Singapore 596224
USA office: 27 Warren Street, Suite 401-402, Hackensack, NJ 07601
UK office: 57 Shelton Street, Covent Garden, London WC2H 9HE

British Library Cataloguing-in-Publication Data
A catalogue record for this book is available from the British Library.

Mathematics, Computing, Language, and Life: Frontiers in Mathematical Linguistics and Language Theory — Vol. 1
PARSING SCHEMATA FOR PRACTICAL TEXT ANALYSIS

ISBN-13 978-1-84816-560-1
ISBN-10 1-84816-560-9

Printed in Singapore.

Preface

This book presents several contributions oriented towards the common goal of bridging the gap between Sikkel's theory of *parsing schemata* and the practical aspects of natural language parser development.

On the practical side, a compiler is presented that can be used to automatically generate an efficient implementation of a parser from its formal description in the form of a parsing schema. This system is then used to obtain implementations of several well-known parsers for context-free grammars and tree-adjoining grammars, test them with practical natural language grammars and then conduct an analysis to determine their empirical performance.

On the theoretical side, two extensions of parsing schemata are introduced, enabling the formalism to describe two kinds of parsers that are useful in practical natural language processing applications, but were not previously supported by this theory.

The first extension is for *error-repair parsers*, which are algorithms able to robustly parse ungrammatical sentences. Apart from the extension itself, a transformation is presented that can be used to automatically obtain error-repair parsers from standard parsers.

The second extension defines a variant of parsing schemata for *dependency parsers*, which are algorithms that represent the structure of sentences as a set of links between their words. This formalism is used to compare and relate several well-known projective and non-projective dependency parsers, as well as to solve the problem of efficiently parsing *mildly non-projective dependency structures* by defining novel algorithms for several sets of these structures.

Put together, the results in this book provide the parser developer with a common formal framework that can be used to design, analyse and

v

compare different kinds of parsing algorithms, including error-repair and dependency-based parsers; as well as practical tools to automatically obtain efficient implementations of these parsers directly from their formal representation.

This book is based on my Ph.D. thesis, completed in 2009 at the University of Corunna. However, extensive changes, additions and improvements have been made to make it useful to a wider range of readers. Many of the contributions presented here were originally published as journal articles or papers in conference proceedings, as can be seen in the references. Thus, first and foremost, I would like to acknowledge and thank my co-authors in these publications (Miguel A. Alonso, John Carroll, Jesús Vilares, Manuel Vilares and David Weir) for their valuable contributions and collaboration. I am also grateful to Víctor J. Díaz, Joakim Nivre, Giorgio Satta and Leo Wanner for the helpful comments and suggestions that they provided as reviewers of the thesis; as well as to the anonymous referees that reviewed the earlier draft of this book and the publications from which it draws. I am also indebted to Klaas Sikkel, not only for his helpful comments on the draft, but also for developing the theory of parsing schemata which is the starting point and foundation of this book. The research reported in the book has been supported in part by grants from the Spanish *Ministerio de Educación y Ciencia* and *FEDER*[1] and *Xunta de Galicia*.[2]

The book can be read by researchers, graduate students and post-graduates interested in computational linguistics and natural language engineering. The reader is assumed to have an elementary background in mathematics and computing, as provided by undergraduate computer science programs. Previous knowledge of parsing or computational linguistics is helpful but by no means required, since all the concepts needed are presented either in the introductory chapter or in the parts of the book where they are relevant. Thus, the book may be used as teaching material for a course on natural language parsing, by starting with the first part and then choosing among the other parts depending on the desired goals, since they can be read independently of each other.

Carlos Gómez-Rodríguez

[1] Projects TIN2004-07246-C03-01, HUM2007-66607-C04-03 and Progr. de Becas FPU.
[2] Grants PGIDIT05PXIC10501PN, PGIDIT07SIN005206PR, Estadías do programa de RRHH da Dirección Xeral de I+D+i, Redes Galegas de Procesamento da Linguaxe e Recuperación de Información e de Lingüística de Corpus.

Contents

Compiling and Executing Parsing Schemata 35

Parsing Schemata for Error-Repair Parsers   101

Parsing Schemata for Dependency Parsers   161

List of Figures

PART 1
Introduction and Preliminaries

Chapter 1

Introduction

This book provides several theoretical and practical tools that extend the applicability of Sikkel's theory of parsing schemata (Sikkel, 1997) in several different directions.

First, a compilation technique is defined that can be used to obtain efficient implementations of parsers automatically from their corresponding schemata. This makes it possible to use parsing schemata to prototype and test parsing algorithms, without the need of manually converting the formal representation to an efficient implementation in a programming language.

Second, the range of parsing algorithms that can be defined by means of schemata is extended with the definition of new variants of the formalism that can deal with error-repair parsers and dependency-based parsers.

Apart from these tools themselves, the book also introduces several research results that have been obtained by using them. The compilation technique is used to obtain implementations of different parsers for context-free grammars and tree-adjoining grammars, and perform an empirical analysis of their behaviour with real-sized grammars. The extension of parsing schemata for error-repair parsing is used to define a transformation that can be employed to automatically add error-repair capabilities to parsers that do not have them. Finally, the extension of parsing schemata for dependency parsing is used to find formal relationships between several well-known dependency parsers, as well as to define novel algorithms for mildly non-projective dependency structures.

1.1 Motivation

Parsing schemata, introduced by Sikkel (1997), are high-level, declarative descriptions of parsing algorithms. A parsing schema describes a set of

3

intermediate results that can be obtained by a parser and a set of operations that it can use to generate new results from existing ones, but it imposes no constraints on the order in which to execute the operations or the data structures in which to store the results. We could say that schemata are descriptions of *what* to do, but they abstract away from *how* to do it.

This high abstraction level makes parsing schemata a useful tool to describe, analyse and compare different parsing algorithms: schemata provide simple and uniform descriptions of the parsers, and allow us to focus on their logic without worrying about implementation details. However, if we wished to apply the schemata formalism to practical parsing of natural language text, we would find several problems, and is it these problems that are addressed in this monograph:

- First of all, the high abstraction level of parsing schemata, which makes them useful from a theoretical standpoint, also rules out the possibility of executing them on a computer. If we wish to test an algorithm that we have defined by means of a schema, we must first implement it in a programming language, filling in the control structures and implementation details that were omitted in the schema. Therefore, schemata are useful as a formal framework for defining parsers and analysing their formal properties but not for prototyping them and studying their empirical behaviour.

- Parsing schemata can be used to represent algorithms that analyse input sentences with respect to a given grammar, so that they only will produce a complete analysis of an input sentence if it is grammatical. However, it is common in practical applications to find sentences that do not conform to the constraints of our grammar, since it is not possible to build a grammar that will recognise every possible structure that can appear in a natural language. Therefore, it is interesting to be able to define *robust* parsers that are able to obtain a complete, albeit approximate, analysis for ungrammatical sentences. The formalism of Sikkel (1997) does not allow the relaxation of grammar constraints in order to define this kind of parsers, since it is based on the assumption that all the possible intermediate results are parts of grammatically valid trees.

- The formalism of Sikkel (1997) is formally linked to *constituency-based* parsing, in which the structure of sentences is expressed by dividing them in blocks (*constituents*) which are, in turn, divided into smaller constituents. However, in recent years, there has been a surge of interest in *dependency-based parsers*, in which the structure of a sentence is represented as a set of binary links (*dependencies*) between its words. Although many current state-of-the-art parsers are based on this assumption, dependency parsers cannot be represented by the formalism of Sikkel (1997).

The purpose and contribution of this monograph is to solve these problems, by defining a set of extensions and tools to make parsing schemata more useful in practice. In addition to this, research results obtained by using these extensions and tools are also presented.

1.2 Background

In this section, the contributions of this book are put into context by briefly introducing the problem of parsing natural language sentences and the formalism of parsing schemata.

1.2.1 *Parsing natural language*

In the context of computational linguistics, the process of *parsing*, or syntactic analysis, consists of finding the grammatical structure of natural language sentences. Given a sentence represented as a sequence of symbols, each corresponding to a word, a *parsing algorithm* (or simply *parser*) will try to find and output a representation of the syntactic structure of the sentence. The nature of this representation depends on the linguistic theory that the parser uses to describe syntax. In *phrase structure parsers*, or *constituency parsers*, sentences are analysed by dividing them into meaningful segments called *constituents*, which are, in turn, broken up into smaller constituents. The result of a constituency analysis can be represented with a *phrase structure tree* (or *constituency tree*), as can be seen in Figure 1.1a. On the other hand, in *dependency-based parsers*, the structure of a sentence is represented by a set of directed links (*dependencies*) between their words, which form a graph as can be seen in Figure 1.1b.

Parsing is a fundamental process in any natural language processing pipeline, since obtaining the syntactic structure of sentences provides us with information that can be used to extract meaning from them: constituents correspond to units of meaning, and dependency relations describe the ways in which they interact, such as who performed the action described in a sentence or which object is receiving the action. Thus, we can find

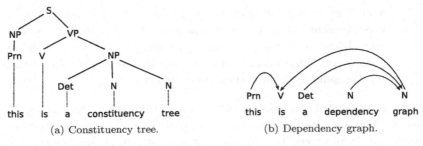

(a) Constituency tree. (b) Dependency graph.

Fig. 1.1 Constituency and dependency structures.

parsers applied to many practical problems in natural language processing where some degree of semantic analysis is necessary or convenient, such as information retrieval (Vilares *et al.*, 2008), information extraction (Surdeanu *et al.*, 2003), machine translation (Chiang, 2005; Shen *et al.*, 2008), textual entailment (Herrera *et al.*, 2005), or question answering (Bouma *et al.*, 2005; Amaral *et al.*, 2008).

The practical importance of parsing natural language text has motivated the development of a diverse range of algorithms for this purpose. Different parsers are better suited to different situations, so the question of which parser is better for a practical application depends on many factors, such as the language, domain, application goal or availability of linguistic resources.

According to the linguistic resources that they use, we can broadly classify parsing techniques into two categories: grammar-driven and data-driven approaches (Nivre, 2006b). In *grammar-driven* parsing, the set of valid sentences in a given language is represented by a *grammar*, which is a set of formal rules that describe the kinds of structures that can appear in the language. In a *data-driven* approach, no formal grammar is needed: instead, some learning technique is used to automatically infer linguistic knowledge from (possibly annotated) texts, that can later be used to parse other texts. However, most of the systems used in practice are not purely grammar-driven or data-driven: instead, they combine features of both approaches. For example, a formal grammar can be annotated with statistical information obtained from a corpus of annotated text, or a system may induce a grammar automatically from text data.

In parsers that use grammars, the kinds of rules that can be used to describe syntactic structures and the ways in which they are used to form sentences depend on the particular *grammatical formalism* that we use.

In the field of constituency parsing, *context-free grammars* (CFGs) are a widely-used formalism, since they are simple and can be parsed efficiently, in cubic time with respect to the length of the input (Younger, 1967; Earley, 1970). However, it has been shown that CFGs are not powerful enough to represent natural languages, since some linguistic phenomena (such as Dutch cross-serial dependencies) are not context-free (Joshi, 1985). This led to the development of *mildly context-sensitive* grammar formalisms (Joshi, 1985; Joshi *et al.*, 1991), which are formalisms that are general enough to account for linguistic phenomena that cannot be handled by CFGs, yet restricted enough to still be parsable in polynomial time. An example of this type of formalism is *tree-adjoining grammars* (TAGs), which are parsable in $O(n^6)$, where n is the length of the input (Vijay-Shanker and Joshi, 1985).

In the case of dependency-based parsing, it is also possible to use a grammar. For example, dependency grammars can be defined with the formalism by Hays (1964) and Gaifman (1965) or as bilexical grammars (Eisner, 2000). However, many dependency parsers (Yamada and Matsumoto, 2003; Nivre *et al.*, 2007b) are purely data-driven, and do not use a grammar at all.

1.2.2 *Robustness in grammar-driven parsers*

One of the biggest difficulties that arise when using grammar-driven approaches to process natural language sentences in practical domains is the problem of achieving *robustness*. Robustness can be defined as the capacity of a parser to analyse any input sentence (Nivre, 2006b), and it is a highly desirable property for any system dealing with unrestricted natural language text. The problem is that, when a parser that employs a formal grammar is used to analyse unrestricted text, it is likely to find sentences that do not belong to the formal language defined by the grammar. This can happen because of several reasons, including insufficient coverage (the sentence is syntactically correct, but our grammar is not detailed enough to recognise it) or errors in the sentence itself (not all the sentences in real texts are syntactically correct).

The methods that have been proposed to solve this problem fall mainly into two broad categories: those which try to parse well-formed fragments of the input when an analysis for the complete sentence cannot be found – partial parsers, like the one by Kasper *et al.* (1999) – and those that try to provide a complete parse for the input sentence by relaxing the constraints imposed by the grammar. One of the approaches to achieve the latter is that of *error-repair parsers* (McKenzie *et al.*, 1995), which are algorithms that are able to find complete parse trees for sentences not covered by their grammar, by supposing that ungrammatical strings are versions of valid strings in which there are a number of errors. Under this assumption, the generation of an analysis for an ungrammatical sentence is based on the analysis of the grammatical sentence that produced it under this error model.

1.2.3 *Parsing schemata*

The formalism of *parsing schemata* (Sikkel, 1997) is a theoretical framework that can be used to describe different parsers in a simple and uniform way. Parsing schemata are based on the idea of considering the parsing process as a deduction process, which proceeds by generating intermediate results called *items*. This is similar to the view of parsing as deduction by Shieber *et al.* (1995), with the difference that Sikkel's framework formally defines items and related concepts, providing a mathematical basis that can be used to reason about formal properties of parsers. In particular, items in parsing schemata are sets of partial constituency trees that are licensed by the rules of a given grammar. Note that this means that parsing schemata are only applicable to grammar-based constituency parsers, and not to data-driven or dependency-based parsers. In fact, Sikkel's examples were focused in CFG parsers only, but parsing schemata have subsequently been used to describe TAG parsers as well (Alonso *et al.*, 1999, 2004).

In order to describe a parser by means of a parsing schema, we need to provide the following:

- A set of *initial items*, or *hypotheses*, which are obtained directly from each input sentence.
- A set of inference rules called *deduction steps*, that can be used to derive new items from existing ones. A parsing schema specifies these inference rules as a set, but makes no claim about the order in which they are to be executed. The set of deduction steps in a schema is given as a function of the rules in our grammar, so that the same parsing strategy will produce different results with different grammars, as expected.
- A set of *final items*, which are items that contain a full parse tree for the input or allow us to obtain it.

A given sentence belongs to the language defined by a grammar if a final item can be obtained from the initial items by some sequence of inferences using deduction steps. A generic deductive procedure as the one described by Shieber *et al.* (1995) can be used to try all the possible inferences in order to find final items, and the sequences of inferences that produce final items can be used to recover parse forests (Billot and Lang, 1989).

Items in parsing schemata are formally defined as sets of partial constituency trees, members of the quotient set of some equivalence relation between trees. Additionally, items can be augmented with additional information. For example, probabilities can be included in items to describe statistical parsers, or feature structures to describe unification-based parsers.

Parsing schemata are a useful theoretical tool to describe and study parsers for several reasons:

- They provide a simple and declarative way to represent parsing algorithms. A representation of a parser by means of a parsing schema is typically much more compact than, for example, a pseudocode representation. Properties of parsers such as their time and space computational complexities are easy to infer from their schemata.

- They represent parsers in a uniform way, and allow us to find and prove relationships between different algorithms. The mathematical framework provided by parsing schemata can also be used to prove the correctness of parsers, and proofs of correctness can be transferred between some parsers by using the formal relationships between them.

- They are at a high abstraction level, so that they focus on the semantics of the parser (what the parser does) and abstract away from implementation details (the particular data and control structures used by the algorithm). Note that this means that there is not a direct correspondence between parsing schemata and algorithms: a schema describes a parsing strategy that can sometimes be realised by different algorithms.

1.3 Outline of the book

The fundamental goal of this book is to provide theoretical and practical tools to extend the applicability of parsing schemata in practical natural language text parsing. In what follows, we list the main research contributions presented in this work, and then outline the contents of each chapter of the book.

1.3.1 *Contributions*

(1) A compiler is presented that automatically converts parsing schemata into efficient executable implementations of their corresponding parsing algorithms. The system is tested by compiling schemata for several well-known CFG parsers and running them on grammars from real-life corpora.

(2) The parsing schemata compiler is used to conduct an empirical study of the performance of several TAG parsing strategies on a real-life, feature-based LTAG (Lexicalised Tree Adjoining Grammar): the XTAG English Grammar (XTAG Research Group, 2001). Note that previous comparative studies of TAG parsers in the literature were done with "toy" grammars, but there were no such studies with real-life, wide-coverage grammars. Additionally, the performance of TAG parsers is also compared to that of CFG parsers, and the empirical overhead introduced when using TAGs to parse context-free languages is quantified.

(3) A theoretical extension of parsing schemata is defined to allow robust parsers under the error-repair paradigm to be described with schemata.

(4) A transformation is defined that can be used to automatically add error-repair capabilities to the schemata of parsers that do not have them. By using this transformation, robust parsers and their implementations can be obtained automatically from non-robust parsing schemata.

(5) A variant of the parsing schemata formalism is defined for dependency-based parsing, and used to describe and formally relate several well-known projective and non-projective dependency parsers in the literature. Parsing schemata are also given for the formalism of link grammar.

(6) Novel parsing algorithms are defined for different sets of mildly non-projective dependency structures, including a new set of *mildly ill-nested* structures that includes all the sentences present in a number of dependency treebanks.

1.3.2 *Structure of the book*

This book is structured in five parts. The first part is introductory, containing this chapter which summarises the main goals and contributions of the monograph, and a chapter defining the formalism of parsing schemata, that will be used throughout the book. The second part presents a compiler for parsing schemata and several empirical studies of constituency-based parsers conducted with it. The third part introduces an extension of parsing schemata that can be used to describe error-repair parsers. The fourth part is devoted to a variant of schemata for dependency-based parsers. Finally, the fifth part summarises conclusions and discusses future work.

A chapter-by-chapter breakdown of the parts follows:

1.3.2.1 *Part 1*

CHAPTER 2 formally introduces the framework of parsing schemata, which will be used throughout the book. The formalism is described here as defined by Sikkel (1997), serving as a starting point for the novel extensions presented in subsequent chapters. The definitions are complemented by concrete examples based on the Cocke-Younger-Kasami (CYK; Kasami, 1965; Younger, 1967) and Earley (1970) parsing algorithms, which will also be used recurringly through the rest of the chapters.

1.3.2.2 *Part 2*

CHAPTER 3 presents a compiler able to automatically transform parsing schemata into efficient Java implementations of their corresponding algorithms. The input to this system is a simple representation of a schema, practically coincident with the formal notation commonly used to denote them, as described in Chapter 2. The system performs an analysis of the deduction steps in the input schema in order to determine the best data structures and indexes to use, ensuring that the generated implementations are efficient. The system described is general enough to handle all kinds of schemata for different grammar formalisms, and it provides an extensibility mechanism allowing the user to define custom notational elements.

In CHAPTER 4, the compiler presented in Chapter 3 is used to generate implementations of three well-known CFG parsing algorithms and compare their empirical performance on several grammars taken from real-life corpora. These results show how different parsing algorithms are better suited to different grammars. Implementations are also generated for four TAG parsing algorithms, and used to analyse sentences with the XTAG grammar, a real-life, wide-coverage feature-based TAG. In order to be able to generate XTAG parsers, some transformations are made to the grammar, and TAG parsing schemata are extended with feature structure unification support and a simple tree filtering mechanism. The data obtained is used to compare the empirical performance of these algorithms, being the first comparison of TAG parsers on a large-scale, wide-coverage grammar: previously to this work, existing comparisons were limited to "toy" grammars with a small number of rules. The results obtained from CFG and TAG parsers on real-life grammars are then complemented by studies performed on artificially-generated grammars, which allow us to evaluate the influence of string and grammar size in empirical computational complexity, as well as to the overhead caused by using TAG to parse context-free languages.

1.3.2.3 *Part 3*

CHAPTER 5 introduces error-repair parsing schemata: an extension of parsing schemata which can be used to define parsers that can robustly handle sentences with errors or inconsistencies. As the original theory of parsing schemata is based on the assumption that items are sets of partial constituency trees that follow the rules of a given grammar, the underlying concepts behind schemata have to be redefined in order to support these robust parsers. This extension of the parsing schema framework allows us to describe and compare error-repair parsers in a simple and uniform way, and provides a formal basis for proving their correctness and other properties. In addition, this framework is used to develop a generic technique for obtaining efficient error-correcting parsers based on regional error repair, and empirical performance results are provided.

In CHAPTER 6, the framework of error-repair parsing schemata is used to define a general transformation technique to automatically obtain robust, error-repair parsers from standard non-robust parsers. If our method is applied to a correct parsing schema verifying certain conditions, the resulting error-repair parsing schema is guaranteed to be correct. The required conditions are weak enough to be fulfilled by a wide variety of popular parsers used in natural language processing, such as CYK, Earley and Left-Corner. The schemata obtained from the transformation can be implemented with global, regional or local error-repair techniques, so that we may choose to obtain more efficient robust parsers by sacrificing the guarantee of obtaining all the optimal solutions.

1.3.2.4 *Part 4*

In CHAPTER 7, a variant of parsing schemata is defined that can be used to describe, analyse and compare dependency parsing algorithms. This extension is used to establish clear relations between several existing projective dependency parsers and prove their correctness. Parsing schemata for non-projective dependency parsers are also presented. A variant of the formalism to represent parsers based on link grammar (Sleator and Temperley, 1991, 1993) is also shown, including examples of how some existing dependency parsers can be adapted to produce parsers for link grammar.

In CHAPTER 8, parsing schemata are used to solve the problem of efficiently parsing mildly non-projective dependency structures. Polynomial time parsing algorithms are presented for various mildly non-projective dependency formalisms, including well-nested structures with gap degree bounded by a constant k, and a new class of *mildly ill-nested* structures for gap degree k. The latter class includes all the gap degree k structures in a number of dependency treebanks.

1.3.2.5 *Part 5*

Finally, CHAPTER 9 contains a summary of the main conclusions derived from the research described in this book, as well as a discussion of possible lines for future research.

Note that the material in Part 1 (especially Chapter 2) is required to understand the rest of the parts, since it introduces notation that will be used throughout the book. Parts 2, 3 and 4 can be read or skipped independently of each other, but the material in the first chapter of each of these parts is required to understand the rest of the part.

Chapter 2

Preliminaries

In this chapter, we introduce some basic concepts about parsing algorithms and grammars, as well as the formalism of *parsing schemata*, which will be used throughout this book.

2.1 Context-free grammars

A *language* is a set of sequences (strings) of symbols from a finite set called an *alphabet*.

A *grammar* is a precise definition of a language by means of a set of rules. One of the most widely used types of grammar is context-free grammars.

Definition 2.1. A *context-free grammar* (CFG) is a 4-tuple $G = (N, \Sigma, P, S)$ where:

- Σ is an alphabet of symbols called *terminal symbols*, which will be the components of the strings in the language associated with G,
- N is an alphabet of auxiliary symbols called *nonterminal symbols*, which will not appear in the strings of the language,
- $S \in N$ is a special nonterminal symbol called the *initial symbol* or *axiom* of G,
- $P \subseteq N \times (\Sigma \cup N)^*$ is a set of *production rules* of the form $A \to \alpha$, where A is a nonterminal symbol and α is a string that may contain both terminal and nonterminal symbols.

From now on, we will follow the usual conventions (Hopcroft *et al.*, 2006) by which we use the lower case letters $a, b \ldots$ to represent terminal symbols, the upper case letters $A, B \ldots$ for nonterminal symbols and $X, Y \ldots$ for arbitrary symbols; and Greek letters $\alpha, \beta \ldots$ for strings of terminals and nonterminals.

The language associated with a grammar $G = (N, \Sigma, P, S)$, denoted $L(G)$, is the set of strings of terminal symbols in Σ that can be obtained by starting with the initial symbol S and applying a sequence of productions in P. A production of the form $A \to \alpha$ can be applied to any string containing the nonterminal A, and is applied by changing one appearance of A in the string to α. We write $\beta \Rightarrow \gamma$ to denote that we can obtain the string γ by applying a production to the string β. We write $\beta \Rightarrow^* \gamma$ to denote that γ can be obtained by applying a sequence of zero or more productions to the string β. Thus, we can write the language associated with the grammar $G = (N, \Sigma, P, S)$ as $L(G) = \{\alpha \in \Sigma^* \mid S \Rightarrow^* \alpha\}$.

Example 2.1. Suppose that we have a CFG $G = (N, \Sigma, P, S)$ defined by the following:

- $\Sigma = \{\text{the, dog, barks}\}$
- $N = \{S, NP, VP, N, V, Det\}$
- $P = \{S \to NP\ VP, NP \to Det\ N, VP \to V, Det \to \text{the}, N \to \text{dog}, V \to \text{barks}\}$

This is a typical example of a fragment of a CFG used for parsing a natural language, in this case English. Of course, this is an extremely simplified "toy" grammar whose associated language $L(G)$ contains a single sentence ("the dog barks"); nevertheless, the larger grammars used in real-life applications often have the same structure: nonterminal symbols correspond to syntactic structures — such as noun phrases (NP) or verb phrases (VP) — and production rules express the valid ways in which these structures can combine into larger ones. Terminal symbols can denote concrete words, as in this example, or part-of-speech tags (such as N or Det). The latter option is common when a parser is used as one of the steps in a natural language processing pipeline, receiving its input from a *part-of-speech tagger* module which maps the words in input sentences to these tags.

We can check that the sentence "the dog barks" is in fact in $L(G)$ by obtaining it as a result of applying a sequence of productions to the initial symbol S, as explained before:
$$S \Rightarrow NP\ VP \Rightarrow Det\ N\ VP \Rightarrow Det\ N\ V \Rightarrow \text{the}\ N\ V \Rightarrow \text{the dog}\ V \Rightarrow$$
the dog barks.

If we represent the derivations we have just made as a tree, where each application of a rule $A \to \alpha$ is represented by adding nodes labelled with the

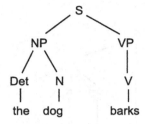

Fig. 2.1 Parse tree for a simple sentence.

symbols in α as children of the node A, we obtain a *parse tree* (or syntax tree) for the sentence, which is shown in Figure 2.1.[1]

Given a CFG G, the problem of *recognition* consists of determining whether a given string $a_1 \ldots a_n$ belongs to the language $L(G)$ by finding a sequence of derivations for it, or by ensuring that none exists. The problem of *parsing* consists of finding all the possible parse trees for the string $a_1 \ldots a_n$ under the grammar G. Parsing with CFGs is a particular instance of grammar-driven parsing, as explained in Section 1.2.1.

Note that, in more complex grammars than the one shown in this example, there may be several different valid parse trees for a single sentence. For example, in a larger natural language grammar, the parsing of the sentence "John saw a man with a telescope" could result in two different trees (shown in Figure 2.2), the former corresponding to the interpretation "a man having a telescope was seen by John", and the latter corresponding to "John used a telescope to see a man". In this case, we say that both the grammar and the sentence are *ambiguous*. Parsers for natural language sentences should be able to handle ambiguity, as it is a common phenomenon in human languages.

---

[1]This particular kind of tree obtained from CFGs is called a *constituency tree*, since it divides sentences into smaller units called *constituents*. A constituency tree is one of several possible ways to represent the syntactic structure of a sentence; a well-known alternative are dependency-based representations, which have been shown in Figure 1.1b and will be further explained in Chapter 7. By default, references to "parse trees" or "syntax trees" in this book should be understood as referring to constituency trees unless the opposite is explicitly stated.

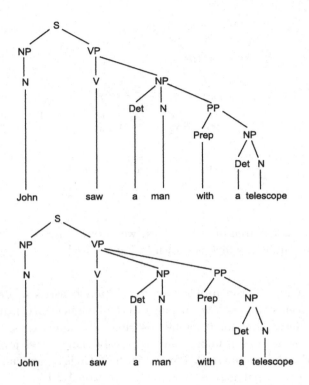

Fig. 2.2   Two alternative parse trees for an ambiguous sentence.

2.2   Parsing algorithms and schemata

The process of parsing is an important step in natural language analysis, as it provides us with hierarchical representation of sentences that we can use to extract meaning from them. This has motivated the development of various parsing algorithms in recent decades. As an example, two of the most widely used parsing algorithms for CFGs are the CYK algorithm (Kasami, 1965; Younger, 1967) and Earley's algorithm (Earley, 1970).

The CYK algorithm is a bottom-up parser, meaning that it starts building a parse tree from the smallest constituents (the leaves) and proceeds by grouping them into larger constituents, building the tree upwards until it finds its root. This algorithm can only be used to parse with CFGs $G = (N, \Sigma, P, S)$ in *Chomsky Normal Form* (Chomsky, 1959), which roughly means that productions in P must be of the form $A \rightarrow BC$ or $A \rightarrow a$.

This poses no problem in practice, as every CFG can be converted to this normal form. CYK is traditionally described as a dynamic programming algorithm that is implemented by means of a table traversed by three nested loops: nonterminal symbols in our grammar G are assigned an index ($N = \{R_1 \ldots R_r\}$), and the parsing table is a boolean array of dimensions $[n, n, r]$ where n is the length of the string. The algorithm works as described by the pseudocode in Figure 2.3: during the traversal of the table, a cell $a[j, i, a]$ is enabled if there exists a tree with root R_a whose yield is the substring of the input that has length i and begins at position j. At the end of execution, if the start symbol of G has the index s, we know whether the input sentence belongs or not to $L(G)$ by checking if the cell $a[1, n, s]$ has been enabled. Note that this pseudocode corresponds to a CYK recogniser, but it can be easily transformed to a parser by making it add pointers from each table cell (line 12) to the pairs of cells that have been used to enable it (line 11). Following these pointers back from the cell $a[1, n, s]$, we obtain a forest of parse trees (Billot and Lang, 1989).

```
1   a = array [n,n,r] of boolean initialised to false;

3   for i = 1 ... n //consider subsequences of length 1
        for each rule R_j → a_i
5          a[i,1,j] = true;

7   for i = 2 ... n //consider subsequences of length i
        for j = 1 ... n-i+1 //j = beginning of subsequence
9          for k = 1 ... i-1 //k = partition of subsequence
               for each rule R_a → R_b R_c
11                 if ( a[j,k,b] = true ∧ a[j+k,i-k,c] = true )
                       a[j,i,a] = true; //apply rule
13
        if ( a[1,n,s] = true ) return true; //string ∈ L(G)
15  else return false; //string does not belong to L(G)
```

Fig. 2.3 Pseudocode for the CYK parsing algorithm.

On the other hand, the algorithm by Earley (1970) was originally described as in the pseudocode in Figure 2.4. Contrary to CYK, Earley's algorithm can work with any CFG, not necessarily in Chomsky Normal Form. Given a string of length n, the algorithm creates $n + 1$ state sets

$(S_0, \ldots, S_n)$. The parser reads the string from left to right and fills these sets with states, which are tuples of the form $(A \to \alpha, j, k)$. $A \to \alpha$ in such a state represents the rule currently being used for recognition, j the amount of already recognised symbols in its right-hand side, and k the final position of the recognised part of the input string (the corresponding initial positions are given by the indexes associated to state sets). The state sets are filled in order, starting with a state $(S \to \alpha, 0, 0)$ in S_0 and proceeding from left to right with three operations (*Predictor*, *Completer* and *Scanner*) as can be seen in the pseudocode in Figure 2.4. At the end of the execution, we know that the input sentence belongs to the language defined by our grammar if $(S \to \alpha, |\alpha|, 0) \in S_n$. Analogously to the CYK case, although this pseudocode describes a recogniser, it can be adapted to build a parse forest by adding back pointers when new states are explored (lines 14, 20 and 25).

By looking at the pseudocode for these two algorithms, we could conclude that they are totally different, unrelated approaches to the problem of parsing with a CFG. Not only do they differ in the way in which they build a parse tree (*bottom-up* in CYK, starting with the leaves and building upwards towards the initial symbol, and *top-down* in Earley, starting with the initial symbol and progressing downwards to the leaves) but they also differ in the data and control structures that they use in the process. While CYK is a classical dynamic programming algorithm that traverses and fills a table with partial results, Earley is a transition-based parser that reads the input from left to right, and will reach a goal state if it can be parsed successfully.

However, the parsing schemata formalism allows us to relate these two algorithms and represent them in a uniform notation. *Parsing schemata*, introduced by Sikkel (1997), are based on the idea of seeing parsing as a deduction process, which proceeds by generating intermediate results called *items*. An initial set of items (*hypotheses*) is directly obtained from the input sentence, and the parsing process consists of the application of inference rules (*deduction steps*) which produce new items from existing ones. Each item contains a piece of information about the sentence's structure, and a successful parsing process will produce at least one *final item* containing a full parse tree for the sentence or guaranteeing its existence.

As examples, the parsing schemata for CYK and Earley's parsing algorithms can be seen in Figures 2.5 and 2.6. We can informally understand how parsing schemata work by studying the semantics of these schemata.

```
1   S = array [0..n] of state sets;
    for i = 0 ... n { S[i] = ∅; } //initialise the sets to ∅
3   for each rule S → α ∈ P //initialise S[0]
      S[0] = S[0] ∪ {(S → α,0,0)};
5
    for i = 0 ... n { //process state sets
7     process the members of S[i] in order, executing
      each of these operations on each state (A → α,j,f)
9     until no more of them can be applied:
        1) Predictor:
11        X = j+1th symbol in α;
          if X exists and is a nonterminal
13          for each production of the form X → β in P
              S[i] = S[i] ∪ {(X → β,0,i)};
15        2) Completer:
          if X does not exist //(j+1 > |α|)
17          for each state (B → β,l,g) in S[f] {
              Y = l+1th symbol in β;
19            if Y exists ∧ Y = A
                S[i] = S[i] ∪ {(B → β,l+1,g)};
21          }
        3) Scanner:
23        if X exists and is a terminal
            if X = a_{i+1}
25            S[i+1] = S[i+1] ∪ {(A → α,j+1,f)};
    }
27
    //check whether string belongs to language L(G)
29  if S[n] contains a state of the form (S → γ,|γ|,0)
      return true;
31  else
      return false;
```

Fig. 2.4 Pseudocode for Earley's parsing algorithm.

Item set:
$$\mathcal{I} = \{[A, i, j] \mid A \in N \wedge 0 \le i < j\}$$

Initial items (hypotheses):
$$\mathcal{H} = \{[a_i, i - 1, i] \mid 0 < i \le n\}$$

Deduction steps:

UNARY: $\dfrac{[a, i - 1, i]}{[A, i - 1, i]} \quad A \to a \in P$

BINARY: $\dfrac{[B, i, j] \qquad [C, j, k]}{[A, i, k]} \quad A \to BC \in P$

Final items:
$$\{[S, 0, n]\}$$

Fig. 2.5   A parsing schema specifying the CYK parsing algorithm.

Item set:
$$\mathcal{I} = \{[A \to \alpha \bullet \beta, i, j] \mid A \to \alpha\beta \in P \wedge 0 \le i \le j\}$$

Initial items (hypotheses):
$$\mathcal{H} = \{[a_i, i - 1, i] \mid 0 < i \le n\}$$

Deduction steps:

INITTER: $\dfrac{}{[S \to \bullet\alpha, 0, 0]} \quad S \to \alpha \in P$

SCANNER: $\dfrac{[A \to \alpha \bullet a\beta, i, j] \qquad [a, j, j + 1]}{[A \to \alpha a \bullet \beta, i, j + 1]}$

PREDICTOR: $\dfrac{[A \to \alpha \bullet B\beta, i, j]}{[B \to \bullet\gamma, j, j]} \quad B \to \gamma \in P$

COMPLETER: $\dfrac{[A \to \alpha \bullet B\beta, i, j] \qquad [B \to \gamma\bullet, j, k]}{[A \to \alpha B \bullet \beta, i, k]}$

Final items: $\{[S \to \gamma\bullet, 0, n]\}$

Fig. 2.6   A parsing schema specifying Earley's parsing algorithm.

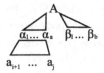

Fig. 2.7   Form of the trees associated with the Earley item $[A \to \alpha \bullet \beta, i, j]$.

Items in the CYK parsing schema are tuples of the form $[A, i, j]$, where A is a symbol and i, j are integer numbers denoting positions in the input string. The meaning of such an item can be interpreted as follows: "There exists a parse tree with root labelled A, licensed by the rules in the grammar, such that its leaf nodes form the substring $a_{i+1} \ldots a_j$ of the input sentence." The algorithm will produce a valid parse for the input sentence if an item of the form $[S, 0, n]$ is generated. According to the said interpretation, this item guarantees the existence of a parse tree with root S whose leaves are labelled $a_1 \ldots a_n$, i.e., a complete parse tree for the sentence.

As the Earley parsing algorithm constructs different intermediate trees than CYK, the item set for its corresponding schema is not the same. In this case, items are tuples of the form $[A \to \alpha \bullet \beta, i, j]$, where $A \to \alpha \bullet \beta$ is a grammar rule with a special marker (dot) added at some position in its right-hand side, and i, j are integer numbers denoting positions in the input string. The meaning of such an item can be interpreted as follows: "There exists a valid parse tree with its root labelled A, where the direct children of A are labelled with the symbols in the string $\alpha\beta$, the leaf nodes of the subtrees rooted at the nodes labelled α form the substring $a_{i+1} \ldots a_j$ of the input, and the nodes labelled β are leaves." Such a tree can be seen on Figure 2.7. Note that this item format and semantics is linked to the top-down, left-to-right strategy that the Earley parser uses to find parse trees for sentences.

A deduction step $\frac{\eta_1 \ldots \eta_m}{\xi} \Phi$ allows us to infer the item specified by its consequent ξ from those in its antecedents $\eta_1 \ldots \eta_m$. *Side conditions* (Φ) specify the valid values for the variables appearing in the antecedents and consequent, and may refer to grammar rules (as in these examples) or specify other constraints that must be verified in order to infer the consequent.

In the particular case of CYK, the UNARY and BINARY steps use the rules of the grammar to join partial parse trees in a bottom-up way, producing larger trees. In particular, the UNARY step uses a rule of the form $A \to a$

to put together the tree $A(a)^2$, while the BINARY step employs a binary rule $(A \to BC)$ to link two partial parse trees rooted at the nonterminals B and C into a new partial parse tree rooted at A.

In the Earley parsing schema, the INITTER and PREDICTOR steps are used to initialise the analysis by generating items with the dot in the left-most position of their associated production's right-hand side. These items represent the application of a production without having recognised any input symbols yet. As we have seen, the dot in productions marks the region of their right-hand side which has been recognised, and the SCANNER and COMPLETER steps allow us to enlarge this region by shifting the dot to the right. The SCANNER step reads and recognises a single terminal symbol from the input, while COMPLETER recognises a nonterminal symbol and joins two partial parse trees into a larger one.

If we now look at Earley's algorithm as described in Figure 2.4, we can see that it is nothing but a particular implementation of this schema. The deduction of an item $[A \to \alpha \bullet \beta, i, j]$ in the schema is implemented by adding a state $(A \to \alpha\beta, |\alpha|, i)$ to the set S[j], and the *Predictor, Completer* and *Scanner* operations in the code correspond to the deduction steps in the schema. The loop and the structure used to hold the state sets impose a particular order on the execution of these operations, which guarantees that the state $(S \to \gamma, |\gamma|, 0)$ will be generated if the input is a valid sentence according to the grammar.

Similar observations can be made about the pseudocode for the CYK parsing algorithm, where the deduction of an item $[N_x, i, j]$ in the schema is implemented by enabling the cell $a[i + 1, j - i, x]$ in the algorithm. Note that the same schema can be implemented by different algorithms: for example, we could write an alternative implementation of CYK processing subsequences from right to left (i.e. reversing the loop on the variable j).

As we can see, a parsing schema specifies a set of operations that must be executed and a set of intermediate results that must be obtained when parsing a sentence, but makes no claim about the order in which to execute the operations or the data structures to use for storing the results. As a result, a parsing schema captures the *logic* of a parsing algorithm (the ways in which the algorithm combines partial parse trees to form larger trees), while abstracting away the implementation details (the data and control structures used to build and store the trees). Thus, parsing schemata are

---

[2]Throughout the book we will use parenthetical notation to represent trees, where we write $X(T_1 \ldots T_k)$ for the tree formed by linking a root node labelled X to the subtrees $T_1 \ldots T_k$.

located at a higher abstraction level than algorithms, and it can be said that a parsing algorithm is a particular implementation of a schema.

2.3 The formalism of parsing schemata

Now that the concept of parsing schemata has been informally introduced, a precise theoretical formulation will be given, which is a summary of the main concepts defined by Sikkel (1997).

From now on, apart from the notational conventions mentioned in Section 2.1, we will use $\mathbb{N}$ as a notation to refer to the set of natural numbers, and ϵ to denote an empty string. We will refer to the root of a tree τ as $root(\tau)$, and to its yield (list of frontier nodes, ordered from left to right) as $yield(\tau)$. We will use the notation $\wp(X)$ to refer to the power set of X.

2.3.1 *Deduction systems*

Definition 2.2. Let X be a set of entities, and $\mathcal{H}$ a set of hypotheses. A *deduction step* is a pair (Y, x), with $x \in X$, where $Y \subseteq \mathcal{H} \cup X$ is a finite set.

In a deduction step of the form $(\{y_1, \ldots, y_k\}, x)$, the entities $y_1 \ldots y_k$ are called *antecedents*, and x is the *consequent*.

Definition 2.3. A *deduction system* $\mathbb{D}$ is a tuple $(X, \mathcal{H}, D)$ where:

- X is a set of entities called the *domain* of $\mathbb{D}$,
- $\mathcal{H}$ is a set of hypotheses,
- $D \subseteq \wp(\mathcal{H} \cup X) \times X$ is a finite set of deduction steps.

Let $\mathbb{D} = (X, \mathcal{H}, D)$ be a deduction system.

Definition 2.4. We define the *inference relation* $\vdash \subseteq \wp(\mathcal{H} \cup X) \times X$ as:
$Y \vdash x$ if $(Y', x) \in D$ for some $Y' \subseteq Y$.

It will also be useful to define the relations:

- $Y \vdash^0 x$ if $x \in Y$,
- $Y \vdash^1 x$ if $Y \vdash x$,
- $\forall n \in \mathbb{N}, Y \vdash^{n+1} x$ if $\exists x_1 \in X$ such that $(Y \vdash x_1 \wedge (Y \cup \{x_1\}) \vdash^n x)$,
- $Y \vdash^* x$ if $\exists n \in (\mathbb{N} \cup \{0\})$ such that $Y \vdash^n x$.

Definition 2.5. We define the set of *valid entities* for $\mathbb{D} = (X, \mathcal{H}, D)$ as
$\mathcal{V}(\mathbb{D}) = \{x \in X \mid \mathcal{H} \vdash^* x\}$.

Thus, the set of valid entities associated with a deduction system is the set of all the entities that can be inferred from the hypotheses by applying a sequence of deduction steps.

Definition 2.6. An *enhanced deduction system* $\mathbb{E}$ is a tuple $(X, \mathcal{H}, \mathcal{F}, \mathcal{C}, D)$ where X, $\mathcal{H}$ and D have the same meaning as in a standard deduction system, $\mathcal{F} \subseteq X$ is a set of *final* entities, and $\mathcal{C} \subseteq \mathcal{F}$ is a set of *correct final* entities.

From a formal standpoint, the definition of the sets $\mathcal{C}$ and $\mathcal{F}$ is arbitrary. In practice, they will be defined according to semantic criteria depending on what the deduction system is used for. The sets $\mathcal{C}$ and $\mathcal{F}$ allow us to establish the correctness of a deduction system; we say that an enhanced deduction system $\mathbb{E} = (X, \mathcal{H}, \mathcal{F}, \mathcal{C}, D)$ is:

- *sound*, if all valid final entities are correct: $\mathcal{F} \cap \mathcal{V}(\mathbb{E}) \subseteq \mathcal{C}$,
- *complete*, if all correct final entities are valid: $\mathcal{C} \subseteq \mathcal{F} \cap \mathcal{V}(\mathbb{E})$,
- *correct*, if it is sound and complete.

In the particular context of parsing, a parser is said to be sound if all the parse trees that it outputs are licensed by the grammar, and complete if every such tree is obtained by the parser. Thus, the set of correct final entities will contain those entities corresponding to full syntax trees licensed by the grammar, as explained in more detail below.

2.3.2 *Parsing systems and parsing schemata*

Parsing schemata are a particular case of deduction systems, where the entities of X and the hypotheses of $\mathcal{H}$ are called *items* and represent sets of partial parse trees in a given grammar.

Definition 2.7. Let G be a grammar, belonging to some class of grammar $\mathcal{CG}$. We will refer to the set of partial constituency trees licensed by G as the set of *valid trees* for G, denoted $Trees(G)$.[3]

For example, if $G = (N, \Sigma, P, S)$ is a CFG, the set $Trees(G)$ is defined by Sikkel as the set of finitely branching finite trees in which children of a node have a left-to-right ordering, every node is labelled with a symbol

---

[3]Note that the definitions given in this chapter correspond to the traditional, grammar-driven formulation of parsing schemata. Throughout the book, this theory will always be used as a starting point, but we will depart from it. In Chapter 5 we will relax the constraints related to valid trees, and in Chapter 7 we will define schemata for data-driven parsers that do not use a grammar at all.

in $N \cup \Sigma \cup (\Sigma \times \mathbb{N}) \cup \{\epsilon\}$, and every node u satisfies one of the following conditions:

- u is a leaf,
- u is labelled A, the children of u are labelled $X_1, \ldots, X_n$ and there is a production $A \to X_1 \ldots X_n \in P$,
- u is labelled a and u has a single child labelled (a, j) for some j.

The pairs (a, j) will be referred to as *marked terminals*, and when we deal with a string $a_1 \ldots a_n$, we will usually write $\underline{a}_j$ as an abbreviated notation for (a_j, j). The natural number j is used to indicate the position of the word a in the input, so that the input sentence $a_1 \ldots a_n$ can be viewed as a set of trees of the form $a_j(\underline{a}_j)$ rather than as a string of symbols. From now on, we shall refer to trees of this form as *pseudo-productions*.

Sets of valid trees for other classes of constituency grammars different from CFG can be defined in an analogous way.

Definition 2.8. The set of *marked parse trees* associated with a grammar G, for strings of length n over an alphabet Σ, is the set:

$$\mathcal{P}_G^{(n)} = \{\tau \in Trees(G) \mid \exists a_1 \ldots a_n \in \Sigma^* : root(\tau) = S \wedge yield(\tau) = \underline{a}_1 \ldots \underline{a}_n\}.$$

If the yield of a marked parse tree τ is $yield(\tau) = \underline{a}_1 \ldots \underline{a}_n$, we will say that τ is a marked parse tree for the string $a_1 \ldots a_n$.

Note that a marked parse tree can be defined as a standard parse tree (under the canonical definition found in the parsing literature, as in Aho *et al.* (1986)) for a string of terminal symbols that have been annotated with their positions (i.e., marked terminals). For example, in the particular case of a CFG, we can write pseudo-productions $a_j(\underline{a}_j)$ as context-free productions $a_j \to \underline{a}_j$ (hence their name). With this, we can define the set of marked parse trees associated with G as the set of parse trees for an augmented grammar $G' = (N \cup \Sigma, \underline{\Sigma}, P \cup \underline{P}, S)$, where $\underline{\Sigma} = \Sigma \times \mathbb{N}$ is an alphabet of marked terminals and $\underline{P}$ is the set of all pseudo-productions.

Definition 2.9. Let $Trees(G)$ be the set of trees for some grammar G. An *item set* is any set $\mathcal{I}$ such that $\mathcal{I} \subseteq \Pi(Trees(G)) \cup \{\varnothing\}$, where Π is a partition of the set $Trees(G)$. Each of the elements of an item set is called an *item*. If the item set contains $\varnothing$ as an element, we call this element the *empty item*.

Therefore, items are sets of valid trees for a grammar G.

Definition 2.10. Let G be a grammar, and Π a partition of *Trees*(G). We define the set of *final items* for strings of length n, denoted $\mathcal{F}_{G,\Pi}^{(n)}$, as:

$$\mathcal{F}_{G,\Pi}^{(n)} = \{\iota \in \Pi(\text{ }\text{Trees}(G)) \mid \iota \cap \mathcal{P}_G^{(n)} \neq \varnothing\}$$

Thus, an item is final for strings of length n if it contains a marked parse tree for some string of that length. If we fix a particular string of length n, we can define a set of *correct final items* for that string:

Definition 2.11. Let G be a grammar, Π a partition of *Trees*(G), and $a_1 \ldots a_n$ a string over Σ. The set of *correct final items* for $a_1 \ldots a_n$ is defined by:

$$\mathcal{CF}_{G,\Pi}^{(a_1 \ldots a_n)} = \{\iota \in \mathcal{F}_{G,\Pi}^{(n)} \mid \iota \text{ contains a marked parse tree}$$

$$\text{for the string } a_1 \ldots a_n\}.$$

Definition 2.12. Let G be a grammar, $a_1 \ldots a_n$ a string over an alphabet Σ. An *instantiated parsing system* for G and $a_1 \ldots a_n$ is a deduction system $(\mathcal{I}, \mathcal{H}, D)$ where:

- $\mathcal{I}$ is an item set,
- $\mathcal{F}_{G,\Pi}^{(n)} \subseteq \mathcal{I}$,
- The tree $a_i(\underline{a}_i) \in \mathcal{H}$ for every $i = 1 \ldots n$.

Definition 2.13. Let G be a grammar, Σ an alphabet of terminals. An *uninstantiated parsing system* for G is a triple $(\mathcal{I}, \mathcal{K}, D)$ where $\mathcal{K} : \Sigma^* \to \wp(\wp(\text{Trees}(G)))$ is a function such that $(\mathcal{I}, \mathcal{K}(a_1 \ldots a_n), D)$ is an instantiated parsing system for each $a_1 \ldots a_n \in \Sigma^*$.

In practice, the parsing systems defined here will always use the same function $\mathcal{K}$, in particular:

$$\mathcal{K}(a_1 \ldots a_n) = \{\{a_i(\underline{a}_i)\} \mid 1 \leq i \leq n\}. \tag{2.1}$$

We will use the notation $[a, i-1, i]$ to refer to the items of the form $\{a_i(\underline{a}_i)\}$ that will be used as hypotheses in parsing schemata.

Definition 2.14. A *parsing schema* for a class of grammars $\mathcal{CG}$ is a function that maps each grammar $G \in \mathcal{CG}$ to an uninstantiated parsing system for that grammar.

In practice, to give a precise definition of a parser in terms of a parsing schema, we will need to define the uninstantiated parsing system $(\mathcal{I}, \mathcal{K}, D)$ to which it maps each given grammar G. This implies defining the item set $\mathcal{I}$, the hypotheses-generating function $\mathcal{K}$ and the set of deduction steps D. However, as the function $\mathcal{K}$ is always the same in practice (Equation 2.1), we will often omit it when defining schemata, providing only $\mathcal{I}$ and D explicitly. For clarity, when defining D, we will normally refer to sets of steps of the form:

$$\{((\{y_1,\dots,y_n\},x) \mid Q(y_1,\dots,y_n,x)\}$$

(where Q is a constraint defined over the values of $y_1,\dots,y_n,x$), with the inference rule notation

$$\text{STEP NAME: } \frac{y_1 \quad \cdots \quad y_n}{x} \; Q(y_1,\dots,y_n,x)$$

where the items y_i are called the antecedent items, x is the consequent item and $Q(y_1,\dots,y_n,x)$ is a *side condition*. Side conditions usually refer to grammar productions, being used to link parsing systems to grammars in the definition of a schema.

This notation will be used in all chapters except in Chapter 6, where, due to the frequent use of deduction step expressions in the proofs, we will employ the more compact representation:

$$\{y_1,\dots,y_n \vdash x \mid Q(y_1,\dots,y_n,x)\}.$$

It should also be noted that, in all chapters except Chapter 6, we often use the term "deduction step" to refer to a set of deduction steps expressed by a common inference rule. For example, in Section 2.2, the term "SCANNER step" has been used to refer to the inference rule:

$$\text{SCANNER: } \frac{[A \to \alpha \bullet a\beta, i, j] \quad [a, j, j+1]}{[A \to \alpha a \bullet \beta, i, j+1]}$$

which, strictly speaking, corresponds to a set of deduction steps (see Definition 2.2), one for each possible combination of concrete values for the variables $(a, i, j \dots)$ that appear in its expression. However, making this distinction explicit is only needed for the proofs in Chapter 6 so, for simplicity, the term "step" will be used loosely in the rest of the chapters.

Examples of parsing schemata are those for CYK and Earley's parsing algorithms, which have been given in Figures 2.5 and 2.6. Note that the sets of hypotheses and final items are given for clarity. In general it is not needed to give any of these sets explicitly, as the set of hypotheses comes from the standard function $\mathcal{K}$, and the set of final items can be obtained by applying the general definition of final item given above (Definition 2.10).

2.3.3   *Correctness of parsing schemata*

Apart from providing us with a simple and compact way to represent parsers, as can be seen in these examples, parsing schemata can also be used to prove the correctness of parsers and to establish formal relations between them.

To prove the correctness of a parser, we can define the soundness, completeness and correctness of a parsing schema in terms of that of its resulting deduction systems for different grammars and strings:

Definition 2.15. A parsing schema $ for a class of grammars $\mathcal{CG}$ is said to be *sound (complete, correct)* if, for every grammar $G \in \mathcal{CG}$, $\$(G)$ is an uninstantiated parsing system of the form $(\mathcal{I}, \mathcal{K}, D)$ such that, for every string $a_1 \ldots a_n \in \Sigma^*$, the enhanced deduction system $(\mathcal{I}, \mathcal{K}(a_1 \ldots a_n), \mathcal{F}_{G,\Pi}^{(n)}$, $\mathcal{CF}_{G,\Pi}^{(a_1 \ldots a_n)}, D)$ is sound (complete, correct).

By Definition 2.6, this means that a parsing schema $ is:

- sound: if, in every instantiated parsing system obtained from $, all valid final items are correct,
- complete: if, in every instantiated parsing system obtained from $, all correct final items are valid,
- correct: if it is both sound and complete.

In practice, correctness of parsers will usually be proven by defining a set of *correct items* for every string $a_1 \ldots a_n$, which will contain trees licensed by the grammar and allowed by the parser for that particular string. This set will always be defined so that its intersection with $\mathcal{F}_{G,\Pi}^{(n)}$ is $\mathcal{CF}_{G,\Pi}^{(a_1 \ldots a_n)}$. Under these conditions, soundness and completeness can be shown by proving the stronger (but often easier to prove) claims that all valid items are correct and all correct items are valid. A complete proof of correctness for the Earley parser (Figure 2.6) can be found in Sikkel (1998).

2.3.4   *Relations between parsing schemata*

The formalism of parsing schemata can also be used to establish formal relations between parsers by means of their underlying schemata. These relations can be used not only to compare parsers, but also to transfer formal properties (such as soundness and completeness) from one parser to another.

Sikkel (1994) defines several kinds of relations between schemata, which fall into two broad categories: *generalisation* relations, which are used to obtain more fine-grained versions of parsers or to extend them to a larger class of grammars, and *filtering* relations, which can be seen as the reverse of generalisation and are used to reduce the number of items and/or deduction steps needed in the parsing process. Thus, a generalisation can be used to add functionality to a parser or to obtain more information from it, while filtering can be employed to obtain an optimised variant and reduce time and space requirements.

As with the properties related to correctness, relations between schemata can be defined by first defining relations between parsing systems, and then extending the concept to schemata. We say that an instantiated parsing system $\mathbb{P}_1 = (\mathcal{I}_1, \mathcal{H}_1, D_1)$ can be *generalised* into an instantiated parsing system $\mathbb{P}_2 = (\mathcal{I}_2, \mathcal{H}_2, D_2)$ by the following transformations:

Definition 2.16. (item refinement): We say that $\mathbb{P}_1 \xrightarrow{ir} \mathbb{P}_2$ ($\mathbb{P}_2$ is an item refinement of $\mathbb{P}_1$) if there exists a surjective function $f : \mathcal{I}_2 \to \mathcal{I}_1$ that preserves deduction sequences, i.e., if $f(X_1) \vdash f(X_2) \vdash \ldots \vdash f(X_k)$ in $\mathbb{P}_1$, then $X_1 \vdash X_2 \vdash \ldots \vdash X_k$ in $\mathbb{P}_2$.

Informally, we say that $\mathbb{P}_2$ is an item refinement of $\mathbb{P}_1$ if there is a mapping between items in both parsers such that each item in P_1 is broken into multiple items in P_2, and deductions are preserved.

Definition 2.17. (step refinement): We say that $\mathbb{P}_1 \xrightarrow{sr} \mathbb{P}_2$ ($\mathbb{P}_2$ is a step refinement of $\mathbb{P}_1$) if $\mathcal{I}_1 \subseteq \mathcal{I}_2$ and $\vdash_1^* \subseteq \vdash_2^*$.

Note that a sufficient condition for $\mathbb{P}_1 \xrightarrow{sr} \mathbb{P}_2$ is that $\mathcal{I}_1 \subseteq \mathcal{I}_2$ and $D_1 \subseteq \vdash_2^*$, i.e., $\mathbb{P}_1$ is a step refinement of $\mathbb{P}_2$ if the item set of $\mathbb{P}_1$ is a subset of that of $\mathbb{P}_2$ and every single deduction step in $\mathbb{P}_1$ can be emulated by a sequence of inferences in $\mathbb{P}_2$.

The item and step refinement relations can be extended to parsing schemata: a schema $\mathbb{S}_2$ is an (item, step) refinement of a schema $\mathbb{S}_1$ if, for every grammar G and string $a_1 \ldots a_n$, the instantiated parsing system obtained from $\mathbb{S}_2$ is an (item, step) refinement of that obtained from $\mathbb{S}_1$.

Sikkel (1994) defines a third kind of generalisation relation called extension, that we will not treat here, and shows that generalisation relations are transitive and reflexive.

On the other hand, we say that an instantiated parsing system $\mathbb{P}_1 = (\mathcal{I}_1, \mathcal{H}_1, D_1)$ can be *filtered* into an instantiated parsing system $\mathbb{P}_2 = (\mathcal{I}_2, \mathcal{H}_2, D_2)$ by the following transformations:

Definition 2.18. (static filtering): We say that $\mathbb{P}_1 \xrightarrow{sf} \mathbb{P}_2$ ($\mathbb{P}_2$ is a static filter of $\mathbb{P}_1$) if $\mathcal{I}_2 \subseteq \mathcal{I}_1$ and $D_2 \subseteq D_1$.

Definition 2.19. (dynamic filtering): We say that $\mathbb{P}_1 \xrightarrow{df} \mathbb{P}_2$ ($\mathbb{P}_2$ is a dynamic filter of $\mathbb{P}_1$) if $\mathcal{I}_2 \subseteq \mathcal{I}_1$ and $\vdash_2 \subseteq \vdash_1$.

Definition 2.20. (item contraction): We say that $\mathbb{P}_1 \xrightarrow{ic} \mathbb{P}_2$ ($\mathbb{P}_2$ is an item contraction of $\mathbb{P}_1$) if $\mathbb{P}_2 \xrightarrow{ir} \mathbb{P}_1$.

Definition 2.21. (step contraction): We say that $\mathbb{P}_1 \xrightarrow{sc} \mathbb{P}_2$ ($\mathbb{P}_2$ is a step contraction of $\mathbb{P}_1$) if $\mathbb{P}_2 \xrightarrow{sr} \mathbb{P}_1$.

Dynamic filtering restricts the set of inferences that a parser can make. This can be achieved, for example, by adding antecedents to steps by taking into account context information. For example, if in a particular parsing system we know that an item ι_c can be valid only if another item ι_a is also valid, we can add ι_a as an antecedent of all deduction steps that generate ι_c. In static filtering, which can be seen as a particular case of dynamic filtering, inferences are constrained by directly removing redundant deduction steps. Item and step contraction are the inverse relations to item and step refinement: in item contraction, multiple items in $\mathbb{P}_1$ are collapsed into a single one in $\mathbb{P}_2$; and in step contraction, a sequence of deduction steps in $\mathbb{P}_1$ is replaced by a single one in $\mathbb{P}_2$. All these filtering relations are extended to parsing schemata in the same way as generalisation relations. Filtering relations are reflexive and transitive.

As an example of a generalisation relation, Sikkel (1994) shows that the CYK parsing schema in Figure 2.5 can be generalised to that of a bottom-up Earley algorithm shown in Figure 2.8.

In turn, the schema for an Earley parser, as shown in Figure 2.6, can be obtained from this one by dynamic filtering.

Relations between schemata can be used to transfer formal properties from a schema to another in correctness proofs. For example, it is easy to check that dynamic filtering preserves soundness, and step refinement preserves completeness.

2.4 Advantages of parsing schemata

The formalism of parsing schemata can be used to describe parsing algorithms in a simple and uniform way. Almost all known parsing algorithms

Item set:
$$\mathcal{I} = \{[A \to \alpha \bullet \beta, i, j] \mid A \to \alpha\beta \in P \land 0 \le i \le j\}$$

Initial items (hypotheses):
$$\mathcal{H} = \{[a_i, i-1, i] \mid 0 < i \le n\}$$

Deduction steps:

BU-INITTER: $\dfrac{}{[A \to \bullet\alpha, i, i]} \; A \to \alpha \in P$

SCANNER: $\dfrac{[A \to \alpha \bullet a\beta, i, j] \quad [a, j, j+1]}{[A \to \alpha a \bullet \beta, i, j+1]}$

COMPLETER: $\dfrac{[A \to \alpha \bullet B\beta, i, j] \quad [B \to \gamma\bullet, j, k]}{[A \to \alpha B \bullet \beta, i, k]}$

Final items: $\{[S \to \gamma\bullet, 0, n]\}$

Fig. 2.8 A parsing schema specifying the bottom-up Earley parsing algorithm.

may be described by a schema (nonconstructive parsers, such as those based on neural networks, are exceptions). Representations of algorithms in the form of parsing schemata are more compact than the corresponding pseudocode representations, and they more directly reflect properties of parsers such as their time and space computational complexities.[4]

Parsing schemata are based in the notion of the parsing process as a deduction process, like the "parsing as deduction" approach by Shieber *et al.* (1995); but they add an array of formal concepts and tools that we can use to prove the correctness of parsers and reason about the relations between different algorithms.

Parsing schemata are located in a higher abstraction level than algorithms, since they specify a set of possible operations on intermediate results, but they set no constraints on the order in which to execute these operations or the data structures used to store the results. This high abstraction level makes parsing schemata a useful tool for defining, analysing and comparing different natural language parsers, since we can focus on

---

[4]For example, we can see that the CYK and Earley parsers both run in cubic time with respect to the input length n because their deduction steps handle at most three independent values (i, j and k) ranging from 0 to n.

their logic and study their formal properties while abstracting away from implementation details.

A parsing schema can be seen as a formal specification of a parser's behaviour, which can be implemented in several ways. For example, the pseudocode seen in Figure 2.3 is a simple, ad-hoc implementation of the CYK schema (Figure 2.5). More generally, we can implement any parsing schema following the generic approach of chart parsing (Kay, 1980). However, a generic implementation of a chart parser is not efficient, unless we add indexing structures to provide fast access to items, and these structures need to be specifically tailored to each particular schema. This problem is the focus of the next chapter of this monograph.

PART 2

Compiling and Executing Parsing Schemata

Chapter 3

A compiler for parsing schemata

In this chapter we present a compiler, described by Gómez-Rodríguez *et al.* (2009c), which can be used to automatically obtain efficient Java implementations of parsing algorithms from formal specifications expressed as parsing schemata. The system performs an analysis of the inference rules in the input schemata in order to determine the best data structures and indexes to use, and ensure that the generated implementations are efficient. The system described is general enough to be able to handle all kinds of schemata for different grammar formalisms, such as CFGs and TAGs, and it provides an extensibility mechanism, allowing the user to define custom notational elements. This compiler has proven very useful for analysing, prototyping and comparing natural language parsers in real domains, as will be seen in the empirical studies provided in the following chapters.

3.1 Motivation and goals

Parsing schemata are located at a higher abstraction level than algorithms. As seen in the previous chapter, a schema specifies a set of steps that must be executed and a set of intermediate results that must be obtained when parsing sentences, but it makes no claim about the order in which to execute the steps or the data structures to use for storing the results.

Their abstraction of low-level details makes parsing schemata very useful, allowing us to define parsers in a simple and straightforward way. Comparing parsers, or considering aspects such as their correctness and completeness or their computational complexity, also becomes easier if we think in terms of schemata. However, when we want to test a parser in practice by running it on a computer, we need to implement it in a programming language, so we have to abandon the high abstraction level and worry about implementation details that were irrelevant at the schema level. In this chapter we show how these implementation decisions can be made automatically, making it possible to prototype and test parsers on real grammars and inputs without abandoning the abstraction level provided by the parsing schemata formalism.

To this end, we present a technique that automates the task of implementing parsing schemata, by compiling them to Java language implementations of their corresponding parsers. The input to the compiler is a simple and declarative representation of a parsing schema, which is practically equal to the formal notation that we used previously. For example, a valid schema file describing the Earley parser will be:

```
@goal [ S -> alpha . , 0 , length ]

@step EarleyInitter
----------------------- S -> alpha
[ S -> . alpha , 0 , 0 ]

@step EarleyScanner
[ A -> alpha . a beta , i , j ]
[ a , j , j+1 ]
---------------------------------
[ A -> alpha a . beta , i , j+1 ]

@step EarleyCompleter
[ A -> alpha . B beta , i , j ]
[ B -> gamma . , j , k ]
---------------------------------
[ A -> alpha B . beta , i , k ]

@step EarleyPredictor
[ A -> alpha . B beta , i , j ]
------------------------- B -> gamma
[ B -> . gamma , j , j ]
```

Comparing this file with Figure 2.6, it can be seen that the input to the compiler is a straightforward encoding of the inference rule representation of the schema. Given this input, the system will produce an efficient implementation of the underlying parser (Earley's parser in this case).

This enables us to save a lot of work, since we can test parsing algorithms and check their results and performance just by writing their specification, which is compact, declarative, highly readable and easy to understand and modify, and without having to implement them. This can be useful both for designing new algorithms and for testing existing ones to determine which is the best for a particular application.[1]

3.1.1 *Design goals*

Three main design goals have been taken into account during the development of this system:

- *Declarativity:* The input format for representing schemata to be compiled by the system should be highly declarative, and similar to the formal notation commonly used to represent them. The system should encompass all the operations needed to transform this formal, abstract notation into a functional implementation of the corresponding parser. This allows the parser designer to focus on the semantics of the schema while abstracting from any implementation detail.
- *Generality:* The system should be able to handle all kinds of parsing schemata for CFGs and other formalisms. Note that this requirement is not trivial, since the formal notation for parsing schemata is open, so that any mathematical object could potentially appear in a schema.
- *Efficiency:* Implementations generated by the system should be efficient. Of course, we cannot expect the generated parsers to be as efficient in terms of runtime or memory usage as ad hoc implementations programmed by hand, but they should at least be equivalent in terms of computational complexity.

The declarativity goal has been achieved by defining a simple language to represent schemata, practically equal to the formal notation normally used in the literature, and using it as a starting point to generate Java code, which can in turn be compiled. Therefore, our system works in a similar fashion to parser generators such as Yacc (Johnson, 1975) or JavaCC (Viswanadha, 2006).

The generality goal has been achieved by means of an extensibility mechanism: since it would be impossible to support by default all the different

---

[1]The source code and binaries of the system described in this chapter can be freely downloaded from http://www.grupocole.org/software/COMPAS/

kinds of object that could appear in schemata, we allow the user to easily define and add new object types, which can be handled by the code generator in the same way as the predefined ones.

Finally, the efficiency goal has been achieved by having our system perform a static analysis of input schemata in order to determine the data structures and indexes needed to provide constant-time access to items, and generate code for these indexes.

3.1.2   *Related work*

Although some previous work has been done on systems and techniques that can be used to implement parsing schemata for natural languages, the existing alternatives do not fulfill the features enumerated in Section 3.1.1. The Dyna language (Eisner *et al.*, 2004) can be used to implement some kinds of dynamic programs, but its notation is not as close to the formal notation commonly used to represent schemata as ours. The DyALog system (de la Clergerie, 2005) can be used to compile and run tabular parsers for several grammatical formalisms, but the specifications are based on logical push-down automata and can be complex and unnatural, especially for purely bottom-up parsers which do not use a left-to-right strategy to process the input string. None of these systems is specifically oriented to the implementation of parsing schemata.

Shieber *et al.* (1995) introduce a technique to execute parsing schemata with a deductive parsing engine programmed in Prolog. However, this requires the conversion of items and deduction steps to the Prolog language. Moreover, if we want the implementations generated with this technique to be efficient, we need to provide item indexing code by hand, so we have to abandon the abstraction level of schemata and take implementation details into account. Without this indexing system, the Prolog interpreter will perform a large amount of CALL and REDO operations, distorting the results when working with large grammars (Alonso and Díaz, 2003b; Díaz and Alonso, 2000).

Basic parsing schemata can also be implemented in Datalog, a variant of Prolog commonly used for deductive databases. The subject of obtaining efficient implementations of Datalog programs has been studied in the literature (McAllester, 1999; Liu and Stoller, 2003). However, the constraints imposed by Datalog disallow some useful extensions to parsing schemata, such as feature structure unification (Carpenter, 1992), that can be used in this system.

3.2   System architecture

Our parsing schemata compiler is composed of several different subsystems:

- The "sparser" (schema parser) subsystem reads input parsing schemata, parses them and transforms them into an internal tree representation, which will be the input to the code generation step. This subsystem is a compiler generated by the JavaCC parser generator (Viswanadha, 2006).

- The "generator" (code generator) subsystem is the most complex part of the schema compiler. This subsystem takes the tree representation produced by "sparser" as input, and uses it to generate the Java classes implementing the algorithm described by the schema. This subsystem is divided into several parts, and each of them is used to generate a part of the implementation: deduction step execution, item management, indexing, etc.

- The "eparser" (element parser) subsystem guarantees the *generality* property discussed previously by providing an extensibility mechanism which can be used to compile schemata with non-predefined elements. As explained above, parsing schemata have an open notation, so any mathematical object could appear as part of an item. Therefore, it would be impossible for our system to recognise *a priori* any kind of item that could potentially appear in an arbitrary schema. The "eparser" subsystem allows the user to define her own kinds of notational elements and use them in schemata, the use of Java's dynamic class loading facilities eliminating the need for recompilation in order to add new element types.

These three systems interact to transform a parsing schema into an executable parser: the "sparser" constructs a tree representation of the schema file, calling the "eparser" for help whenever it needs to parse an user-defined element. The "generator" then takes this tree and transforms it into Java source code, which includes a buildfile to compile it to bytecode. The result of this compilation is a Java executable which can read a grammar from a file and parse input sentences with that grammar, using the algorithm described in the schema.

More details about each of the subsystems will be given in the following sections.[2]

3.3 Generated code

Before going into detail about the design of our code-generating system, we first need to think about the design of the code it will have to generate. The structure of this code must be generic enough to be applicable to any schema, but it must also allow us to include particular optimisations for each schema, to enable us to achieve the efficiency goal.

A deductive parsing engine such as the one described by Shieber *et al.* (1995) fulfills the first condition, providing a generic means of implementing any parsing schema. However, it is not efficient unless we can access items in constant time, and the way to achieve this is different in each particular schema. The idea of compiling parsing schemata allows us to generate schema-specific code to attain efficiency.

In particular, our compilation process proceeds according to the following principles:

- A class is generated for each deduction step. The classes for deduction steps implement a common interface with an `apply` method which tries to apply the step to a given item. If the step is in fact applicable to the item, the method returns the new items obtained from the inference. In order to achieve this functionality, the method works as follows: initially, it checks if the given item matches any of the step's antecedents. For every successful match found, the method searches for combinations of previously-generated items in order to satisfy the rest of the antecedents. Each combination of items satisfying all antecedents corresponds to an instantiation of the step variables which is used to generate an item from the consequent.
- Code is generated to read an input grammar and create an instance of a deduction step class for each possible set of values satisfying its side conditions. For example, a distinct instance of the Earley Predictor step will be created at runtime for each grammar rule of the form $B \rightarrow \gamma \in P$, which is specified in the step's side condition. Deduction step instances

---

[2] A high-level description of the system is provided here, as low-level design and implementation issues fall outside the scope of this book. Readers interested in a more detailed description, including samples of generated code, should refer to Gómez-Rodríguez *et al.* (2009c)

are lightweight objects, so large grammars needing a large amount of instances can be handled.

- The execution of deduction steps in the generated code is coordinated by a deductive parsing engine, which can be seen as an implementation of the dynamic programming approach that underlies chart parsing (Kay, 1980). Since this is a generic algorithm, the parsing engine will always be the same and we do not need to generate it. The engine works as described by the pseudocode in Figure 3.1.

```
     steps = set { deduction step instances };
  2  itemSet = set { initial items };
     agenda = list [ initial items ];
  4  for each deduction step with an empty
     antecedent (s) in steps
  6    result = s.apply ([]);
       for each item (ι) in result
  8      if ι ∉ itemSet
           add ι to itemSet;
 10        enqueue ι into agenda;
       remove s from steps;
 12  while agenda not empty
       currentItem = agenda.removeFirst ();
 14    for each deduction step applicable
       to currentItem (p) in steps
 16      result = p.apply (currentItem);
         for each item (ι) in result
 18        if ι ∉ itemSet
             add ι to itemSet;
 20          enqueue ι into agenda;
     return itemSet;
```

Fig. 3.1 Pseudocode for the generic deductive engine.

The algorithm works with the set of all items that have been generated (either as initial hypotheses or as a result of the application of deduction steps) and an agenda, implemented as a queue, containing the items with which we have not yet tried to trigger new deductions. When the agenda is emptied, all possible items will have been generated, and the presence or absence of final items in the item set at this point indicates

whether or not the input sentence belongs to the language defined by
the grammar.

- An **ItemHandler** class is generated to provide efficient access to items.
  This class contains indexing code specific to each schema, since the best
  choice of indexes will depend on the particular features of each. Additionally, a **StepHandler** class is generated to provide efficient access to
  deduction steps.

3.4   Reading schemata

As explained above, the goal of the "sparser" subsystem is reading an input
file with the description of a parsing schema and converting it to an internal
tree representation holding the data that will be passed to the next subsystem, the code generator. The notation used to describe schemata is very
simple, and practically identical to the formal notation commonly used to
define them. More concretely, the schema file format is the one described
by the Extended Backus-Naur Form (EBNF) grammar in Figure 3.2. Note
that C-style comments (of the form /* ... */) are also allowed in schema
files, although not reflected in the EBNF grammar.

As we can see, there are two symbols in the EBNF grammar (*element*
and *element_definition*) which are undefined. This is because their definition will vary depending on the custom notational elements defined by
the user. Actually, from the point of view of the "sparser", the definition
of these symbols is a generic regular expression accepting any string without spaces or commas which cannot be confused with other components of
the schema file. When the "sparser" finds one of these strings in a position where an *element* or *element_definition* is expected, it will delegate its
analysis to the "eparser" module, which deals with elements and element
definitions. In the remainder of this chapter, we will use the word *element*
to refer to any object that can appear as part of an item.

The general structure of a schema file consists of an optional section
with *element definitions*, a second optional section containing *options*, a
series of *deduction steps*, and a series of *goals* or final items. An example
of a schema file containing all these sections is shown in Figure 3.3.

As we can see, the element definition section is used to define the types of
element that will appear in the parsing schema's deduction steps. Element

Schema ::= [ElementDefinitionList] [OptionList]
    { StepName StepDescription }
    { "**@goal**" GoalDescription }
ElementDefinitionList ::=
    "**@begin_elements**" { ElementDefinition } "**@end_elements**"
ElementDefinition ::= *element_definition*
OptionList ::=
    { "**@begin_options**" Option "**@end_options**" }
Option ::= "**@option**" key value
StepName ::= "**@step**" ID
StepDescription ::=
    Antecedent Separator Conditions Consequent
GoalDescription ::= Antecedent
Antecedent ::= { ItemDescription }
Separator ::= { "-" }
Consequent ::= ItemDescription
ItemDescription ::= "[" ElementList "]"
ElementList ::= [ElementWrapper { , ElementWrapper }]
ElementWrapper ::= Element
Conditions ::= ElementList
Element ::= *element*

Fig. 3.2　EBNF grammar for parsing schema files.

definitions map regular expressions to Java classes and methods. For example, the element definition

element.StringPosition:nonGroundFromString:[i–n]

means that, whenever a lower case letter in the range $i \ldots n$ is found in an item, an instance of the `StringPosition` class must be created by invoking the method with signature `public static StringPosition nonGroundFromString(String s)` in the `element.StringPosition` class. This job is done by the "eparser", as mentioned earlier. Note that the reference to "non-ground" in the method name means that the generated instance will represent a variable. Constant (ground) string positions are defined in the example by a different regular expression (`[0-9]+`).

In this case, element definitions are shown only for explanatory purposes as all the elements used in the Earley schema are already predefined in the system, so we do not need to explicitly redefine them. Explicit element definitions are only needed to include new kinds of elements defined by the

@begin_elements
element.Symbol:nonGroundFromString:[A–RT–Za–ho–z]
element.Symbol:groundFromString:S
element.RuleWrapper:fromString:[A–Za–z \.]+->[A–Za–z \.]*
element.StringPosition:nonGroundFromString:[i–n]
element.StringPosition:groundFromString:[0–9]+
element.SumOfPositionsExpression:fromString:[0–9i–k\+\–]+
element.SymbolSequence:fromString:((alpha)|(beta)|(gamma))
element.SpecialElement:fromString:\.
@end_elements

@begin_options
@option outputItems allItems
@end_options

@step EarleyInitter
------------------------------ S -> alpha
[S -> . alpha , 0 , 0]

@step EarleyScanner
[A -> alpha . a beta , i , j]
[a , j , j+1]

[A -> alpha a . beta , i , j+1]

@step EarleyCompleter
[A -> alpha . B beta , i , j]
[B -> gamma . , j , k]

[A -> alpha B . beta , i , k]

@step EarleyPredictor
[A -> alpha . B beta , i , j]
-------------------------------- B -> gamma
[B -> . gamma , j , j]

@goal [S -> alpha . , 0 , length]

Fig. 3.3   A schema file.

user, or for overriding the default regular expressions associated with the predefined elements.

The options section is used to parametrise the resulting parser. In the example in Figure 3.3, we pass an option to the system indicating that we want the generated parser to output all items obtained for each sentence (if no option were used, only the goal items would be output). Options can also be used to dynamically change the type of agenda or deductive engine. For example, for error-repair parsing, we could need an agenda implemented as a priority queue instead of a standard queue, so that the items with smaller error count could be used first. In order to use such an agenda, we would use a line

@option agendaClass agenda.PriorityQueueAgenda

and define an `agenda.PriorityQueueAgenda` class implementing a simple `Agenda` interface. The content of `@option` lines is also accessible via a simple API from the generated code, so that user-defined classes such as this agenda can also use `@option` lines for further parametrisation.

After these optional sections, we define the deduction steps of our schema in the simple notation mentioned in Section 3.1, and then specify the format of the final items with one or more `@goal` lines. If items matching a `@goal` specification are found by the generated parser, the parsing process is considered to have been successful and these final items are output.

To implement the "sparser" subsystem, the JavaCC (Viswanadha, 2006) compiler compiler has been used. This tool generates an LL(k) compiler from a grammar annotated with Java code. In this case the code is simple, since it only has to build a tree which will be passed as input to the code generator. One of the advantages of using an LL(k)-based compiler compiler such as JavaCC is that it provides helpful error messages by default, thus making it easy to locate syntax errors in parsing schema files.

The tree produced by the "sparser" is nothing more than a hierarchical representation of the schema, where the schema itself, deduction steps, antecedents, etc. are represented by tree nodes. The leaf nodes in this tree are the components of items that we have called *elements*, and are instantiated by the "eparser".

3.5   The code generation process

The "generator" subsystem is the most complex and important component of the parsing schema compiler. From a tree representation of a parsing schema generated by the "sparser" and "eparser", this component generates Java code for the classes implementing the corresponding algorithm. For the sake of simplicity, we will use the parsing schema corresponding to the CYK (Kasami, 1965; Younger, 1967) bottom-up parser in some of the code generation examples. This schema, which has been shown in Figure 2.5, is one of the simplest that we can find in practice, having fewer steps and fewer kinds of element than Earley's, and can be defined in the compiler as follows:

```
@step  Unary
[ a , i , i+1 ]
--------------------- A -> a
[ A , i , i+1 ]

@step  Binary
[ B , i , j ]
[ C , j , k ]
--------------------- A -> B C
[ A , i , k ]

@goal  [S,0,length]
```

3.5.1   *Element types*

As we have seen in the previous section, the leaf nodes of a schema tree contain the basic components of items, called elements. Since we want our system to be able to work with all kinds of parsing schemata, and any mathematical object could potentially appear in the representation of an item, we have implemented an extensibility mechanism that allows the user to define custom elements if the predefined element classes do not suffice to represent a particular schema. This extensibility mechanism works by allowing the user to define regular expressions to represent new kinds of elements, and associate them with Java classes. The problem is that the code generator should be able to handle these user-defined elements and use them successfully to generate efficient code. In order to achieve this, our system requires element classes to follow a simple contract, providing the services needed by the code generator. This basic contract comes from the idea that any element appearing in a schema can be classified into one of four basic types:

- *Simple Elements:* Atomic, unstructured elements which can be instantiated or not in a given moment. When simple elements are instantiated, they take a single value from a set of possible values, which may be bounded or not. Values can be converted to indexing keys. Examples of simple elements are grammar symbols, integers, string positions, probabilities, the dot in Earley items, etc.

  In order to define a new simple element class, the user must implement a `SimpleElement` interface, providing a method to obtain a Java code representation of the element's value, if it has one. For example, the Java code representation of an element representing a string position and holding the value 1 is the string "StringPosition.groundFromValue(1)", which calls a static method returning an integer element with the value 1.[3] In addition to this method, simple element classes should implement a method returning an integer indexing key, so that the corresponding elements can be used for item indexing.

- *Expression Elements:* These elements denote expressions which take simple elements or other expressions as arguments. For example, i+1 is an expression element representing the addition of two string positions. Feature structures and logic terms are also represented by this kind of element. When all simple elements in an expression are instantiated to concrete values, the expression will be treated as a simple element whose value is obtained by applying the operation it defines (for example, summation). For the code generator to be able to do this, a Java expression must be provided as part of the expression element type definition, so that, for example, sums of string positions appearing in schemata can be converted to Java integer sums in the

---

[3]Using a static method such as this one instead of creating a new instance ("new StringPosition(1)") is an optimisation. A parser may use millions of items, each of them with several elements, so all the predefined element classes are programmed in such a way that the generated code uses multiple references to the same instances instead of multiple instances. Apart from the memory saved with this optimisation, it must also be noted that item comparison is one of the main performance bottlenecks in generated parsers, and this optimisation allows such comparisons to be performed at the reference level, which is much faster than dereferencing the elements and comparing their values.

generated implementation. Expressions have been used to implement unification of feature structures (Carpenter, 1992), left-corner relations (Rosenkrantz and Lewis II, 1970), etc.

- *Composite Elements:* Composite elements represent sequences of elements whose length must be finite and known. Composite elements are used to structure items. For instance, the Earley item $[A \rightarrow \alpha \bullet B\beta, i, j]$ is represented as a composite element with three components, the first being in turn a composite element representing a grammar rule.

  The interface for this kind of element only requires the user to provide methods returning the number of children (sub-elements) of a composite, and to get the ith child.

- *Sequence Elements:* These elements denote sequences of elements of any kind whose length is finite, but only becomes known when the sequence is instantiated to a concrete value. The strings α, β and γ appearing in the Earley schema are examples of sequence elements, being able to represent symbol strings of any length.

  The interface `SequenceElement` only requires the user to provide a method returning a type (class) for the elements in the sequence. It is possible to define sequences holding elements of multiple types by returning a common superclass of the allowed element classes.

3.5.2 *Deduction step classes*

Each of the deduction steps in the schema, represented by `@step` specifications in the input file, produces a class implementing the `DeductionStep` interface. Goal specifications (`@goal`) also produce deduction step classes, as if they were steps with a single antecedent and no consequent, since in this way the indexing and matching techniques used to find items matching antecedents can be reused to find the goal items in an item set.

The main function of deduction step classes is to provide a method that, given a particular item, generates all the items that the step can deduce using that item as an antecedent, and previously generated items for the rest of the antecedents. This functionality is provided by a

List apply (Object[] item)

method in the `DeductionStep` interface, which will be implemented by each concrete deduction step class created by the code generator.

3.5.3 *Deduction step code generation*

The two most complex methods in a deduction step class are the constructor and the aforementioned `apply` method. If a deduction step has a production rule as a side condition, the constructor must check if a rule passed as a parameter matches the condition, and initialise the corresponding variables. Therefore, the constructor of the step

```
@step Binary
[ B , i , j ]
[ C , j , k ]
---------------------- A -> B C
[ A , i , k ]
```

will check whether the parameter is an array of length 3, and initialise the variables A, B and C in the step to the concrete values found in the parameter. Therefore, if the initialisation parameter is the concrete rule $S \to NP \ \ VP$, the constructor will assign $A = S$, $B = NP$ and $C = VP$.

On the other hand, the `apply` method returns all the items which can be generated using the one passed as a parameter as an antecedent, and previously generated items for the rest of the antecedents. As an example, suppose that we have the instance of the Binary step created with the rule $S \to NP \ \ VP$, and we receive the item $[NP, 0, 2]$ as a parameter. The operations needed to implement the `apply` method are the following:

- Match the given item with the specification $[B, i, j]$ where the value of B must be NP and i, j can take any value.
- If it matches, assign particular values to the variables i and j (in this case, the matching is successful, and we assign $i = 0$ and $j = 2$).
- Search for *all* the items in the item set that are of the form $[C, j, k]$ where the value of C is VP and the value of j is 2. That is, search for the items of the form $[VP, 2, ?]$.
- For each of these, generate a conclusion item $[S, 0, k]$ with the corresponding value of k.
- Repeat all the steps for the other antecedent, i.e., match the given item with the specification $[C, j, k]$ and then search for items satisfying $[B, i, j]$. In our particular case, the item $[NP, 0, 2]$ does not match the second antecedent.

Putting it all together, in order to generate code for the constructor and `apply` methods, we need a way to obtain code for the following operations:

- Match a given item with a specification. The specification may come from an antecedent or a side condition, and is known at schema compile time, while the item is only known at runtime.
- Search for all items matching a specification known at compile time.
- Use a specification to initialise step variables to values taken from an item.
- Generate a conclusion item from step attribute values.

The code for all these operations can be generated in a similar way if we take into account that all of them traverse an item and are directed by a specification. We have used the Visitor design pattern (Gamma *et al.*, 1995) to structure this part of the code generator. Code generating visitors traverse the parts of the schema tree corresponding to item specifications. There is a different visitor for each basic operation in the generated code (matching, assigning values, etc.) and each visitor has a different behaviour for each kind of node (`SimpleElement`, `ExpressionElement`...) in the specification. We also need to keep track of which variables in specifications have a concrete value at each part of the code and which are uninstantiated, so this information is kept by an external structure which can be queried by the visitor.

The visitors themselves are also stateful, since they keep code for accessing parts of items as an internal state. This is because some information generated when matching an element can be needed to generate the matching code for subsequent elements.

3.5.4 *Search specifications*

In the previous section we mentioned that one of the operations the `apply` method needs to perform is to search for all the items matching a specification known at compile time. While the rest of the operations that we have mentioned work on a single item, this one must access the item set. This operation is not really implemented by the deduction step classes, but in an `ItemHandler` class that provides efficient access to items by using indexes specifically generated for each schema.

The `ItemHandler` class provides three services: adding an item to the item set including it in the corresponding indexes; checking whether a given item is present or not in the item set; and returning all items verifying certain characteristics. All of these methods need indexing techniques in order to work efficiently.

In order to call the third method, which is the one used by `apply` to search for antecedent items, we need a way of specifying constraints on items, such as the constraint specifying that only items of the form $[VP, 2, ?]$ must be returned by the search in our previous example. A simple and efficient way to do this is by representing search constraints like items, but using `null` values as placeholders for the unconstrained elements. We call such a representation of constraints on items a *search specification*.

3.6 Indexing

If we wish our generated parsers to achieve the efficiency goal mentioned in Section 3.1.1, access to items and deduction steps must be efficient (Gómez-Rodríguez *et al.*, 2007a). As we have seen in the previous section, when we execute a step we often need to search the item set for all the items satisfying a given specification. In order to maintain the theoretical complexity of parsing schemata, we must provide constant-time access to items. In this case, each single deduction takes place in constant time, and the worst-case complexity is bounded by the maximum possible number of deduction step executions: all complexity in the generated implementation is inherent to the schema.

As an example, the theoretical complexity of the CYK parsing algorithm is $O(n^3)$, where n is the length of the input. This is because the most complex step in this algorithm is

```
@step Binary
[ B , i , j ]
[ C , j , k ]
---------------------- A -> B C
[ A , i , k ]
```

which can be executed on at most $O(n^3)$ combinations of antecedents, since positions i, j and k take values between 0 and n and symbols A, B, C come from a finite set.

As we have seen, the `apply` method that executes this step in the generated code matches the item received as a parameter with the specification $[B, i, j]$ and then searches for all items in the item set of the form $[C, j, k]$ for fixed values of C and j. If we can obtain a list of these items in constant time, the `apply` method will run in $O(n)$ (since we have to traverse this list and generate a conclusion for each of the items),[4] and it will generate $O(n)$ items. Since the total number of items generated in a CYK parser is $O(n^2)$ (items have two indexes ranging from 0 to n), this `apply` method will be invoked $O(n^2)$ times during the execution of the parser. Therefore, the total complexity is $O(n^2) \times O(n) = O(n^3)$, matching the theoretical computational complexity of CYK. However, if we had no indexing and the search for items were sequential, the `apply` method would run in $O(n^2)$ (there are $O(n^2)$ items to search among) and the generated implementation for CYK would be $O(n^4)$.

3.6.1 *Static analysis and index descriptors*

Generating indexes that can provide constant-time access to items is not a trivial task, since a generic indexing technique does not suffice. The elements by which we should index items in order to achieve efficiency vary among schemata. For example, the CYK parser's deduction steps perform two different kinds of searches for items: searches for items of the form $[C, j, ?]$ (where ? can take any value) and searches for items of the form $[B, ?, j]$. Thus, in order to ensure that these searches access items in constant time, we need at least two indexes: one by the first and second components and another one by the first and third. Different parsing schemata, as well as different steps in the same schema, will have different needs. Therefore, in order to generate indexing code, we must take the distinct features of each schema into account.

Two distinct kinds of item indexes are generated for each schema. Situations like the one just mentioned as an example, where it is necessary to search for items conforming to a given specification, are handled by *search indexes*. On the other hand, *existence indexes* are used to efficiently check whether an item exists in the item set.

To illustrate how the adequate indexes can be determined by a static analysis of the schema that can be performed at compilation time (Gómez-Rodríguez *et al.*, 2007c), we analyse the general case where we have a deduction step of the form

---

[4] In this reasoning about complexity, we are only taking into account the first part of the `apply` method, which matches the parameter item with the first specification and then searches for items conforming to the second. However, if we apply an analogous reasoning to the second part of the method (i.e. applying matching to the second specification and searching to the first), we obtain that the second part is also $O(n)$, so the method is globally $O(n)$.

$$\frac{[a,d,e,g] \qquad [b,d,f,g]}{(consequent)} \; c \; e \; f \; g$$

where each lower case letter represents the set of elements (be them grammar symbols, string positions or other entities) appearing at particular positions in the step, so that a stands for the set of elements appearing only in the first antecedent item, e represents those appearing in the first antecedent and side condition, g those appearing in both antecedents and side condition, and the rest of the letters represent the other possible combinations as can be seen in the step. Note that any deduction step with two antecedent items can be represented in this way (taking into account that some of the element sets a, b... may be empty, and that the ordering of elements inside items is irrelevant to this discussion). In this example, we consider only two antecedents for the sake of simplicity, but the technique is general and can be applied to deduction steps with an arbitrary number of antecedents.

In this case, the following indexes are needed:

- One search index for each antecedent, using as keys the elements appearing in that antecedent which are also present in the side condition *or* in the other antecedent. Therefore, a search index is generated by using (d,e,g) as keys in order to recover items of the form $[a,d,e,g]$ when d, e and g are known and a can take any value; and another index using the keys (d,f,g) is generated and used to recover items of the form $[b,d,f,g]$ when d, f and g are known. The first index allows us to efficiently search for items matching the first antecedent when we have already found a match for the second, while the second one can be used to search for items matching the second antecedent when we have started our deduction by matching the first one.

- One existence index using as keys all the elements appearing in the consequent, since all of them are instantiated to concrete values when the step successfully generates a consequent item. This index is used to check whether the generated item already exists in the item set before adding it.

As this index generation process must be applied to all deduction steps in the schema, the number of indexes needed to guarantee constant-time access to items increases linearly with the number of steps. However, in practice we do not usually need to generate all of these indexes, since many of them are repeated or redundant. For example, if we suppose that the sets e and f in our last example contain the same number and type of elements, and elements are ordered in the same way in both antecedents, the two search indexes generated would in fact be the same, and our compiler would detect this fact and generate only one. In practical cases, the items used by different steps of a parsing schema usually have the same structure (see, for example, the first antecedents of SCANNER, COMPLETER and PREDICTOR, or the consequents of SCANNER and COMPLETER, on the Earley schema shown in Figure 2.6). Thus, in more complex schemata, indexes can usually be shared among several deduction steps, so the amount of indexes generated is kept small.

The static analysis that has just been explained in an abstract way is carried out in a more procedural fashion by the compiler, by gathering information during deduction step code generation. To decide which search indexes are needed, a data structure called a *search descriptor* is generated whenever the system generates the code for searching items by specification in a deduction step's `apply` method. For example, when the code generator produces the code for a search in the CYK parser using the search specification $[C, j, null]$, it will also internally create a tree structure of the form [`Symbol` , `StringPosition` , `null`]. This structure, called a *search descriptor*, specifies the structure of the items that are searched for and the positions and classes of elements which take concrete values in the search specification.

Note that components of search specifications and descriptors take null or non-null values depending on which of the sets $(a,b\ldots)$ seen in the abstract description contains the element that generated each of them. However, the code generator does not need to reason with these sets explicitly. Instead, it works with the list of variables that have been assigned concrete values in each point of the `apply` method where a search is needed. The division into the aforementioned sets arises in a natural way from this procedure.

Search descriptors from all the deduction steps in the input schema are gathered into a list, and used to decide which indexes to create. It will be convenient to create indexes by non-null components of search descriptors that can be used for indexing (i.e. belonging to a class that provides a method to obtain an indexing key, see Section 3.5.1). The simplest way to do this, and the one corresponding to the general description provided above, is by creating an index for every search descriptor, indexing by all components meeting these conditions. With this approach, the presence of our search descriptor [`Symbol` , `StringPosition` , `null`] means that we should generate an index on the first and second components of items, and the other search descriptor obtained from the same step (which is [Symbol , null , StringPosition]) means that we should generate an index on the first and third components.

The decisions that the system makes about the indexes it needs to create are encoded into objects called *index descriptors*, which are lists containing the positions of elements used for indexing and the type of indexes that are going to be used. For example, an index descriptor for our first index in this case could be [0:hash,1:hash], meaning that we are going to use the elements in positions 0 and 1 as keys for hash indexes.[5] The decision as to which particular data structures to use for indexes (hashes, arrays...) can be configured as an option, either by setting a global default or by configuring it for each particular element class.

3.6.2 *Generation of indexing code*

Once we have index descriptors for all the search indexes we will need, we can proceed to generate indexing code. This code is located in the ItemHandler class which, as mentioned in section 3.5.4, provides three services: finding all items verifying a given specification (getBySpecification); checking whether a given item exists in the set (exists); and adding an item to the set (add).

The getBySpecification service uses *search indexes*, which are obtained from index descriptors computed as described in the previous section. The exists service uses *existence indexes*. These are obtained in the same way as search indexes, but their search descriptors come from a full consequent item instead of from a search specification, and have no null values. The add service must use both search indexes and existence indexes, since every item added to the set must be accessible to the other two services.

Although the functionality of each of the three services is different, their implementation can be done in such a way that a significant part of the code is common to all of them, and we can take advantage of this fact during code generation. In particular, we can describe the three methods with the high-level pseudocode in Figure 3.4.

---

[5] Note that items are trees, not lists, so in a general case the position of an element cannot be denoted by a single integer. Positions are represented by lists of integers. For example, when working with Earley items of the form $[A \to \alpha \bullet B\beta, i, j]$, we can have a search descriptor [[null,null,null,Symbol,null],null,IntElement], and the corresponding index descriptor for an index by B and j would be [[0,3]:hash,[2]:hash].

```
method ( item or specification )
{
        test whether parameter conforms to search
        descriptor associated with index 1;
        if it does
        {
                access index 1 using parameter;
                process obtained list;
        }
        (...)
        test whether parameter conforms to search
        descriptor associated with index d;
        if it does
        {
                access index d using parameter;
                process obtained list;
        }
}
```

Fig. 3.4 Pseudocode of the services provided by the item handler.

Note that, although we mention search descriptors in the pseudocode, search descriptors are not accessible from the code, they are only used to generate it. Each of the d tests in the pseudocode corresponds to a different series of conditional statements that check if the parameter conforms to the structure expressed by a search descriptor, but they do not use the descriptor itself as its constraints are directly compiled into code. Also note that, although the conditions and bodies of the **if** statements are expressed in an uniform way in the pseudocode, they are different in the code, since they are generated from different search descriptors. This is the reason why the pseudocode is expressed as a series of conditional statements, and not as a loop.

The main conceptual difference between the three methods is the meaning of "process obtained list". In the case of **add**, processing the list means initialising it if it is null and adding the parameter item to it. In the case of **exists**, it consists of checking if the list is empty. Finally, in the case of **getBySpecification**, the method will simply return the obtained list.

In reality, the parts appearing as common in the pseudocode are also slightly different, but the differences are small enough to allow us to reuse most of the generator code.

The strategy for generating the code for these methods is similar to the one used in step classes. In this case, instead of traversing an element tree, we traverse a search descriptor, generating code at each node. We do not use the Visitor design pattern because the behaviour at each node depends on its content rather than its class. The generation of index addressing code has a quite complex implementation, due to the support for various data structures, nested indexes and the handling of null values. A description of these implementation details is outside the scope of this book, information about them can be found in Gómez-Rodríguez *et al.* (2009c); Gómez-Rodríguez (2009).

3.6.3 *Deduction step indexing*

Apart from the indexes on items explained above, our system also includes *deduction step indexes* in the generated parsers. These indexes are used to optimise the process of deciding which deduction step instances can be applicable to a given item. Instead of blindly trying to apply every step and let the pattern-matching processes discard those not matching the processed item, we use the index to obtain a set of potentially applicable step instances, the rest (which are known not to be useful) being directly discarded.

As particular instances of deduction steps in a schema are usually tied to grammar rules, deduction step indexes do not improve computational complexity with respect to string length (which is already optimised by item indexing), but they can improve complexity with respect to grammar size. This is usually an important factor for performance in natural language applications, since it is common to use grammars with thousands of rules.

Deduction step indexes are generated by taking into account step variables which take a value during the creation of a step instance, i.e. variables appearing on side conditions. For instance, for the general deduction step shown in section 3.6.1, one deduction step index would be created for each antecedent, using as keys the elements appearing both in the side condition *and* in that particular antecedent. Therefore, two indexes are generated using the values (e, g) and (f, g). These indexes are used to restrict the set of deduction step instances applicable to items. As each instance corresponds to a particular instantiation of the side conditions, in this case each step instance will have different values for c, e, f and g. When the deductive engine asks for the set of steps applicable to a given item $[w, x, y, z]$, the deduction step handler will use the values of (y, z) as keys in order to return only instances with matching values of (e, g) or (f, g). Instances of the steps where these values do not match can be safely discarded, as we know that our item will not match any of both antecedents. Note that it is not necessary to use the value c as an indexing key. Since it does not appear on any of the antecedents, it will not affect the applicability of the step to any item.

3.7 Discussion

In this chapter, we have described the design and implementation of a working compiler which is able to automatically transform formal specifications of parsing algorithms (expressed as parsing schemata) into efficient implementations of the corresponding parsers. The system's source code can be downloaded from http://www.grupocole.org/software/COMPAS/.

The compiler takes a simple representation of a parsing schema as input and uses it to produce optimised Java code for the parsing algorithm it describes. The system performs a static analysis of the input schema in order to determine the adequate indexes and data structures that will provide constant-time access to items, ensuring the efficiency of the generated implementation.

The system is general enough to be applicable to different grammatical formalisms, and has been used to generate parsers for CFGs and TAGs. In addition, we provide an extensibility mechanism that allows the user to add new kinds of elements to schemata apart from the predefined ones. This same mechanism has been used to provide predefined extensions like those for feature structure unification and probabilistic parsing.

The ability to easily produce parsers from schemata is very useful for the design, analysis and comparison of parsing algorithms, as it allows us to test them and check their results and performance without having to implement them in a programming language. The implementations generated by our system are efficient enough to be used as prototypes in real-life domains (Gómez-Rodríguez *et al.*, 2007d), so they provide a quick means of evaluating several parsing algorithms in order to find the best one for a particular application. This is especially useful in practice, since different parsing algorithms can be better suited to different grammars and application domains.

The following chapters of this book provide practical examples of how the described system can be used to prototype, test and evaluate parsing algorithms: we use it to generate implementations of different parsers for CFGs and TAGs, and to perform empirical comparisons of these algorithms on real-sized grammars.

Chapter 4

Practical complexity of constituency parsers

In the last chapter, we presented a compiler able to automatically obtain efficient implementations of parsing algorithms from their formal specifications expressed as parsing schemata. In this chapter, we show how this system can be used to prototype different parsing algorithms for constituency-based grammar formalisms. We evaluate these algorithms empirically, both on practical grammars and corpora, and on artificially-generated examples.

First, implementations are generated for three well-known parsing algorithms for CFGs, and they are compared by using them to parse sentences with three different grammars taken from real-life corpora. The obtained results show how the choice of the most suitable algorithm for a particular application depends on the characteristics of the particular grammar being used (Gómez-Rodríguez et al., 2006d).

Second, implementations are also generated with our system for four different TAG parsers, and they are used to analyse natural language sentences under the XTAG English Grammar (XTAG Research Group, 2001). This allows us to compare the empirical performance of these algorithms under a real-life, wide-coverage feature-based TAG (Gómez-Rodríguez et al., 2006b). To the best of our knowledge, this is the first such empirical comparison of TAG parsers as previous studies in the literature (Díaz and Alonso, 2000) are based on "toy" grammars with a small number of rules, so their results are hardly extrapolable to practical applications.

The claim that performance results for small TAGs do not predict those for large grammars will be further substantiated in the last part of the chapter, where we use experiments based on artificially-generated grammars to provide an evaluation of the influence of grammar size on the performance of TAG parsers (Gómez-Rodríguez et al., 2006a,c), as well as a study of the practical overhead caused by using TAGs to parse context-free languages.

Table 4.1   Information about the CFGs used in the experiments: total
number of symbols, nonterminals, terminals, production rules, distribution
of rule lengths and average length of the right-hand side of productions.

	SUSANNE	ALVEY	DELTRA
Symbols ($|N \cup \Sigma|$)	1,921	498	310
Nonterminals ($|N|$)	1,524	266	282
Terminals ($|\Sigma|$)	397	232	28
Rules ($|P|$)	17,633	1,485	704
Epsilon rules	0.00%	0.00%	15.48%
Unary rules	5.26%	10.64%	41.05%
Binary rules	22.98%	50.17%	18.18%
Other rules	71.76%	39.19%	25.28%
Average rule length (RHS)	3.54	2.40	1.74

4.1   Parsing natural language with CFGs

As a first example of the use of the compilation technique presented in
Chapter 3 to prototype parsing algorithms and test them with different
natural language grammars, we have used the compiler to generate implementations of three popular parsing algorithms for CFGs: CYK (Kasami,
1965; Younger, 1967), Earley (Earley, 1970) and Left-Corner (Rosenkrantz
and Lewis II, 1970).

The schemata we have used describe recognisers, and therefore their generated implementation only checks sentences for grammaticality by launch-
ing the deductive engine and testing for the presence of final items in the
item set.   However, these schemata can easily be modified to produce a
parse forest as output (Billot and Lang, 1989). If we want to use a probabilistic grammar in order to modify the schema so that it produces the
most probable parse tree, this requires slight modifications of the deductive
engine, since it should only store and use the item with the highest proba-
bility when several items differing only in their associated probabilities are
found (Manning and Schütze, 1999).

The three algorithms have been tested with sentences from three different natural language grammars: the English grammar from the Susanne
corpus (Sampson, 1994); the Alvey grammar (Carroll, 1993) (which is
also an English-language grammar); and the Delta grammar (Schoorl and
Belder, 1990), which generates a fragment of Dutch. The Alvey and Delta
grammars are unification-based grammars, which were converted to plain

CFGs by removing their arguments and feature structures.[1] The test sentences were randomly generated by starting with the axiom and randomly selecting nonterminals and rules to perform expansions, until valid sentences consisting only of terminals were produced. Note that, as we are interested in measuring and comparing the performance of the parsers, not the coverage of the grammars, randomly-generated sentences are a good input in this case: by generating several sentences of a given length, parsing them and averaging the resulting runtimes, we get a good idea of the performance of the parsers for sentences of that length. Table 4.1 summarises some facts about the three grammars, where by "Rule Length" we mean the average length of the right-hand side of a grammar's production rules.

For Earley's algorithm, we have used a schema file similar to the one given in Section 3.1, but slightly modified by dividing the PREDICTOR step into different steps for different lengths of the associated production's right side (0, 1, 2 or more symbols). This modification of the schema makes existence indexing more effective and thus reduces execution times, without affecting computational complexity.

For the CYK algorithm, grammars were converted to Chomsky normal form (CNF), since this is a precondition of the algorithm. In the case of the Delta grammar, which is the only one of our test grammars containing epsilon rules, we have used a weak variant of CNF allowing epsilon rules and the CYK variant described by the schema file in Figure 4.1, which can handle them.

Left-Corner parsing (Rosenkrantz and Lewis II, 1970) can be seen as an optimisation of Earley parsing which takes advantage of information obtained from the grammar, in the form of so-called left-corner relations between nonterminal symbols. If we define a relation $First(A, B)$ between nonterminals such that $First(A, B)$ is true if an only if there is a production of the form $A \to B\alpha$ in the grammar, the transitive and reflexive closure of the *First* relation is called the left-corner relation. A parsing schema for Left-Corner parsing (Sikkel, 1997) can be obtained from that for a standard Earley parser by using this left-corner information to contract its deduction steps and avoid the generation of unnecessary items.

In particular, the schema used for the Left-Corner parser in the experiments in this book is the *sLC* variant described by Sikkel (1997), where

---

[1]Note that, although the compiler can handle feature structure unification, it has not been used in this study, since the goal was to compare the three grammars under homogeneous conditions. For experiments where feature structures are used, see the comparisons performed with the XTAG English Grammar in Section 4.5.

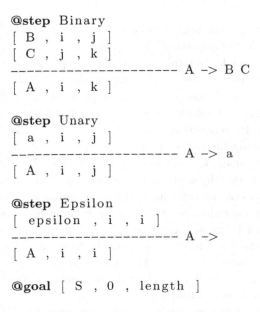

```
@step Binary
[ B , i , j ]
[ C , j , k ]
---------------------- A -> B C
[ A , i , k ]


@step Unary
[ a , i , j ]
---------------------- A -> a
[ A , i , j ]


@step Epsilon
[ epsilon , i , i ]
---------------------- A ->
[ A , i , i ]


@goal [ S , 0 , length ]
```

Fig. 4.1   Schema file for the CYK parser used in the experiments.

side conditions containing boolean expression elements are used to evaluate left-corner relations. Side conditions of this kind are compiled to code that prevents the steps from generating results if the corresponding predicates do not hold. This code is inserted in such a way that the predicates are checked as soon as the referenced variables are instantiated. By aborting the steps as soon as possible when predicates do not hold, we avoid unnecessary calculations. A schema file for *sLC* is shown in Figure 4.2.[2]

Performance results[3] (Gómez-Rodríguez *et al.*, 2007c) for all these algorithms and grammars are shown in Table 4.2. The following conclusions can be drawn from the measurements:

- The empirical computational complexity of the three algorithms is below their theoretical worst-case complexity of $O(n^3)$, where n denotes

---

[2]This is a slightly simplified version of the actual *sLC* schema file used in the tests, which can be found in the long version of Gómez-Rodríguez *et al.* (2006d). However, the differences are merely notational and both versions are equivalent in terms of performance.

[3]The machine used for these tests was a standard end-user computer in 2006, a laptop equipped with an Intel 1500 MHz Pentium M processor, 512 MB RAM, Sun Java Hotspot virtual machine (version 1.4.2_01-b06) and Windows XP.

@step SimplifiedLCInitter
------------------------------ S -> gamma
[S -> . gamma , 0 , 0]

@step SimplifiedLCNonterminal
[E , i]
[A -> alpha . , i , j]
------------------------------ B -> A beta / LC(E;B)
[B -> A . beta , i , j]

@step SimplifiedLCTerminal
[E , i]
[A , i , i+1]
------------------------------ B -> A beta / LC(E;B)
[B -> A . beta , i , i+1]

@step SimplifiedLCEpsilon
[E , i]
------------------------------ B ->
[B -> . , i , i]

@step SimplifiedLCSummariser
[C -> gamma . E delta , k , i]

[E , i]

@step SimplifiedLCScanner
[A -> alpha . B beta , i , j]
[B , j , j+1]

[A -> alpha B . beta , i , j+1]

@step SimplifiedLCCompleter
[A -> alpha . B beta , i , j]
[B -> gamma . , j , k]

[A -> alpha B . beta , i , k]

@goal [S -> alpha . , 0 , length]

Fig. 4.2 Schema file for the Left-Corner parser used in the experiments. LC(E;B) denotes the left-corner relation between nonterminals E and B.

Table 4.2   Performance measurements for CFG parsers.

Grammar	String length	Time Elapsed (s)			Items Generated		
		CYK	Earley	LC	CYK	Earley	LC
Susanne	2	0.000	1.450	0.030	28	14,670	330
	4	0.004	1.488	0.060	59	20,945	617
	8	0.018	4.127	0.453	341	51,536	2,962
	16	0.050	13.162	0.615	1,439	137,128	7,641
	32	0.072	17.913	0.927	1,938	217,467	9,628
	64	0.172	35.026	2.304	4,513	394,862	23,393
	128	0.557	95.397	4.679	17,164	892,941	52,803
Alvey	2	0.000	0.042	0.002	61	1,660	273
	4	0.002	0.112	0.016	251	3,063	455
	8	0.010	0.363	0.052	915	7,983	1,636
	16	0.098	1.502	0.420	4,766	18,639	6,233
	32	0.789	9.690	3.998	33,335	66,716	39,099
	64	5.025	44.174	21.773	133,884	233,766	170,588
	128	28.533	146.562	75.819	531,536	596,108	495,966
Deltra	2	0.000	0.084	0.158	1,290	1,847	1,161
	4	0.012	0.208	0.359	2,783	3,957	2,566
	8	0.052	0.583	0.839	6,645	9,137	6,072
	16	0.204	2.498	2.572	20,791	28,369	22,354
	32	0.718	6.834	6.095	57,689	68,890	55,658
	64	2.838	31.958	29.853	207,745	282,393	261,649
	128	14.532	157.172	143.730	878,964	1,154,710	1,110,629

the length of the input string. In the case of the Susanne grammar, the measurements we obtain are close to being linear with respect to string size. In the other two grammars, the measurements grow faster with string size (approximately $O(n^2)$), but are still far below the cubic worst-case bound.

- CYK is the fastest algorithm in all cases, and it generates less items than the other ones. This may come as a surprise at first, as CYK is generally considered slower than Earley-type algorithms, particularly than Left-Corner. However, these considerations are based on time complexity relative to string size, and do not take into account complexity relative to grammar size. In this aspect, CYK is better than Earley-type algorithms, providing linear - $O(|P|)$ - worst-case complexity with respect to grammar size, while Earley is $O(|P|^2)$.[4] Therefore, the fact that CYK outperforms the other algorithms in our tests is not so surprising, as the grammars we have used have a large number of productions. The greatest difference between CYK and the other two algorithms in terms of the amount of items generated appears with the Susanne grammar, which has the largest number of productions. It is also worth noting that the relative difference in terms of items generated tends to decrease when string length increases, at least for Alvey and Deltra, suggesting that CYK could generate more items than the other algorithms for larger values of n.

- Left-Corner is notably faster than Earley in all the experiments, except for some short sentences when using the Deltra grammar. The Left-Corner parser always generates fewer items than the Earley parser, since it avoids unnecessary predictions by using information about left-corner relations. The Susanne grammar seems to be very well suited for Left-Corner parsing, since the number of items generated decreases by an order of magnitude with respect to Earley. On the other hand, the Deltra grammar's left-corner relations seem to contribute less useful information than the others, since the difference between Left-Corner and Earley in terms of items generated is small when using this grammar. In some of the cases, Left-Corner's runtimes are a bit slower than Earley's because this small difference in items is not enough to compensate for the extra time required to process each item due to the extra steps in the schema, which make Left-Corner's matching and indexing code more complex than Earley's.[5]

- The parsing of the sentences generated using the Alvey and Deltra grammars tends to require more time, and the generation of more items, than that of the Susanne sentences. This happens in spite of the fact that the Susanne grammar has more rules. The probable reason is that the Alvey and Deltra grammars have more ambiguity, since they are

---

[4]It is possible to reduce the computational complexity of Earley's parser to linear with respect to grammar size by defining a new set of intermediate items and transforming prediction and completion deduction steps accordingly. Even in this case, CYK performs better than Earley's algorithm due to the lower amount of items generated: $O(|N \cup \Sigma| n^2)$ for CYK vs. $O(|G| n^2)$ for Earley's algorithm, where $|G|$ denotes the size of the grammar measured as $|P|$ plus the summation of the lengths of all productions.

[5]From a theoretical point of view, our indexing mechanisms should make performance results invariant to the number and size of deduction steps and items. However, in practice, there are many aspects (memory allocation, object packaging, ...) that make execution time dependent on the number and size of steps and items.

designed to be used with their arguments and feature structures, and information has been lost when these features were removed from them. On the other hand, the Susanne grammar is designed as a plain CFG and therefore its symbols contain more information.

- Execution times for the Alvey grammar quickly grow for sentence lengths above 16 words. This is because sentences generated for these lengths tend to be repetitions of a single terminal symbol, and are highly ambiguous.

4.2　Parsing with TAGs

Up to now, all the schemata that we have seen correspond to parsers for CFGs. However, as mentioned in Section 2.3.2, it is also possible to define parsing schemata for other constituency-based grammar formalisms. All the definitions in Section 2.3.2 can be applied to any grammar class CG as long as we can define a set of valid constituency trees $Trees(G)$ for every grammar $G \in CG$.

In this section, our schema compiler is used to obtain implementations of parsers for TAGs (Joshi and Schabes, 1997), and test their empirical performance by parsing natural language sentences with a real-sized grammar: the XTAG English Grammar (XTAG Research Group, 2001). To this end, we first provide a brief introduction to the formalism of TAG.

4.2.1　*Tree-adjoining grammars*

CFGs are one of the most widely used formalisms for defining the syntax of natural languages, since they are relatively simple to define and can be parsed efficiently. As we have seen, several parsers for CFGs have a cubic worst-case complexity with respect to input length, and their behaviour is typically better than cubic in practical cases (see Section 4.1). However, it has been shown that CFGs are not expressive enough to cover all the linguistic phenomena present in natural languages. Some constructions present in human languages are context-sensitive, and thus cannot be adequately modelled by a CFG. For instance, Huybregts (1984) and Shieber (1985) show that certain variants of German contain constructions that can only be modelled by formalisms that generate the *copy language* ($\{\alpha\alpha \mid \alpha \in \Sigma^*\}$), which is not context-free. Another known linguistic phenomenon that lies outside the generative capacity of CFGs is that of cross-serial dependencies, present in languages like Dutch (Joshi, 1985). Cross-serial dependencies appear in sentences of the form $a_1 a_2 \ldots a_k b_1 b_2 \ldots b_k$, where each a_i depends on the corresponding b_i.

Thus, it is clear that CFGs are not enough to model natural language: if we want a formalism that can successfully express the range of syntactic constructions used in human languages, we need a class of grammars with greater generative capacity than CFG, i.e., one that generates a strict superset of the set of context-free languages. However, for our formalism to be useful, this superset should not be too large. For example, the smallest strict superset of context-free languages described in the classical formal language hierarchy defined by Chomsky (1956, 1959), which is the set of *context-sensitive languages*, allows expressing constraints that are considered more complex than those in natural languages (for instance, the language $\{a^p \mid p$ is a prime number$\}$ is context-sensitive), and the parsing problem is PSPACE-complete for this class of languages.

For these reasons, researchers have devoted considerable efforts to search for grammar formalisms that are general enough to be able to model all the known constructions present in human languages, yet restricted enough to be parsable in polynomial time. The formalisms satisfying these conditions are called *mildly context-sensitive* (Joshi, 1985; Joshi *et al.*, 1991), and the languages they generate are known as *mildly context-sensitive languages*. Several mildly context-sensitive formalisms have been proposed, ones generating larger sets of structures than others. For example, among the most general of these formalisms we have linear context-free rewriting systems (Vijay-Shanker *et al.*, 1987; Weir, 1988), and among the most restrictive we have TAGs (Joshi and Schabes, 1997).

TAGs are an extension of CFGs, first described by Joshi *et al.* (1975), and later refined by Joshi (1987). The languages generated by these grammars, called tree-adjoining languages (TAL), are only slightly more expressive than context-free languages, yet expressive enough to model linguistic phenomena like cross-serial dependencies or those derived from the copy language. This, together with the fact that TAG parsers run in $O(n^6)$ time in the worst case (Vijay-Shanker and Joshi, 1985), makes them an interesting formalism for natural language processing.

Definition 4.1. A *tree-adjoining grammar* (TAG) is a 5-tuple $G = (N, \Sigma, \mathbb{I}, \mathbb{A}, S)$ where:

- Σ is an alphabet of symbols called terminal symbols,

- N is an alphabet of auxiliary symbols called nonterminal symbols, satisfying $\Sigma \cap N = \varnothing$,
- $S \in N$ is a distinguished nonterminal symbol called the initial symbol or axiom of the grammar G,
- $\mathbb{I}$ is a finite set of trees called *initial trees*, and
- $\mathbb{A}$ is a finite set of trees called *auxiliary trees*.

The meaning of N and Σ is the same as in CFG (see Section 2.1): terminal symbols (Σ) are those that appear in strings of the language generated by the grammar, nonterminals (N) are auxiliary symbols used to derive strings. As in CFG, the initial symbol S will be the root node of parse trees. On the other hand, the initial and auxiliary trees in $\mathbb{I} \cup \mathbb{A}$ (together called *elementary trees*) are used to derive trees (and from them, strings), although the derivation operations are different from those in CFG.

Given a CFG G, we saw in Section 2.1 that the strings of its associated language $L(G)$ can be obtained by starting with the initial symbol S and applying a series of derivations (licensed by a set of production rules) to it. However, if instead of strings we focus on parse trees, we could equivalently define $L(G)$ as the set of yields of the trees obtained by starting with the tree with a single node labelled S, and applying a series of operations consisting of adding nodes labelled with the symbols of a string α as children of a frontier node labelled A if there is a production $A \to \alpha$ in the grammar, until all the frontier nodes in our tree are labelled with terminals.

The general idea of derivation in TAGs is a generalisation of this tree-based derivation concept for CFG. In this case, the starting point is any initial tree in the set $\mathbb{I}$ rooted at a node labelled S, not necessarily a trivial tree with a single node, and new trees can be obtained by combining elementary trees, using two combination operations: *substitution* and *adjunction*. Substitution consists of inserting a complete initial tree, rooted at a node labelled A, in the place of a frontier node also labelled A: note that this is the same operation done in CFG derivations, but adding the possibility of inserting trees of arbitrary depth, instead of the trees with two levels represented by CFG productions. On the other hand, adjunction is the operation that provides TAG with their extra generative power, and it roughly consists of inserting an auxiliary tree $t \in \mathbb{A}$, verifying certain constraints, in the place of an *inner* node of another tree, which has been marked as an adjunction node. The original tree containing the adjunction node is split into two parts, with the said node appearing in both, and the auxiliary tree being used to link them.

4.2.2   *Substitution and adjunction*

To define TAG derivations in more detail, we first need to define initial and auxiliary trees. Initial trees are trees whose non-leaf nodes are labelled with symbols in N, and whose leaf nodes can be labelled with any symbol in $N \cup \Sigma \cup \{\epsilon\}$. Auxiliary trees have the same form as initial trees, with the exception that exactly one of their frontier nodes must be marked as a *foot node*. The foot node must be labelled with a nonterminal symbol, and it must have the same label as the root. The path from the root to the foot node of an auxiliary tree is referred to as its *spine*.[6]

Elementary trees in $\mathbb{I} \cup \mathbb{A}$ can be combined among themselves to form *derived trees*, which can in turn be combined with other derived trees or elementary trees to form larger derived trees. Trees can be combined by using the adjunction and substitution operations.

The *adjunction* operation combines an auxiliary tree β with another tree γ, which can be an initial, derived or auxiliary tree. For an adjunction to be possible, there must be an inner node in the tree γ (called an *adjunction node*) whose label is the same as that of the root and foot of the auxiliary tree β. Under this assumption, the derived tree is assembled as follows (Figure 4.3):

(1) Let γ_2 be the subtree of γ rooted at the adjunction node. We call γ_1 the tree obtained by removing all the nodes in γ_2, except for the adjunction node, from γ. Note that both γ_1 and γ_2 contain a copy of the adjunction node (these copies act as a frontier node of γ_1 and the root of γ_2).

(2) The derived tree is obtained by linking the tree β to the trees γ_1 and γ_2 by collapsing the copy of the adjunction node in γ_1 and the root of β into a single node, and by collapsing the copy of the adjunction node in γ_2 and the foot node of β into a single node.

---

[6]We are defining TAG with the adjunction and substitution operations, since the XTAG English grammar that will be used in our experiments allows these operations. However, it should be noted that it is also possible to define TAG where only adjunction is allowed. In this case, there are additional constraints on the sets $\mathbb{I}$ and $\mathbb{A}$: the root of initial trees must be labelled S, and no leaf nodes of elementary trees can be labelled with nonterminal symbols except for the foot nodes of auxiliary trees. TAG without substitution are formally simpler than those described here and have the same generative power; however, substitution is usually allowed in practical grammars since it simplifies the description of elementary trees.

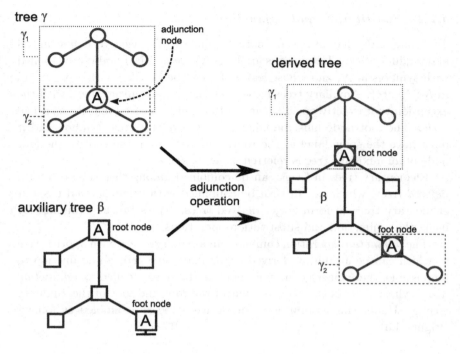

Fig. 4.3   Adjunction operation in TAG.

In simple variants of TAG, any non-leaf node is allowed to act as an adjunction node as long as its label matches that of the root and foot nodes of the auxiliary tree which is being adjoined. In practice, it is often convenient to add further restrictions to adjunction operations: a node in an elementary tree can be associated with a (possibly empty) set of auxiliary trees that may adjoin into it, so that adjunctions of other trees into that node are forbidden even if their labels match. It is also possible to add obligatory adjunction constraints to nodes, forcing certain nodes to be expanded by adjunction operations. In the case of the XTAG English grammar, adjunction constraints are not represented explicitly, but they are enforced by the feature structures (Carpenter, 1992) associated with nodes in its elementary trees. An adjunction operation is forbidden if it produces feature structures that do not unify.

The *substitution* operation combines an initial tree β with another tree γ, which can be an initial, derived or auxiliary tree. For a substitution to be possible, there must be a non-foot node in the frontier of γ whose label

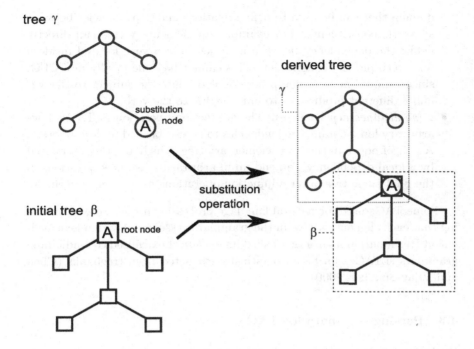

Fig. 4.4 Substitution operation in TAG.

is the same as that of the root of β. We call such a node a *substitution node*. Under this assumption, the derived tree is obtained as in Figure 4.4: β is linked to γ by collapsing the substitution node in γ and the root node of β into a single node.

Given these two operations, we can define the set of valid trees associated to a TAG $G = (N, \Sigma, \mathbb{I}, \mathbb{A}, S)$, denoted *Trees(G)*, as the set of all trees that can be derived from an initial tree whose root is labelled S by applying the adjunction and substitution operations using trees from $\mathbb{I} \cup \mathbb{A}$.

4.2.3 *Properties of TAG*

TAGs have some interesting properties that make them a useful formalism to describe the structure of natural language sentences:

- *Extended domain of locality*: In CFGs, syntax trees are assembled from productions of the form $A \to \alpha$. In contrast, in TAGs, the basic building blocks are elementary trees of arbitrary depth. This enlarges the domain that can be used to define relations and dependencies between syntactic constituents. For example, an elementary tree can directly define the dependency between a subject and a verb located inside a *VP* (verb phrase) constituent. This cannot be done locally in a CFG, since we need at least one production to relate the subject to the *VP* and a different production to link the *VP* to the verb.

- *Long-distance dependencies*: The adjunction operation in TAG allows arbitrary long-distance dependencies to be established in derived trees. A pair of nodes in the same elementary tree, which are directly related by a local dependency, can end up in arbitrarily distanced positions in the final parse tree, after adjunction operations have been performed.

Some TAGs used for natural language processing are *lexicalised*, meaning that each elementary tree in the grammar is associated with a lexical element (terminal) in its frontier, called its *anchor*. Lexicalised tree-adjoining grammars (LTAG) can be automatically extracted from treebanks (Chen and Vijay-Shanker, 2000).

4.3   Parsing schemata for TAG

With the definition of valid trees for a TAG G, given at the end of Section 4.2.2, we can apply all the definitions in Section 2.3.2 to TAG, including that of parsing schema (2.14). Thus, the formalism of parsing schemata can be used to describe TAG parsers.

As in the case of CFG, describing a TAG parser by means of a schema implies establishing a mapping that assigns an uninstantiated parsing system to each particular grammar G. In the case of CFG, we usually do this by writing inference rules, each representing a set of deduction steps, and (possibly) linked to the grammar by a side condition requiring the presence of a particular kind of production rule (Section 2.3.2). For example, in the schema for Earley's CFG parser, one of such rules is:

$$\text{PREDICTOR: } \frac{[A \to \alpha \bullet B\beta, i, j]}{[B \to \bullet\gamma, j, j]} \; B \to \gamma \in P$$

where the condition $B \to \gamma \in P$ restricts the values of the variables B and γ depending on the productions (P) of the grammar.

Since TAGs use elementary trees instead of productions, it could seem appropriate to use elementary trees as side conditions for TAG parsing schemata. However, it is usually not necessary to use complete trees to define deduction steps, since a smaller context is enough to describe their logic. In particular, it is common in the literature (Nederhof, 1997, 1999; Alonso *et al.*, 1999) to use a representation based on representing each elementary tree γ as a set of context-free productions $P(\gamma)$, and using these productions as side conditions. This notation, called *multi-layer* representation (Díaz *et al.*, 1998), is simple and compact, and it makes the relations between TAG and CFG parsers easy to understand.

Given a TAG $G = (N, \Sigma, \mathbb{I}, \mathbb{A}, S)$, and a tree $\gamma \in (\mathbb{I} \cup \mathbb{A})$, we denote by $P(\gamma)$ the set of productions of the form $N^\gamma \rightarrow N_1^\gamma N_2^\gamma \ldots N_r^\gamma$, such that N^γ is an inner node of the tree γ, and $N_1^\gamma N_2^\gamma \ldots N_r^\gamma$ is the ordered sequence of direct children of N^γ. Additionally, we will use the notation $\mathbf{R}^\gamma$ for the root node of a tree γ, and $\mathbf{F}^\gamma$ for the foot node of γ.

An example of a parsing schema for TAG is the schema corresponding to the CYK-based algorithm by Vijay-Shanker and Joshi (1985), which can be found in Alonso *et al.* (1999). This schema is defined as a function that maps each TAG $G = (N, \Sigma, \mathbb{I}, \mathbb{A}, S)$ to a deduction system whose domain is the item set:

$$\{[N^\gamma, i, j, p, q, adj]\}$$

verifying that N^γ is a tree node in an elementary tree $\gamma \in (\mathbb{I} \cup \mathbb{A})$, i and j $(0 \leq i \leq j)$ are string positions, p and q may be undefined or instantiated to positions $i \leq p \leq q \leq j$ (the latter only when $\gamma \in \mathbb{A}$), and $adj \in \{true, false\}$ is a flag indicating whether an adjunction has been performed on node N^γ.[7]

The positions i and j indicate that a substring $a_{i+1} \ldots a_j$ of the string is being recognised, and positions p and q denote the substring dominated by γ's foot node. The final item set is:

$$\{[\mathbf{R}^\alpha, 0, n, -, -, adj] \mid \alpha \in I\}$$

for the presence of such an item would indicate that there exists a valid parse tree with yield $a_1 a_2 \ldots a_n$ and rooted at R^α, the root of an initial tree, and therefore there exists a complete parse tree for the sentence.

The deduction steps for this schema are as follows:

$$\text{SCANNER:} \frac{[a, i, i+1]}{[N^\gamma, i, i+1, -, -, \text{false}]} \quad a = \text{label}(N^\gamma)$$

$$\text{EPSILON:} \frac{}{[N^\gamma, i, i, -, -, \text{false}]} \quad \epsilon = \text{label}(N^\gamma)$$

---

[7]The standard TAG formalism that we consider here does not allow multiple trees to adjoin into a single node, although some extensions do (Alonso and Díaz, 2003a).

The steps SCANNER and EPSILON are used to start the bottom-up parsing process by recognising a terminal symbol in the input string, or none if we are using a tree with an epsilon node.

$$\text{UNARY:} \frac{[M^\gamma, i, j, p, q, adj]}{[N^\gamma, i, j, p, q, \text{false}]} \quad N^\gamma \to M^\gamma \in \mathcal{P}(\gamma)$$

$$\text{BINARY:} \frac{\begin{array}{c} [M^\gamma, i, k, p, q, adj1], \\ [P^\gamma, k, j, p', q', adj2] \end{array}}{[N^\gamma, i, j, p \cup p', q \cup q', \text{false}]} \quad N^\gamma \to M^\gamma P^\gamma \in \mathcal{P}(\gamma)$$

The BINARY step (where the operation $p \cup p'$ returns p if p is defined, and p' otherwise) represents the bottom-up parsing operation which joins two subtrees into one, and is analogous to the BINARY step of the CYK parser for CFG (Figure 2.5). The UNARY step is used to handle unary branching productions.

$$\text{FOOT:} \frac{[N^\gamma, i, j, p, q, \text{false}]}{[\mathbf{F}^\beta, i, j, i, j, \text{false}]} \quad \beta \in \text{adj}(N^\gamma)$$

$$\text{ADJUNCTION:} \frac{\begin{array}{c} [\mathbf{R}^\beta, i', j', i, j, adj], \\ [N^\gamma, i, j, p, q, \text{false}] \end{array}}{[N^\gamma, i', j', p, q, \text{true}]} \quad \beta \in \text{adj}(N^\gamma)$$

FOOT and ADJUNCTION implement the adjunction operation, where a tree β is adjoined into a node N^γ. Their side condition $\beta \in \text{adj}(N^\gamma)$ means that β must be adjoinable into the node N^γ (which involves checking that N^γ is an adjunction node, comparing its label to $\mathbf{R}^\beta$'s and verifying that no adjunction constraint disallows the operation, if the grammar contemplates such constraints).

$$\text{SUBSTITUTION:} \frac{[\mathbf{R}^\alpha, i, j, -, -, adj]}{[N^\gamma, i, j, -, -, \text{false}]} \quad \alpha \in \text{subs}(N^\gamma)$$

Finally, the SUBSTITUTION step implements the substitution operation in grammars supporting it.

4.4 Parsing schemata for the XTAG English grammar

By using parsing schemata like the above example or the ones described by Alonso *et al.* (1999) and Nederhof (1999) as an input to the system described in Chapter 3, we can easily obtain efficient implementations of several TAG parsing algorithms. Additionally, if we extend them with support for feature structure unification, the generated parsers can be used with feature-based TAGs like the XTAG English grammar (XTAG Research Group, 2001), although further additions, such as tree filtering, are highly convenient in order to obtain good performance results with this grammar (Gómez-Rodríguez *et al.*, 2006b).

In this section, we describe how we have dealt with the particular characteristics of the XTAG English grammar in order to make it compatible with our generic compilation technique. We also provide empirical results which allow us to compare the performance of several different TAG parsing algorithms in the practical case of the XTAG grammar. It should be noted that previous comparisons of TAG parsers in the literature (Díaz and Alonso, 2000) use much smaller grammars, such as simplified subsets of the XTAG English grammar, instead of the whole XTAG grammar with all its trees and feature structures. Therefore, our comparison provides valuable information about the behaviour of various parsers on a complete, large-scale natural language grammar. This behaviour is very different from the one that can be observed on small grammars, since grammar size becomes a dominant factor in computational complexity when large grammars like XTAG are used to parse relatively small natural language sentences (see the experiments by Sarkar (2000), and the empirical evaluation of the impact of grammar size in complexity that will be presented in Section 4.6).

4.4.1 *Grammar conversion*

The first step we undertook in order to generate parsers for the XTAG English grammar was a full conversion of the grammar to an XML-based format, a variant of the TAG markup language (TAGML) (Bonhomme and Lopez, 2000). In this way we had the grammar in a standard, well-defined format, easier to parse and modify than the original, ad-hoc format. This is highly convenient since grammar preprocessing or conversion is often necessary (an example is the binarisation required in order to use the CYK algorithm) and standard APIs for XML make it fast and easy to perform such transformations.

During this conversion, the relationships between features that were expressed as unification equations in the original XTAG grammar were transformed to links to symbolic variables, so that two features that should take equal values were linked to the same variable.

Additionally, the trees' anchor nodes were duplicated, so that every anchor node in the original XTAG grammar was transformed to an adjunction node with a single child labelled as an anchor node, with both nodes taking their label and feature structures from the original node. This transformation was necessary in order to work around a peculiar characteristic of the XTAG grammar. While the generic TAG formalism does not allow adjunction at anchor nodes, the XTAG grammar does. By applying this transformation to the grammar, we can parse it with our generic parsers without needing to modify them in order to contemplate this variation from the standard definition of TAGs, since we can perform adjunctions at the new adjunction nodes that we add to the trees and the effect is equivalent to that of adjoining on the anchor.

4.4.2 Feature structure unification

The XTAG trees include feature structures (Carpenter, 1992; Vijay-Shanker and Joshi, 1988) associated with each of its nodes. Feature structures contain information about how nodes may interact with each other, and they may impose constraints on the adjunction and substitution operations, where the feature structures in the involved nodes must unify.

Two strategies may be used in order to take unification into account in parsing: feature structures can be unified after parsing or during parsing. The first strategy consists of parsing the sentence just as in a grammar without feature structures, ignoring unification, and then recovering the parse forest and performing unification only on the final parse trees, eliminating trees that violate unification constraints. The second strategy consists of performing unification as a part of the parsing process, so that feature structures are unified during operations like adjunction or substitution.

At first sight, each of these strategies has its advantages and disadvantages. By performing unification during parsing, we are considering the constraints imposed by feature structures earlier, so we avoid the generation of unnecessary trees violating these constraints. On the other hand, by unifying after parsing, we are only performing unification on the items needed to build the final parse trees, so we avoid unification operations on items that lead to incomplete parses.

Therefore, none of the methods is better than the other in absolute terms: the convenience of one or the other will depend on the way feature structures are used in the grammar.

Table 4.3 Runtimes in milliseconds of an Earley-based TAG parser using two different unification strategies: unification during and after parsing. The following data are shown: mean, trimmed means (10 and 20%), quartiles, standard deviation, and p-value for the Wilcoxon paired signed-rank test (the p-value of 0.4545 indicates that no statistically significant difference was found between the medians).

	DURING PARSING	AFTER PARSING
Mean	108,270	412,793
Trimmed Mean 10%	12,614	10,710
Trimmed Mean 20%	7,812	10,019
1st Quartile	1,585	2,123
Median	4,424	9,023
3rd Quartile	9,671	19,073
Standard Deviation	388,010	14,235
Wilcoxon p-value	0.4545	

In the particular case of the XTAG English grammar, we have compared the two strategies with a parsing schema for the Earley algorithm for TAGs without the valid prefix property described by Schabes (1994) (the extensions made to the schema in order to support unification are described later) by using 16 sample sentences taken from the XTAG distribution. An analysis of the runtimes provides the results in Table 4.3.

Although the means of both samples seem very different, they are not highly significant, as they are influenced by huge outliers. Trimmed means, which are insensitive to outliers, are fairly similar. The Wilcoxon two-sample paired signed-rank test (Wilcoxon, 1945) (whose p-value is shown in the last row) does not find significant difference between both methods, so we cannot conclude that any of them is better than the other for parsing the XTAG grammar. We can, however, conclude that unification during parsing performs better for *most* sentences (cf. the quartiles) although it performs much worse for some particular cases.

If we measure the number of items generated instead of execution time, we conclude that if we unify during parsing we generate significantly fewer items (Wilcoxon p-value = 0.0174). This means that the amount of items we avoid to generate thanks to failed unification operations exceeds the amount of extra items generated when we have situations where several items differ only in their associated feature structures.

From now on, we will focus on the strategy that performs unification during parsing. In order to generate implementations of parsing algorithms that support this strategy with our parsing schemata-based system, we must extend our schemata in order to support unification. This has been done in the following way:

- Items are extended so that they hold a feature structure in addition to the rest of the information they include.
- We define two operations on feature structures: the unification operation and the "keep variables" operation. The "keep variables" operation is a transformation of feature structures that takes a feature structure as an argument, which may contain features, values, symbolic variables and associations between them. The operation returns a feature structure containing only the variable-value associations related to a given elementary tree, ignoring the variables and values not associated through these relations, and completely ignoring features.
- During the process of parsing, feature structures that refer to the same node, or to nodes that are taking part in a substitution or adjunction and are going to collapse into a single node in the final parse tree, must be unified. For this to be done, the test that these nodes must unify is added as a side condition to the steps that must handle them, and the unification results are included in the item generated by the consequent. Of course, considerations about the different role of the top and bottom feature structures in adjunction and substitution (Vijay-Shanker and Joshi, 1988) must be taken into account when determining which feature structures must be unified.
- Feature structures that are included in items must only hold variable-value associations for the symbolic variables appearing in the tree to which the structures refer, for these relationships hold the information that we need in order to propagate values according to the rules specified in the unification equations. Variable-value associations referring to different elementary trees are irrelevant when parsing a given tree, and feature-value and feature-variable associations are local to a node and cannot be extrapolated to other nodes, so we will not propagate any of this information in items. However, it must be used locally for unification. Therefore, deduction steps perform unification by using the information in their antecedent items and recovering complete feature structures associated to nodes directly from the grammar, and then use

the "keep-variables" operation to remove the information that is not needed in the consequent item.

- In some algorithms, such as the CYK-based algorithm for TAG, a single deduction step deals with several different elementary tree nodes that do not collapse into one in the final parse tree. In this case, several "keep variables" operations must be performed on each step execution, one for each of these nodes. If we just unified the information on all the nodes and called "keep variables" at the end, we could propagate information incorrectly.

- In Earley-type algorithms, we must make a decision about how predictor steps handle feature structures. Two options are possible: one is propagating the feature structure in the antecedent item to the consequent, and the other is discarding the feature structure and generating a consequent whose associated feature structure is empty. The first option has the advantage that violations of unification constraints are detected earlier, thus avoiding the generation of some items. However, in scenarios where a predictor is applied to several items differing only in their associated feature structures, this approach generates several different items while the discarding approach collapses them into a single consequent item. Moreover, the propagating approach favours the appearance of items with more complex feature structures, thus making unification operations slower. In practice, for the XTAG grammar we have found that these drawbacks of propagating the structures overcome the advantages, especially in complex sentences, where the discarding approach performs much better. Therefore, in our comparison of different algorithms we will use this variant, where unification constraints within a tree involving a node are not checked until the node is completed by a Completer step.

4.4.3 Tree filtering

The full XTAG English grammar contains thousands of elementary trees, so parsing performance is not good if we use the whole grammar to parse each sentence. Tree selection filters (Schabes and Joshi, 1991) are used to select a subset of the grammar, discarding the trees which are known not to be useful given the words in the input sentence.

To emulate this functionality in our parsing schema-based system, we have used its extensibility mechanism to define a function *Selects-tree(a, T)* that returns *true* if the terminal symbol *a* selects the tree *T*.

The implementation of this function is a Java method that looks for this information in XTAG's syntactic database. Then the function is inserted in a filtering step on our schemata:

$$\frac{[a, i, j]}{[Selected, \alpha]} \; \alpha \in Trees/Selects\text{-}tree\,(a; \alpha)$$

The presence of an item of the form $[Selected, \alpha]$ indicates that the tree α has been selected by the filter and can be used for parsing. In order for the filter to take effect, we add $[Selected, \alpha]$ as an antecedent to every step in our schemata introducing a new tree α into the parse (such as initters, substitution and adjoining steps). In this way we guarantee that no trees that do not pass the filter will be used for parsing.

Note that the *Selects-tree* function can be defined to return *true* by default when we are working with a generic non-lexicalised TAG without such a filter, so we can preserve the genericity of the schemata while allowing them to take advantage of lexicalisation to improve performance with the XTAG grammar.

4.4.3.1 *Example*

An example of two of the steps in the parsing schemata shown in Section 4.3 (BINARY and FOOT), written in the input notation used as input to our schemata compiler, is shown in Figure 4.5, where:

- **Union** represents the operation that we have denoted as ∪ in the schema in Section 4.3,
- **Tfoot** is a special convenience node that we add as a daughter of foot nodes in elementary trees, with the only function of marking them as the foot node (as in Nederhof (1999)),
- **Symbol-of** returns the label of a given node, and **Tree-of** the tree to which it belongs,
- **Identity** is a comparison operation that returns true if their operands are the same object,
- **Adjoinable** checks whether an auxiliary tree can be adjoined into a given node, by comparing the node's label to those associated with the root and foot nodes of the auxiliary tree.

@step CYKBinary
```
[ Node1 , i , k , p , q , adj  ]
[ Node2 , k , j , p1 , q1 , adj2  ]
-------------------------------------------- Node3 -> Node1
    Node2
[ Node3 , i , j , Union(p;p1) , Union(q;q1) , false ]
```

@step CYKFoot
```
[ Node1 , i , j , p , q , false ]
------------------------------------------ Node2 -> Node3 /
    Identity ( Symbol-of( Node3 ) ; Tfoot ) , Adjoinable (
    Tree-of( Node2 ) ; Node1 )
[ Node2 , i , j , i , j , false  ]
```

Fig. 4.5   Schema file for some TAG steps.

After extending the steps with the support for tree filtering and feature structure unification, we obtain the file in Figure 4.6, where:

@step CYKBinary
```
[ Node1 , i , k , p , q , adj1 , fs1 ]
[ Node2 , k , j , p1 , q1 , adj2 , fs2 ]
-----------------------------------------------------------
    Node3 -> Node1 Node2 / Not-null ( Keep-vars ( Tree-
    vars( Tree-of ( Node1 ) ) ; Unify ( Top( Node1 ) ;
    Bottom( Node1 ) ; fs1 ; Top( Node2 ) ; Bottom( Node2 )
    ; fs2 ; Bottom( Node3 ) ) ) )
[ Node3 , i , j , Union(p;p1) , Union(q;q1) , false , Unif
    -result ]
```

@step CYKFoot
```
[ Node1 , i , j , p , q , false , fs ]
[ Selected , Tree-of ( Node2 ) ]
--------------------------------------------------- Node2 ->
    Node3 / Identity( Symbol-of( Node3 ) ; Tfoot ) , Not-
    null ( Keep-vars ( Tree-vars( Tree-of ( Node2 ) ) ) ;
    Unify ( Bottom( Node1 ) ; fs ; Bottom( Node2 ) ) ) ) )
[ Node2 , i , j , i , j , false , Unif-result ]
```

Fig. 4.6   Schema file for TAG steps with feature structure unification and tree filtering, usable with the XTAG English Grammar.

- **Keep-vars** calls the "keep variables" operation discussed above, and **Unify** performs feature structure unification,
- **Tree-vars** returns the list of variables associated with a given elementary tree, and is used to specify the variables that must be preserved by **Keep-vars** operations,
- **Top** and **Bottom** return the top and bottom feature structures (Vijay-Shanker and Joshi, 1988) associated to a node in an XTAG elementary tree,
- Unification operations return a null value when feature structures do not unify (which is checked by the **Not-null** predicate used in side conditions). If structures do unify, the variable **Unif-result** used in consequent items stores the feature structure obtained from unification.

4.5 Comparing several parsers for the XTAG grammar

In this section, we make an empirical comparison of several different TAG parsing algorithms on the XTAG English grammar (release 2.24.2001), by using the compiler described in Chapter 3 and the ideas we have explained above. The compared algorithms are the following:

- The CYK-based bottom-up algorithm described by Vijay-Shanker and Joshi (1985), whose parsing schema was shown in Section 4.3.
- The Earley-based parsing algorithm described in Alonso *et al.* (1999) and Alonso *et al.* (2004), inspired by the one by Schabes (1994); which is a version of the Earley parser for CFGs, extended to support adjunction and substitution, that does not satisfy the valid prefix property (VPP).[8]
- The Earley-based parser with the VPP described in Alonso *et al.* (1999), which enforces the said property at the cost of storing an extra index in its items, and thus increasing the computational complexity with respect to the input length to $O(n^7)$ from the $O(n^6)$ of the previous algorithm.

---

[8] A left-to-right parser is said to satisfy the valid prefix property if, at any point in the parsing process, the portion of the input string that has been read so far is guaranteed to be a prefix of some string of the language defined by the grammar. In terms of parsing schemata, this means that if the yield of a tree contained in a valid item in the schema starts with a string of terminals $a_1 \ldots a_k$, then there must be some string of the form $a_1 \ldots a_k b_1 \ldots b_m$ in the language defined by the grammar.

Table 4.4 Test sentences from the XTAG distribution.

1. He was a cow
2. He loved himself
3. Go to your room
4. He is a real man
5. He was a real man
6. Who was at the door
7. He loved all cows
8. He called up her
9. He wanted to go to the city
10. That woman in the city contributed to this article
11. That people are not really amateurs at intellectual duelling
12. The index is intended to measure future economic performance
13. They expect him to cut costs throughout the organization
14. He will continue to place a huge burden on the city workers
15. He could have been simply being a jerk
16. A few fast food outlets are giving it a try

- The algorithm by Nederhof (1999), which splits deduction steps in the previous parser and uses an intermediate set of items to achieve a computational complexity of $O(n^6)$ while maintaining the VPP.

The schemata for these algorithms without unification support can be found in Alonso *et al.* (1999). These schemata were extended as described in the previous sections, and used as input to our system which generated implementations of their corresponding parsers. The parsers were then run on sample sentences taken from the XTAG distribution, which are shown in Table 4.4, obtaining the performance measures (in terms of runtime and number of items generated) that can be seen in Tables 4.5 and 4.6.[9] Note that the sentences are ordered by minimal runtime.

As we can see, the execution times are not as good as the ones we would obtain if we used Sarkar's XTAG distribution parser written in C (Sarkar, 2000). This is not surprising, since our parsers have been generated by a generic tool without knowledge of the grammar, while the XTAG parser has been designed specifically for optimal performance in this particular grammar and uses additional information (such as tree usage frequency data from several corpora, see XTAG Research Group (2001)).

However, our comparison allows us to draw conclusions about which parsing algorithms are better suited for the XTAG grammar. In terms of memory usage, the CYK-based algorithm is the clear winner, since it

[9]The machine used for these tests was an Intel Pentium 4 / 3.40 GHz, with 1 GB RAM and Sun Java Hotspot virtual machine (version 1.4.2_01-b06) running on Windows XP.

Table 4.5   Runtimes for different XTAG parsers on the sentences shown in Table 4.4. Best results for each sentence are highlighted with an asterisk.

Sentence	Runtimes in milliseconds			
	CYK	EARLEY, NO VPP	EARLEY, VPP	NEDERHOF
1	2,985	*750	*750	2,719
2	3,109	1,562	*1,219	6,421
3	4,078	1,547	*1,406	6,828
4	4,266	1,563	*1,407	4,703
5	4,234	1,921	*1,421	4,766
6	4,485	1,813	*1,562	7,782
7	5,469	2,359	*2,344	11,469
8	7,828	4,906	*3,563	15,532
9	10,047	4,422	*4,016	18,969
10	13,641	*6,515	7,172	31,828
11	16,500	*7,781	15,235	56,265
12	16,875	17,109	*9,985	39,132
13	25,859	*12,000	20,828	63,641
14	54,578	*35,829	57,422	178,875
15	*62,157	113,532	109,062	133,515
16	*269,187	3,122,860	3,315,359	

clearly generates fewer items than the other algorithms, and a CYK item does not take up more memory than an Earley item.

On the other hand, if we compare execution times, there is not a single best algorithm, since the performance results depend on the size and complexity of the sentences. The Earley-based algorithm with the VPP is the fastest for the first, "easier" sentences, but CYK gives the best results for the more complex sentences. In the middle of the two, there are some sentences where the best performance is achieved by the variant of Earley that does not verify the VPP. Therefore, in practical cases, we should take into account the most likely kind of sentences that will be passed to the parser in order to select the best algorithm.

Nederhof's algorithm is always the one with the slowest execution time, in spite of being an improvement of the VPP Earley parser that reduces worst-case time complexity. This is probably because, when extending the Nederhof schema in order to support feature structure unification, we get a schema that needs more unification operations than Earley's and has to use items that store several feature structures. Nederhof's algorithm would perhaps perform better in relation to the others if we had used the strategy

Table 4.6   Number of items generated by different XTAG parsers on the sentences shown in Table 4.4. Best results for each sentence are highlighted with an asterisk.

Sentence	Items generated			
	CYK	EARLEY, NO VPP	EARLEY, VPP	NEDERHOF
1	1,341	1,463	*1,162	1,249
2	*1,834	2,917	2,183	2,183
3	*2,149	2,893	2,298	2,304
4	1,864	1,979	*1,534	2,085
5	1,855	1,979	*1,534	2,085
6	*2,581	3,587	2,734	2,742
7	*2,658	3,937	3,311	3,409
8	*4,128	8,058	4,711	4,716
9	*4,931	6,968	5,259	5,279
10	*6,087	8,828	7,734	8,344
11	*7,246	12,068	13,221	13,376
12	*7,123	10,428	9,810	10,019
13	*10,408	12,852	15,417	15,094
14	*20,760	31,278	40,248	47,570
15	*22,115	37,377	38,824	59,603
16	*68,778	152,430	173,128	

of parsing without feature structures and then performing unification on the output parse forest.[10]

Note that the generated implementations used for these executions apply the tree filtering technique discussed in Section 4.4.3, so that the effective grammar size is different for each sentence, hence the high variability in execution times among the different test sentences. Sentences where the filter selects more trees tend to have larger execution times.

4.6   Parsing with artificially-generated TAGs

In this section, we investigate the factors that affect performance of TAG parsers in more detail. While comparing parsers on real natural language grammars provides interesting results about their relative performance in practical settings, this approach is not sufficient if we want to gain insight

---

[10]It should also be noted that the example sentences do not correspond to the worst case in TAG parsing, so the theoretical worst-case performance of the algorithm is not necessarily a good predictor of practical performance. As it is not possible to define an "average case" for TAG parsing, having an homogeneous comparison environment (as provided by the system presented in this book) is useful in determining which algorithms work better in practice.

into the underlying factors that influence performance. As the natural language grammars that we have used are fixed, we cannot use them to evaluate the influence of grammar-related parameters (such as grammar size) in performance.

When studying the complexity of parsing algorithms in theory, it is common to focus mainly on complexity with respect to sentence length. However, other factors such as grammar size can have a significant influence on the practical performance of parsers. In the particular case of TAG parsers, both the results reported by Sarkar (2000) and the experiments in the previous section suggest that the main factor affecting performance in practical settings is not sentence length, but grammar size. This is especially relevant in the case of LTAG parsing, where the effective grammar size for a given sentence depends on the lexicalised trees selected by each of its lexical elements.

In this section, we make a detailed analysis of the influence of both sentence length and grammar size in the empirical performance of several TAG parsers (Gómez-Rodríguez et al., 2006c). As in previous comparisons, the system described in Chapter 3 is used to generate implementations of the parsers, but in this case the algorithms are compared on artificially generated grammars and sentences.

The advantage of using artificially generated grammars is that we can easily see the influence of grammar size on performance. If we test the algorithms on a real-life grammar, as we did in Section 4.5, we cannot get a very precise idea of how the size of the grammar affects performance, since we have no control over this factor. On the other hand, by using artificial grammars, we are able to adjust both string length and grammar size at will in the experiments, making it possible to isolate and analyse the influence of each of these factors.

The algorithms used in this comparison are the same TAG parsers that were used in Section 4.5: the CYK-based algorithm by Vijay-Shanker and Joshi (1985), Earley-like parsers with and without the VPP (Alonso et al., 1999; Schabes, 1994), and the algorithm described by Nederhof (1999).

For the grammars, we will use a grammar size parameter k, in such a way that we can obtain a grammar of size k for each value of k. To define these grammars, we will use bracketed notation to write elementary trees, and $*$ to mark the foot node of auxiliary trees. Given an integer $k > 0$, we define the TAG G_k to be the grammar $G_k = (N, \Sigma, \mathbb{I}, \mathbb{A}, S)$ where:

$$\Sigma = \{a_j \mid 0 \leq j \leq k\},$$
$$N = \{S, B\},$$
$$\mathbb{I} = \{S(B(a_0))\}, \text{and}$$
$$\mathbb{A} = \{B(B(B^* \ a_j)) \mid 1 \leq j \leq k\}.$$

Therefore, for a given k, G_k is a grammar with one initial tree and k auxiliary trees, which parses a language over an alphabet with $k+1$ terminal symbols. The actual language defined by G_k is the regular language $L_k = a_0(a_1 \mid a_2 \mid \ldots \mid a_k)^*$.

It is easy to prove that the grammar G_k is one of the minimal TAGs (in terms of number of trees) whose associated language is L_k. Note that we need at least a tree containing a_0 as its only terminal in order to parse the sentence a_0, and for each $1 \leq i \leq k$, we need at least a tree containing a_i and no other a_j $(j > 0)$ in order to parse the sentence $a_0 a_i$. Therefore, any TAG for the language L_k must have at least $k + 1$ elementary trees.

Note that although the languages L_k are trivial, the grammars G_k are built in such a way that any of the auxiliary trees may adjoin into any other. Therefore these grammars are suitable if we want to make an empirical analysis of worst-case complexity.

Table 4.7 shows the execution time in milliseconds,[11] and Table 4.8 the number of items generated, obtained by running four TAG parsers working with the grammars G_k, for different values of string length (n) and grammar size (k). Input strings were always generated in the same way: as the prefix of length n of $a_0(a_1 a_2 \ldots a_k)^*$.

From the results in Table 4.7, we can observe that both factors (string length and grammar size) have an influence on runtime, and they interact among themselves. The growth rates with respect to one factor are influenced by the other factor, so it is hard to give precise estimates of empirical computational complexity. However, we can get rough estimates by focusing on cases where one of the factors takes high values and the other one takes low values (since in these cases the constant factors affecting complexity will be smaller). We can then test them by checking whether the sequence $T(n, k)/f(n)$ seems to converge to a positive constant for each fixed k (with $T(n, k)$ being the execution time for string length n and grammar size k, and $f(n)$ an estimation of complexity with respect to string length) or whether $T(n, k)/f(k)$ seems to converge to a

---

[11] The machine used for these tests was an Intel Pentium 4 3.40 GHz, with 1 GB RAM and Sun Java Hotspot virtual machine (version 1.4.2_01-b06) running on Windows XP.

Table 4.7 Execution times of four different TAG parsers for artificially-generated grammars G_k. Best results are highlighted with an asterisk.

RUNTIMES IN MS: EARLEY-BASED WITHOUT THE VPP				
	Grammar Size (k)			
String Size (n)	1	8	64	512	4096
2	~0	16	15	*1,156	*109,843
4	~0	31	63	*2,578	*256,094
8	16	31	*172	*6,891	*589,578
16	31	172	*625	*18,735	*1,508,609
32	110	609	*3,219	*69,406	
64	485	2,953	*22,453	*289,984	
128	2,031	*13,875	*234,594		
256	10,000	*101,219			
512	61,266				

RUNTIMES IN MS: CYK-BASED				
	Grammar Size (k)			
String Size (n)	1	8	64	512	4096
2	~0	~0	16	1,344	125,750
4	~0	~0	63	4,109	290,187
8	16	31	234	15,891	777,968
16	*15	*62	782	44,188	2,247,156
32	*94	*312	3,781	170,609	
64	*266	*2,063	25,094	550,016	
128	*1,187	14,516	269,047		
256	*6,781	108,297			
512	*52,000				

RUNTIMES IN MS: NEDERHOF'S ALGORITHM				
	Grammar Size (k)			
String Size (n)	1	8	64	512	4096
2	~0	~0	47	1,875	151,532
4	~0	15	187	4,563	390,468
8	15	31	469	12,531	998,594
16	46	188	1,500	40,093	2,579,578
32	219	953	6,235	157,063	
64	1,078	4,735	35,860	620,047	
128	5,703	25,703	302,766		
256	37,125	159,609			
512	291,141				

RUNTIMES IN MS: EARLEY-BASED WITH THE VPP				
	Grammar Size (k)			
String Size (n)	1	8	64	512	4096
2	~0	~0	31	1,937	194,047
4	~0	16	78	4,078	453,203
8	15	31	234	10,922	781,141
16	31	188	875	27,125	1,787,140
32	125	750	4,141	98,829	
64	578	3,547	28,640	350,218	
128	2,453	20,766	264,500		
256	12,187	122,797			
512	74,046				

Table 4.8 Items generated by four different TAG parsers for artificially-generated grammars G_k. Best results are highlighted with an asterisk.

ITEMS GENERATED: EARLY-BASED WITH AND WITHOUT THE VPP				

String Size (n)	Grammar Size (k)				
	1	8	64	512	4096
2	*20	55	335	2,575	20,495
4	*54	160	944	7,216	57,392
8	*170	*590	3,054	22,766	180,462
16	*594	*2,538	11,290	79,386	624,154
32	*2,210	*10,850	*47,410	298,290	
64	*8,514	*45,138	*226,914	*1,187,426	
128	*33,410	*156,405	*1,152,834		
256	*132,354	*688,053			
512	*526,850				

ITEMS GENERATED: CYK-BASED				

String Size (n)	Grammar Size (k)				
	1	8	64	512	4096
2	23	*44	*212	*1,556	*12,308
4	64	*143	*703	*5,183	*41,023
8	206	605	*2,621	*18,749	*147,773
16	730	2,933	*10,873	*71,801	*559,225
32	2,738	13,349	50,417	*286,961	
64	10,594	57,095	264,673	1,196,513	
128	41,666	236,768	1,442,721		
256	165,250	964,754			
512	658,178				

ITEMS GENERATED: NEDERHOF'S ALGORITHM				

String Size (n)	Grammar Size (k)				
	1	8	64	512	4096
2	22	64	400	3,088	24,592
4	66	215	1,335	10,295	81,875
8	226	877	4,909	37,165	295,213
16	834	3,989	19,545	141,401	1,140,829
32	3,202	17,509	84,145	557,233	
64	12,546	73,733	397,665	2,261,345	
128	49,666	302,917	1,970,949		
256	197,634	1,228,229			
512	788,482				

positive constant for each fixed n (if $f(k)$ is an estimation of complexity with respect to grammar size).

By applying these principles, we find that the empirical time complexity with respect to string length is in the range between $O(n^{2.8})$ and $O(n^3)$ for the CYK-based and Nederhof algorithms, and between $O(n^{2.6})$ and $O(n^3)$ for the Earley-based algorithms with and without the VPP. Therefore, the practical time complexity we obtain is far below the theoretical worst-case bounds for these algorithms, which are $O(n^6)$ (except for the Earley-based algorithm with the VPP, which is $O(n^7)$).[12]

If we focus on the number of items generated in each case (Table 4.8) we obtain that the empirical space complexity with respect to string length is approximately $O(n^2)$ for all the algorithms, also far below the worst-case bounds ($O(n^4)$ and $O(n^5)$).

With respect to the size of the grammar, we obtain a time complexity of approximately $O(|\mathbb{I} \cup \mathbb{A}|^2)$ for all the algorithms. This matches the theoretical worst-case bound, which is $O(|\mathbb{I} \cup \mathbb{A}|^2)$ due to the adjunction steps, which work with pairs of trees. In the case of our artificially generated grammars G_k, any auxiliary tree can adjoin into any other, so it is logical that our times grow quadratically. Note, however, that real-life grammars such as the XTAG English grammar (XTAG Research Group, 2001) have relatively few different nonterminals with respect to their amount of elementary trees, so many pairs of trees are susceptible to adjunction and we cannot expect their behaviour to be much better than this.

Space complexity with respect to grammar size is approximately $O(|\mathbb{I} \cup \mathbb{A}|)$ for all the algorithms. This is an expected result, since each generated item is associated with a given tree node.

An overview of the empirical time and space complexities obtained from these experiments, compared to the corresponding theoretical worst-case complexities, is shown in Table 4.9.

Practical applications of TAG in natural language processing usually fall within the range of values for n and k covered in our experiments (grammars with hundreds or a few thousands of trees are used to parse sentences of several dozens of words). Within these ranges, both string length and grammar size take significant values and have an important influence on

---

[12] Although it is possible to design artificial grammars producing worst-case performance with respect to n, the results for such grammars would have less practical interest, as they would depart from the usual characteristics of practical TAGs. The elementary trees in the grammars G_k have a similar structure to trees found in natural language grammars such as the XTAG English grammar.

Table 4.9 Comparison of the empirical time and space complexities obtained for four TAG parsers with the corresponding theoretical complexities.

TIME COMPLEXITY	CYK	EAR. NO VPP	EAR. VPP	NEDERHOF
Theoretical wrt n	$O(n^6)$	$O(n^7)$	$O(n^6)$	$O(n^6)$
Practical wrt n	$O(n^{2.9})$	$O(n^{2.8})$	$O(n^{2.8})$	$O(n^{2.9})$
Theoretical wrt k	$O(k^2)$	$O(k^2)$	$O(k^2)$	$O(k^2)$
Practical wrt k	$O(k^2)$	$O(k^2)$	$O(k^2)$	$O(k^2)$

SPACE COMPLEXITY	CYK	EAR. NO VPP	EAR. VPP	NEDERHOF
Theoretical wrt n	$O(n^4)$	$O(n^4)$	$O(n^5)$	$O(n^5)$
Practical wrt n	$O(n^2)$	$O(n^2)$	$O(n^2)$	$O(n^2)$
Theoretical wrt k	$O(k)$	$O(k)$	$O(k)$	$O(k)$
Practical wrt k	$O(k)$	$O(k)$	$O(k)$	$O(k)$

execution times, as we can see from the results in the tables. This leads us to note that traditional complexity analysis based on a single factor (string length or grammar size) can be misleading for practical applications, since it can lead us to an incomplete idea of real complexity. For example, if we are working with a grammar with thousands of trees, the size of the grammar is the most influential factor, and the use of filtering techniques (Schabes and Joshi, 1991) to reduce the amount of trees used in parsing is essential in order to achieve good performance. The influence of string length in these cases, on the other hand, is mitigated by the huge constant factors related to grammar size. For instance, in the times shown in the tables for the grammar G_{4096}, we can see that parsing times are multiplied by a factor less than 3 when the length of the input string is duplicated, although the rest of the results have lead us to conclude that the practical asymptotic complexity with respect to string length is at least $O(n^{2.6})$. These interactions between both factors must be taken into account when analysing performance in terms of computational complexity.

Earley-based algorithms achieve better execution times than the CYK-based algorithm for large grammars, although they are worse for small grammars. This contrasts with the results obtained for CFGs in Section 4.1, where CYK worked better for large grammars. When working with CFGs, CYK has a better computational complexity than Earley with respect to grammar size (see Section 4.1), but the TAG variant of the CYK algorithm is quadratic with respect to grammar size and does not have this advantage.

CYK generates fewer items than the Earley-based algorithms when working with large grammars and short strings, and the opposite happens when working with small grammars and long strings.

The Earley-based algorithm with the VPP generates the same number of items as the one without this property, and has worse execution times. The reason is that no partial parses violating this property are generated by any of both algorithms in the particular case of the grammars G_k, so guaranteeing the VPP does not prevent any items from being generated. Therefore, the fact that the variant without the VPP works better in this particular case cannot be extrapolated to other grammars. However, the differences in times between these two algorithms illustrate the overhead caused by the extra checks needed to guarantee the VPP in a particularly bad case.

Nederhof's algorithm has slower execution times than the other Earley variants. Despite the fact that Nederhof's algorithm is an improvement over the other Earley-based algorithm with the VPP in terms of computational complexity, the extra deduction steps it contains make it slower in practice.

Finally, if we compare the runtimes obtained in this section with those obtained with the XTAG English Grammar (Table 4.5), we see that the obtained execution times for the XTAG grammar are in the ranges that we could expect given the artificial grammar results, i.e. they approximately match the times in the tables for the corresponding grammar sizes and input string lengths. The most noticeable difference is that the Earley-like algorithm verifying the VPP generates fewer items than the variant without the VPP in the XTAG grammar, and this causes its runtimes to be faster. But this difference is not surprising, as explained above.

4.7 Overhead of TAG parsing over CFG parsing

The languages L_k that we parsed in the last section were regular languages, so in practice we do not need tree adjoining grammars to parse them, although it was convenient to use them in our comparison. This can lead us to wonder how large is the overhead caused by using the TAG formalism to parse context-free languages (Gómez-Rodríguez *et al.*, 2006c).

Given the regular language $L_k = a_0(a_1 \mid a_2 \mid \ldots \mid a_k)^*$, a CFG that parses it is $G'_k = (N, \Sigma, P, S)$, with:

$$N = \{S\}, \text{and}$$

$$P = \{S \to a_0\} \cup \{S \to Sa_i \mid 1 \le i \le k\}.$$

This grammar minimises the number of rules needed to parse L_k ($k + 1$ rules), but has left recursion. If we want to eliminate left recursion, we can use the grammar $G''_k = (N, \Sigma, P, S)$ with:

$$N = \{S, A\}, \text{and}$$

$$P = \{S \to a_0A\} \cup \{A \to a_iA \mid 1 \le i \le k\} \cup \{A \to \epsilon\},$$

which has $k + 2$ production rules.

The number of items generated by the Earley algorithm for CFGs when parsing a sentence of length n from the language L_k by using the grammar G'_k is $(k+2)n$. In the case of the grammar G''_k, the same algorithm generates $(k + 4)n + \frac{n(n-1)}{2} + 1$ items. In both cases the amount of items generated is linear with respect to grammar size, as with TAG parsers. With respect to string length, the amount of items is $O(n)$ for G'_k and $O(n^2)$ for G''_k, and it was approximately $O(n^2)$ for the TAG G_k. Note, however, that the constant factors behind complexity are much greater when working with G_k than with G''_k, and this reflects on the actual number of items generated (for example, the Earley algorithm generates 16,833 items when working with G''_{64} and a string of length $n = 128$, while the TAG variant of Earley without the VPP generated 1,152,834 items, as seen in Table 4.8).

The execution times for both algorithms appear in Table 4.10. From the obtained times, we can deduce that the empirical time complexity is linear with respect to string length and quadratic with respect to grammar size in the case of G'_k; and quadratic with respect to string length and linear with respect to grammar size in the case of G''_k. So this example shows that, when parsing a context-free language using a TAG, we suffer an overhead both in constant factors (more complex items, more deduction steps, etc.) and in asymptotic behaviour (summarised in Table 4.11), so actual execution times can be several orders of magnitude larger. Note that the way grammars are designed also has an influence, but our tree adjoining grammars G_k are the simplest TAGs able to parse the languages L_k by using adjunction (an alternative would be to write a grammar using the substitution operation to combine trees).

Table 4.10   Runtimes in ms obtained by applying the Earley parser for CFGs to sentences in L_k.

STRING LENGTH (n)	GRAMMAR SIZE (k), GRAMMAR G'_k				
	1	8	64	512	4096
n=2	~0	~0	~0	31	2,062
n=4	~0	~0	~0	62	4,110
n=8	~0	~0	~0	125	8,265
n=16	~0	~0	~0	217	15,390
n=32	~0	~0	15	563	29,344
n=64	~0	~0	31	1,062	61,875
n=128	~0	~0	109	2,083	122,875
n=256	~0	15	188	4,266	236,688
n=512	15	31	328	8,406	484,859

STRING LENGTH (n)	GRAMMAR SIZE (k), GRAMMAR G''_k				
	1	8	64	512	4096
n=2	~0	~0	~0	~0	47
n=4	~0	~0	~0	15	94
n=8	~0	~0	~0	16	203
n=16	~0	~0	~0	46	688
n=32	~0	~0	15	203	1,735
n=64	31	31	93	516	4,812
n=128	156	156	328	1,500	13,406
n=256	484	547	984	5,078	45,172
n=512	1,765	2,047	3,734	18,078	

Table 4.11 Comparison of empirical complexities obtained when parsing the languages L_k with CFGs and TAGs.

COMPLEXITY	TAG G_k	CFG G'_k	CFG G''_k
Time wrt n	$O(n^{2.9})$	$O(n)$	$O(n^2)$
Time wrt k	$O(k^2)$	$O(k^2)$	$O(k)$
Space wrt n	$O(n^2)$	$O(n)$	$O(n^2)$
Space wrt k	$O(k)$	$O(k)$	$O(k)$

4.8 Discussion

In this chapter, we have used the compiler introduced in Chapter 3 to perform empirical comparisons of different constituency-based parsing algorithms. We have compared algorithms for two different constituency grammar formalisms (CFG and TAG) by using them to parse sentences with grammars from well-known natural language corpora, as well as with artificially generated grammars.

In the experiments with natural language grammars, for the case of CFG, the CYK (Kasami, 1965; Younger, 1967), Earley (Earley, 1970) and Left-Corner (Rosenkrantz and Lewis II, 1970) algorithms have been compared on the Susanne (Sampson, 1994), Alvey (Carroll, 1993) and Deltra (Schoorl and Belder, 1990) grammars. For TAG, we have compared a CYK-based algorithm (Vijay-Shanker and Joshi, 1985), Earley-based algorithms with and without the VPP (Alonso *et al.*, 1999; Schabes, 1994), and the algorithm by Nederhof (1999), using the XTAG English Grammar (XTAG Research Group, 2001).

These experiments are an example of how the parsing schemata compiler presented in Chapter 3 can be used to easily obtain implementations of different parsers and test them on real-sized grammars under homogeneous conditions. The measurements obtained in the comparisons show how different parsers can be better or worse suited to a particular task depending on factors related to the size and nature of the grammar and sentences to be parsed. Our system provides a quick way to prototype and evaluate several parsing algorithms in order to find the best one for a particular application.

These studies have been complemented with experiments based on artificially-generated grammars, providing an evaluation of the influence of grammar size on the performance of TAG parsers, as well as a study of the practical overhead caused by using TAGs to parse context-free languages.

The results show that both string length and grammar size can be important factors in performance, and the interactions between them sometimes make their influence hard to quantify. The influence of string length in practical cases is usually below the theoretical worst-case bounds (between $O(n)$ and $O(n^2)$ in our tests for CFGs, and slightly below $O(n^3)$ for TAGs). Grammar size becomes the dominating factor in large TAGs, making tree filtering techniques advisable in order to achieve faster execution times.

Using TAGs to parse context-free languages causes an overhead both in constant factors and in practical computational complexity, thus increasing execution times by several orders of magnitude with respect to CFG parsing.

The results presented in this chapter conclude Part 2 of this book, in which we have defined a practical tool for the development of natural language parsers using parsing schemata, and we have used it to study the empirical behaviour of parsers for CFGs and TAGs. This system can be used to generate an efficient implementation of any parser that can be described as a parsing schema, allowing parser developers to prototype algorithms by specifying them formally, without the need to implement them.

In the following parts, we take a more theoretical approach, in order to extend the theory of parsing schemata to be able to describe two kinds of parsers of practical interest that were not contemplated in the original formalism by Sikkel (1997). In particular, Part 3 defines parsing schemata for error-repair parsers, and Part 4 for dependency-based parsers. In both cases, the definitions of the formalisms are followed by novel results derived from their application.

PART 3

Parsing Schemata for Error-Repair Parsers

Chapter 5

Error-repair parsing schemata

Robustness, the ability to analyse any input regardless of its grammaticality, is a desirable property for any system dealing with unrestricted natural language text. Error-repair parsing approaches achieve robustness by considering ungrammatical sentences as corrupted versions of valid sentences.

The formalism of parsing schemata, as defined by Sikkel (1997) and explained in Chapter 2 of this book, cannot be used to represent this kind of parsing algorithms. In this chapter we present a variant of the formalism (Gómez-Rodríguez *et al.*, 2007b, 2010a) that can be used to define and relate error-repair parsers and study their formal properties, such as correctness. Additionally, we will use this new formalism, together with the parsing schema compiler presented in Chapter 3, to generate and compare implementations of parsers with global and regional error-repair strategies.

5.1   Motivation

When using grammar-driven parsers to process natural language texts in real-life domains, it is common to find sentences that cannot be parsed by the grammar. This may be due to several reasons, including insufficient coverage (the input is well-formed, but the grammar cannot recognise it) and ill-formedness of the input (errors in the sentence or errors caused by input methods). A standard parser will fail to return an analysis in these cases. A robust parser is one that can provide useful results for such extragrammatical sentences.

The methods that have been proposed to achieve robustness in grammar-driven parsing fall mainly into two broad categories: those that try to parse well-formed fragments of the input when a parse for the complete sentence cannot be found (partial parsers, such as the one described by Kasper *et al.* (1999)), and those which try to assign a complete parse to the input sentence by relaxing grammatical constraints. In this chapter we will focus on error-repair parsers, which fall into the second category. An error-repair parser is a kind of robust parser that can find a complete parse tree for sentences not covered by the grammar, by supposing that ungrammatical strings are corrupted versions of valid strings.

In the field of compiler design for programming languages, the problem of repairing and recovering from syntax errors during parsing has received a great deal of attention in the past (see for example the list of references provided in the annotated bibliography of Grune and Jacobs (2008, section 18.2.7)) and also in recent years (see for example van der Spek *et al.* (2005); Corchuelo *et al.* (2002); Kim and Choe (2001); Cerecke (2002)). In the field of natural language parsing, some error-repair parsers have also been described, for example, in Lyon (1974); Mellish (1989), or more recently in Vilares *et al.* (2004) and Perez-Cortes *et al.* (2000).

However, no formalism has been proposed to uniformly describe error-repair parsers, compare them and prove their correctness. In this chapter we propose such a framework as an extension of parsing schemata (Sikkel, 1997). This not only allows us to take advantage of all the theoretical benefits of parsing schemata that have been described in Section 2.4 when defining and studying error-repair parsers, but also to use the compiler introduced in Chapter 3 to obtain efficient implementations of them, as will be described at the end of this chapter. Furthermore, we will show in Chapter 6 how the described formalism can be used to automatically transform standard parsers, like those used in Chapter 4, into robust, error-repair parsers.

5.2   Error repair in parsing schemata

As mentioned above, error-repair parsers are able to analyse ungrammatical sentences by considering them as versions of valid sentences that have been modified by applying a number of *errors* to them. Thus, errors can be seen as transformations on strings: for instance, a typical error could be the omission of a word from a sentence. Here, we will take the more general approach of considering that errors are transformations of constituency parse trees. From this point of view, string transformations can be seen as a particular case of tree transformations where only terminal nodes can be altered.

An error-repair parser will be able to detect errors in sentences, and build a constituency tree for an ungrammatical sentence based on the parse tree for its corresponding grammatical sentence.

The parsing schemata formalism introduced in Chapter 2 does not suffice to define error-repair parsers that can show such a robust behaviour in the presence of errors. By Definition 2.9, items can only contain members of *Trees*(G), which are trees that conform to the constraints imposed by the grammar, but in order to build trees for ungrammatical sentences we need to be able to violate these constraints. What we need is to obtain items containing "approximate parses" if an exact parse for the sentence does not exist. Approximate parses need not be members of *Trees*(G), since they may correspond to ungrammatical sentences, but they should be *similar* to a member of *Trees*(G). This notion of "similarity" can be formalised as a distance function in order to obtain a definition of items allowing approximate parses to be generated.

5.2.1 *The formalism of error-repair parsing schemata*

Given a grammar G with an alphabet Σ of terminal symbols and a set N of nonterminal symbols, we shall denote by *Trees'*(G) the set of finitely branching finite trees in which children of a node have a left-to-right ordering and every node is labelled with an element from $N \cup \Sigma \cup (\Sigma \times \mathbb{N}) \cup \{\epsilon\}$. Note that *Trees*$(G) \subset$ *Trees'*(G), and that nodes labelled with elements of $(\Sigma \times \mathbb{N})$ correspond to *marked terminals* of the form (a, i) (cf. Definition 2.7). We will use the notation $\underline{a}_i$ to abbreviate a marked terminal (a, i) or (a_i, i), depending on the context.

Let $d :$ *Trees'*$(G) \times$ *Trees'*$(G) \to \mathbb{N} \cup \{0, \infty\}$ be a function verifying the following distance axioms:[1]

- For all $t_1, t_2 \in$ *Trees'*(G), $d(t_1, t_2)$ takes non-negative real values or the value $+\infty$ (*non-negativity*),
- For all $t \in$ *Trees'*(G), $d(t, t) = 0$,
- For all $t_1, t_2 \in$ *Trees'*(G), $d(t_1, t_2) = d(t_2, t_1)$ (*symmetry*),
- For all $t_1, t_2, t_3 \in$ *Trees'*(G), $d(t_1, t_3) \leq d(t_1, t_2) + d(t_2, t_3)$ (*triangle inequality*).

---

[1] These are the axioms for an *extended pseudometric*. If, in addition to this, the function d verifies positive definiteness (i.e. if, apart from being non-negative, we have that $d(t_1, t_2) = 0$ if and only if $t_1 = t_2$), then the distance is an *extended metric*. A pseudometric is a generalisation of a metric where we allow distinct entities to be at zero distance, and a (pseudo)metric is called extended if it is allowed to take the value $+\infty$.

We shall denote by $Trees_e(G)$ the set $\{t \in Trees'(G) \mid \exists t' \in Trees(G) : d(t, t') \le e\}$, i.e., $Trees_e(G)$ is the set of trees that have distance e or less to some grammatically valid tree. Note that, by construction, $Trees(G) \subseteq Trees_0(G)$.

Definition 5.1. We define the set of *approximate trees* for a grammar G and a tree distance function d as $ApTrees(G) = \{(t, e) \in (Trees'(G) \times (\mathbb{N} \cup \{0\})) \mid t \in Trees_e(G)\}$.

Therefore, an approximate tree is the pair formed by a tree and an upper bound of its distance to some tree in $Trees(G)$.

This concept of approximate trees allows us to precisely define the problems that we want to solve with error-repair parsers. Given a grammar G, a distance function d and a sentence $a_1 \ldots a_n$, the *approximate recognition problem* is to determine the minimal $e \in (\mathbb{N} \cup \{0\})$ such that there exists an approximate tree $(t, e) \in ApTrees(G)$ where t is a marked parse tree for the sentence. We will call such an approximate tree an *approximate marked parse tree* for $a_1 \ldots a_n$.

Similarly, the *approximate parsing* problem consists of finding the minimal $e \in (\mathbb{N} \cup \{0\})$ such that there exists an approximate marked parse tree $(t, e) \in ApTrees(G)$ for the sentence, and finding all approximate marked parse trees of the form (t, e) for the sentence.

As we can see, while the problem of parsing is a problem of finding trees, the problem of approximate parsing can be seen as a problem of finding approximate trees. In the same way that the problem of parsing can be solved by a deduction system whose items are sets of trees, the problem of approximate parsing can be solved by one whose items are sets of approximate trees.

Definition 5.2. Given a grammar G and a distance function d, we define an *approximate item set* as a set $\mathcal{I}'$ such that:

$$\mathcal{I}' \subseteq \left(\left(\bigcup_{i=0}^{\infty} \Pi_i\right) \cup \{\varnothing\}\right)$$

where each Π_i is a partition of the set $\{(t, i) \in ApTrees(G)\}$.

Each element of an approximate item set is a set of approximate trees, and will be called an *approximate item*. Note that the concept is defined in such a way that each approximate item contains approximate trees with a single value of the distance e. Directly defining an approximate item set using any partition of $ApTrees(G)$ would be impractical, since we need our parsers to keep track of the degree of discrepancy of partial parses with respect to the grammar, and that information would be lost if our items were not associated to a single value of e. This concrete value of e is what we will call the *parsing distance* of an item ι, or $dist(\iota)$:

Definition 5.3. Let $\mathcal{I}' \subseteq ((\bigcup_{i=0}^{\infty} \Pi_i) \cup \{\varnothing\})$ be an approximate item set as defined above, and $\iota \in \mathcal{I}'$. The *parsing distance* associated to the nonempty approximate item ι, $dist(\iota)$, is defined by the (trivially unique) value $i \in (\mathbb{N} \cup \{0\}) \mid \iota \in \Pi_i$. In the case of the empty approximate item $\varnothing$, we will say that $dist(\varnothing) = \infty$.

Having defined approximate item sets that can handle robust parsing by relaxing grammar constraints, error-repair parsers can be described by using parsing schemata that work with these items. They are defined in an analogous way to standard parsing schemata:

Definition 5.4. Let G be a grammar over an alphabet Σ of terminals and an alphabet N of nonterminals, d a distance function, and $\mathcal{I}'$ an approximate item set for that grammar and distance. We define the set of *final approximate items* for strings of length n, denoted $\mathcal{F}'^{(n)}_{G,\mathcal{I}'}$, as:

$$\mathcal{F}'^{(n)}_{G,\mathcal{I}'} = \{\iota \in \mathcal{I}' \mid \exists(t,e) \in \iota : t \in \mathcal{P}^{(n)}_G\}.$$

Thus, an approximate item is final for strings of length n if it contains an approximate marked parse tree for some string of length n. As in the case of standard parsing schemata, we can fix a particular string of length n to define a set of *correct final items* for that string:

Definition 5.5. Let G be a grammar over an alphabet Σ of terminals and an alphabet N of nonterminals, d a distance function, $\mathcal{I}'$ an approximate item set for that grammar and distance, and $a_1 \ldots a_n \in \Sigma^*$. The set of *correct final approximate items* for that string, denoted $\mathcal{CF}'^{a_1 \ldots a_n}_{G,\mathcal{I}'}$, is:

$$\mathcal{CF}'^{a_1 \ldots a_n}_{G,\mathcal{I}'} = \{\iota \in \mathcal{I}' \mid \exists(t,e) \in \iota : t \text{ is a marked parse tree}$$
$$\text{for the string } a_1 \ldots a_n\}.$$

Definition 5.6. Let G be a grammar, Σ an alphabet of terminals, d a distance function, and $a_1 \ldots a_n \in \Sigma^*$ a string.

An *error-repair instantiated parsing system* is a deduction system $(\mathcal{I}', \mathcal{H}, D)$ such that $\mathcal{I}'$ is an approximate item set for G with distance function d, and $\mathcal{H}$ is a set of hypotheses such that $\{a_i(\underline{a_i})\} \in \mathcal{H}$ for each $a_i, 1 \le i \le n$.

Definition 5.7. Let G be a grammar, Σ an alphabet of terminals and d a distance function.

An *error-repair uninstantiated parsing system* is a triple $(\mathcal{I}', \mathcal{K}, D)$ where $\mathcal{K}$ is a function such that $(\mathcal{I}', \mathcal{K}(a_1 \ldots a_n), D)$ is an error-repair instantiated parsing system for each $a_1 \ldots a_n \in \Sigma^*$ (in practice, we will always define this function as $\mathcal{K}(a_1 \ldots a_n) = \{\{a_i(\underline{a}_i)\} \mid 1 \le i \le n\}$).

Definition 5.8. An *error-repair parsing schema* (Gómez-Rodríguez *et al.*, 2010a) for a class of grammars $\mathcal{CG}$ and a distance function d is a function that assigns an error-repair uninstantiated parsing system to each grammar $G \in \mathcal{CG}$.

The concepts of *valid items*, *soundness*, *completeness* and *correctness* are totally analogous to the standard parsing schemata case (Section 2.3.3). Note that, in the particular case of completeness, this means that a complete error-repair parser must be able to infer all correct final items, regardless of their associated parsing distance. However, in practice, only items with a minimal distance need to be used to solve the approximate parsing problem:

Definition 5.9. The *minimal parsing distance* for a string $a_1 \ldots a_n$ in an approximate item set $\mathcal{I}'$ is defined by:

$$MinDist(\mathcal{I}', a_1 \ldots a_n) = min\{e \in (\mathbb{N} \cup \{0\}) \mid \exists \iota \in \mathcal{CF}'^{a_1 \ldots a_n}_{G, \mathcal{I}'} : dist(\iota) = e\}.$$

Definition 5.10. The set of *minimal final items* for a string $a_1 \ldots a_n$ in an approximate item set $\mathcal{I}'$ is defined by:

$$\mathcal{MF}(\mathcal{I}', a_1 \ldots a_n) = \{\iota \in \mathcal{CF}'^{a_1 \ldots a_n}_{G, \mathcal{I}'} \mid dist(\iota) = MinDist(\mathcal{I}', a_1 \ldots a_n)\}.$$

The *approximate recognition* and *approximate parsing* problems that we defined earlier for any string and grammar can be solved by obtaining the set of minimal final items in an approximate item set. Minimal final items can be deduced by any correct error-repair parsing schema, since they are a subset of correct final items.

5.2.2 *A tree distance for edit distance-based repair*

A correct error-repair parsing schema will obtain the approximate parses whose distance to an exact parse is minimal. Therefore, a suitable distance function should be chosen depending on the kind of errors that are more likely to appear in input sentences.

Let us suppose a generic scenario where we would like to repair errors according to edit distance. The edit distance or Levenshtein distance (Levenshtein, 1966) between two strings is the minimum number of insertions, deletions or substitutions of a single terminal needed to transform either of the strings into the other one. Given a string $a_1 \ldots a_n$ containing errors, we would like our parsers to return an approximate parse based on the exact parse tree of one of the grammatical strings whose Levenshtein distance to $a_1 \ldots a_n$ is minimal.

A suitable distance function $\hat{d}$ for this case is given by ignoring the indexes in marked terminals (i.e. two trees differing only in the integer values associated to their marked terminals are considered at zero distance for this definition) and defining the distance as the number of elementary tree transformations that we need to transform one tree into another, if the elementary transformations that we allow are inserting, deleting or changing the label of a marked terminal node in the frontier.

More formally, for each $t \in Trees'(G)$, we define $Insertion(t)$, $Deletion(t)$ and $Substitution(t)$ as the set of trees obtained by inserting a marked terminal node in the frontier, deleting a marked terminal node and changing its associated symbol, respectively. With this, we can define sets of transformations of a given tree t as follows:

$$Trans_0(t) = \{t\} \cup \{t' \mid t' \text{ differs from } t$$
only in integer values associated with marked terminals$\}$,

$$Trans_1(t) = \bigcup_{t' \in Trans_0(t)} Insertion(t') \cup Deletion(t') \cup Substitution(t'),$$

$$Trans_i(t) = \{t' \in Trees'(G) \mid \exists u \in Trans_{i-1}(t) : t' \in Trans_1(u)\}, \text{ for } i > 1,$$
and our distance function $\hat{d}$ as follows:

$$\hat{d} : Trees'(G) \times Trees'(G) \rightarrow \mathbb{N} \cup \{0, \infty\},$$

$$\hat{d}(t_1, t_2) = min\{i \in (\mathbb{N} \cup \{0\}) \mid t_2 \in Trans_i(t_1)\}, \text{ if}$$

$$\exists i \in (\mathbb{N} \cup \{0\}) : t_2 \in Trans_i(t_1),$$

$$\hat{d}(t_1, t_2) = \infty \text{ otherwise.}$$

Note that our distance function $\hat{d}$ satisfies the properties of an extended pseudometric:

- It is symmetrical, since for every $t_1, t_2 \in Trees'(G)$, we have that $t_1 \in Trans_i(t_2)$ if and only if $t_2 \in Trans_i(t_1)$. This is easy to verify if we take into account that $t_1 \in Deletion(t_2) \Leftrightarrow t_2 \in Insertion(t_1)$, $t_1 \in$

Insertion(t_2) $\Leftrightarrow$ t_2 $\in$ *Deletion*(t_1), and t_1 $\in$ *Substitution*(t_2) $\Leftrightarrow$ t_2 $\in$ *Substitution*(t_1),

- Non-negativity is trivial to verify, since $Trans_i(t)$ is only defined for $i \geq 0$,
- $\hat{d}(t,t)$ is always zero because $t \in Trans_0(t)$ by construction,
- The triangle inequality holds because if t_3 $\in$ $Trans_{e2}(t_2)$ and t_2 $\in$ $Trans_{e1}(t_1)$, then we have that t_3 $\in$ $Trans_{e1+e2}(t_1)$; because if we apply to t_1 the $e1$ transformations that turn it into t_2, and then apply the $e2$ transformations that turn t_2 into t_3, we obtain t_3 (note that there may be a way of obtaining t_3 from t_1 with less transformations, hence the inequality).

If we call the string edit distance d_{ed}, then it is easy to see that for any tree t_1 such that $yield(t_1) = \alpha$, and for any string β, there exists a tree t_2 with yield β such that $\hat{d}(t_1,t_2) = d_{ed}(\alpha,\beta)$. This tree is obtained by applying to the frontier nodes of α the elementary transformations that turn α into β.

As we only allow transformations dealing with marked terminal nodes, trees that differ in nodes labelled with other symbols will be considered to be at infinite distance. Therefore, when we define a parser using this distance, the parses (t_2) obtained for an ungrammatical input sentence (β) will be identical, except for marked terminals, to the valid parses (t_1) corresponding to the grammatical sentences (α) whose distance to the input is minimal. As an example, Figure 5.1 shows a marked parse tree t for the grammatical input sentence "The dog barks"; and Figure 5.2 shows the minimal distance trees for ungrammatical sentences obtained by adding, removing and changing a word of the original sentence (we will call these transformations an *insertion error*, *deletion error* and *substitution error*, respectively). Each of the trees in Figure 5.2 is at distance 1 from the tree in Figure 5.1 for the distance function $\hat{d}$.[2]

---

[2]Note that the marked terminal nodes in the figure have been labelled with words (*the*, etc.), instead of with parts-of-speech like the terminal nodes (*Det*, etc.). This has been done for clarity, to show the kind of errors in words and sentences that can be detected. In reality, if the terminal alphabet Σ is a set of parts-of-speech, marked terminals have to contain parts-of-speech as well: thus, for example, the typographical error of typing "do" instead of "dog" could translate into a substitution of an V tag for an N tag in the marked terminal nodes.

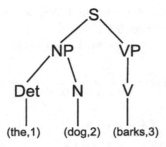

Fig. 5.1 Marked parse tree for a simple grammatical sentence.

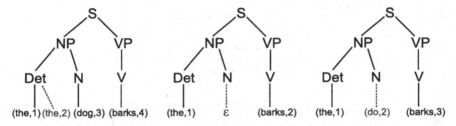

Fig. 5.2 Trees obtained for sentences with one insertion, deletion and substitution error, respectively, under the distance function $\hat{d}$.

5.3 Lyon's error-repair parser

The formalism of error-repair parsing schemata allows us to represent error-repair parsers in a simple, declarative way, making it easy to explore their formal properties and obtain efficient implementations of them. As an example, we will see how this formalism can be used to describe one of the most influential error-repair parsers in the literature, the one described by Lyon (1974).

The schema for Lyon's error-repair parser maps each CFG $G = (N, \Sigma, P, S) \in \mathcal{CFG}$ to a triple $(\mathcal{I}', \mathcal{K}, D)$, where $\mathcal{K}$ has the standard definition given above, and $\mathcal{I}'$ and D are defined as follows:

$$\mathcal{I}'_{Lyon} = \{[A \to \alpha \bullet \beta, i, j, e] \mid A \to \alpha\beta \in P \wedge e \geq 0 \wedge 0 \leq i \leq j\}$$

where we use $[A \to \alpha \bullet \beta, i, j, e]$ as a shorthand notation for the set of approximate trees (t, e) such that t is a partial parse tree with root A where the direct children of A are labelled with the symbols of the string $\alpha\beta$, and the frontier nodes of the subtrees rooted at the symbols in α form the substring $\underline{a}_{i+1} \cdots \underline{a}_j$ of the input string. The distance function d used to define the approximate item set, and therefore conditioning the values of e, is $\hat{d}$ as defined in Section 5.2.2.

The set of deduction steps, D, for Lyon's parser is defined as the union of the following:

$$\text{INITTER:} \quad \frac{}{[S \to \bullet\gamma, 0, 0, 0]} \quad S \to \gamma \in P$$

$$\text{SCANNER:} \quad \frac{[A \to \alpha \bullet x\beta, i, j, e] \qquad [x, j, j+1]}{[A \to \alpha x \bullet \beta, i, j+1, e]}$$

$$\text{COMPLETER:} \quad \frac{[A \to \alpha \bullet B\beta, i, j, e_1] \qquad [B \to \gamma\bullet, j, k, e_2]}{[A \to \alpha B \bullet \beta, i, k, e_1 + e_2]}$$

$$\text{PREDICTOR:} \quad \frac{[A \to \alpha \bullet B\beta, i, j, e_1]}{[B \to \bullet\gamma, j, j, 0]} \quad B \to \gamma \in P$$

$$\text{SCANSUBSTITUTED:} \quad \frac{[A \to \alpha \bullet x\beta, i, j, e] \qquad [b, j, j+1]}{[A \to \alpha x \bullet \beta, i, j+1, e+1]}$$

$$\text{SCANDELETED:} \quad \frac{[A \to \alpha \bullet x\beta, i, j, e]}{[A \to \alpha x \bullet \beta, i, j, e+1]}$$

$$\text{SCANINSERTED:} \quad \frac{[A \to \alpha \bullet \beta, i, j, e] \qquad [b, j, j+1]}{[A \to \alpha \bullet \beta, i, j+1, e+1]}$$

The INITTER, SCANNER, COMPLETER and PREDICTOR steps are similar to those in Earley's algorithm (Figure 2.6 on page 22), with the difference that we have to keep track of the distance associated with the approximate trees in our items.

The SCANSUBSTITUTED, SCANDELETED and SCANINSERTED steps are error-repair steps, and they allow us to read unexpected symbols from the string while incrementing the distance. SCANSUBSTITUTED allows us to repair a substitution error in the string, SCANDELETED repairs a deletion error and SCANINSERTED an insertion error.

Note that the SCANINSERTED step is defined slightly differently from the one in the original formulation by Lyon (1974), which is:

$$\text{SCANINSERTEDLYON:} \quad \frac{[A \to \alpha \bullet x\beta, i, j, e] \qquad [b, j, j+1]}{[A \to \alpha \bullet x\beta, i, j+1, e+1]}$$

This alternative version of SCANINSERTED cannot be used to repair an insertion error at the end of the input, since a repair is only attempted if we are expecting a terminal symbol x and we find another terminal b instead, but not if we are expecting the end of the string. Lyon avoids this problem by extending the grammars used by the schema by changing the initial symbol S to S' and adding the additional rule $S' \rightarrow S\$$, where the character $\$$ acts as an end-of-sentence marker. However, we choose to keep our more general version of the step, and not to extend the grammar with this additional rule.

The set of final items and the subset of correct final items are:

$$\mathcal{F}'_{Lyon} = \{[S \rightarrow \gamma \bullet, 0, n, e]\}$$

$$\mathcal{CF}'_{Lyon} = \{\iota = [S \rightarrow \gamma \bullet, 0, n, e] \mid \exists(t, e) \in \iota :$$
$$t \text{ is a marked parse tree for } a_1 \ldots a_n\}$$

5.3.1 *Lyon is correct*

Once we have defined a parser by means of an error-repair parsing schema, as we have done with Lyon's error-repair parser, we can use the formalism to prove its correctness. As an example, we will show an outline of the proof that the parsing schema for Lyon's algorithm is correct. Note that the proof is not given in full detail since it will be subsumed by a more general result presented in Chapter 6. In that chapter, we will see how any standard parsing schema meeting a certain set of conditions can be systematically transformed to an error-repair parser, in such a way that the correctness of the standard parser implies that the error-repair parser obtained by applying the transformation is also correct. The proof outlined here can be obtained as a particular case of the proof that the aforesaid transformation preserves soundness and completeness, which is described in detail in Section 6.3.

First of all, we observe that the schema for Lyon's parser, as given above, does not guarantee completeness as defined by the parsing schemata formalism: the goal of Lyon's algorithm is to perform a least-errors analysis of the input sentence, and therefore to obtain all the *minimal* correct final items for a given string, rather than the full set of correct final items. However, we can easily obtain a strictly correct version of the schema by adding a deduction step:

$$\text{DISTANCEINCREASER:} \quad \frac{[A \rightarrow \alpha \bullet \beta, i, j, e]}{[A \rightarrow \alpha \bullet \beta, i, j, e + 1]}$$

This DISTANCEINCREASER step is not necessary in practical implementations of the parser, where we are not interested in strict completeness (finding all possible approximate parses) because we only need the minimal-distance parses. However, if we are able to prove that the variant of the parser that includes DISTANCEINCREASER is correct, it immediately follows that the version without it generates all minimal final items, since any sequence of deductions that uses an item $[A \rightarrow \alpha \bullet \beta, i, j, e+1]$ obtained from a DISTANCEINCREASER to produce a minimal final item can also be made directly with $[A \rightarrow \alpha \bullet \beta, i, j, e]$, avoiding the use of this step. Thus, if we call the variant of Lyon's schema with the DISTANCEINCREASER $\$_{Lyon}$, the practical correctness of Lyon's algorithm is implied by the following theorem:

Theorem 5.1. *The parsing schema $\$_{Lyon}$ is correct.*

Proof. In order to prove the correctness of the schema $\$_{Lyon}$, we must prove:

- Soundness: given a grammar and an input string, all valid final items are correct.
- Completeness: given a grammar and an input string, all the correct final items are valid (i.e. can be inferred from the hypotheses). □

5.3.1.1 *Soundness*

By construction, each of the items $[A \rightarrow \alpha \bullet \beta, i, j, e]$ in $\mathcal{I}'_{Lyon}$ represents the set of approximate trees (t, e) such that t is a partial parse tree with root A where the direct children of A are the symbols of the string $\alpha\beta$. We will say that an item $[A \rightarrow \alpha \bullet \beta, i, j, e]$ is *correct* if it contains at least one approximate tree (t, e) such that the leaf nodes of the subtrees rooted at the symbols in α form the substring $\underline{a}_{i+1} \ldots \underline{a}_j$ of the input string[3] (we will call such a tree a *correct tree* for the item). In the particular case of final items, which are of the form $[S \rightarrow \gamma\bullet, 0, n, e]$, correct approximate trees (t, e) trivially verify that t is a marked parse tree for $a_1 \ldots a_n$, and thus a final item containing a correct approximate tree verifies the generic definition of a correct final item.

Proving the soundness of a parsing schema is proving that all valid final items are correct for every grammar G and input string $a_1 \ldots a_n$. To do

---

[3] We are supposing that we have each terminal in the input string annotated with its position, so that our input is a string of marked terminals.

this, we will follow the general procedure described in Section 2.3.3, proving the stronger claim that *all valid items are correct* for every grammar G and input string $a_1 \ldots a_n$. Since hypotheses are trivially correct, it suffices to show that the consequent item of each deduction step in the schema is always correct if its antecedents are. This is proven by reasoning individually about each deduction step, we show the reasoning for some of them as an example:

- Consequents of an INITTER or PREDICTOR step are correct by construction: an item of the form $[B \to \bullet\gamma, j, j, 0]$ contains at least the approximate tree $(B(\gamma), 0)$, which is trivially a correct tree for this item, since $B(\gamma) \in Trees(G)$.

- If the antecedents of a SCANNER are correct, then the consequent is correct: if the item $[A \to \alpha \bullet x\beta, i, j, e]$ is correct, then there exists an approximate tree $(A(\alpha(\ldots)x\beta), e)$ where the yield of α is $\underline{a}_{i+1} \ldots \underline{a}_j$. Since $x \to \underline{x}_{j+1}$ is a legal pseudo-production, we know that adding $\underline{x}_{j+1}$ as only child of x in this tree will not result in an increase of distance to a grammatical tree, so there exists an approximate tree $(A(\alpha(\ldots)x(\underline{x}_{j+1})\beta), e)$ where the yield of α is $\underline{a}_{i+1} \ldots \underline{a}_j$. On the other hand, if the hypothesis $[x, j, j+1]$ is present, then $a_{j+1} = x$. Thus, the approximate tree $(A(\alpha(\ldots)x(\underline{x}_{j+1})\beta), e)$ also verifies the property that the yield of αx is $\underline{a}_{i+1} \ldots \underline{a}_{j+1}$, and thus is a correct approximate tree for the item $[A \to \alpha x \bullet \beta, i, j+1, e]$, so the consequent item is correct.

- If the antecedents of a SCANSUBSTITUTED are correct, then the consequent is correct: if the item $[A \to \alpha \bullet x\beta, i, j, e]$ is correct, then we apply the same reasoning as in the SCANNER to conclude that there exists an approximate tree $(A(\alpha(\ldots)x(\underline{x}_{j+1})\beta), e)$ where the yield of α is $\underline{a}_{i+1} \ldots \underline{a}_j$. On the other hand, if the hypothesis $[b, j, j+1]$ is present, then $a_{j+1} = b$. The tree $A(\alpha(\ldots)x(\underline{b}_{j+1})\beta)$ is trivially in $Trans_1(A(\alpha(\ldots)x(\underline{x}_{j+1})\beta))$, and as we have that $A(\alpha(\ldots)x(\underline{x}_{j+1})\beta)$ is in $Trans_e(t)$ for some $t \in Trees(G)$, we know that the distance from that t to $A(\alpha(\ldots)x(\underline{b}_{j+1})\beta)$ is at most $e+1$. Therefore, there exists an approximate tree $(A(\alpha(\ldots)x(\underline{b}_{j+1})\beta), e+1)$. Since this approximate tree verifies the property that the yield of αx is $\underline{a}_{i+1} \ldots \underline{a}_{j+1}$, it is a correct approximate tree for the consequent item $[A \to \alpha x \bullet \beta, i, j+1, e+1]$, hence this item is correct.

By reasoning similarly about the rest of the deduction steps in $\$_{Lyon}$, we conclude the soundness part of the proof.

5.3.1.2 *Completeness*

Proving completeness for this schema is proving that, given an input string, all correct final items are valid, i.e., they can be inferred from the hypotheses. Therefore, given a string $a_1 \ldots a_n$, we have to prove that every item containing an approximate tree (t, e) such that t is a marked parse tree for $a_1 \ldots a_n$ can be inferred from the hypotheses.

Since final items in this schema are always of the form $[S \to \alpha\bullet, 0, n, e]$, this is equivalent to proving the following proposition:

Proposition 5.1. *Let* $G = (N, \Sigma, P, S)$ *be a CFG, and* $a_1 \ldots a_n \in \Sigma^*$ *a string. Every correct item of the form* $[S \to \alpha\bullet, 0, n, e]$ *is valid in the instantiated parsing system* $(\mathcal{I}'_{Lyon}, \mathcal{K}(a_1 \ldots a_n), D)$ *obtained from applying* $\$_{Lyon}$ *to* G *and* $a_1 \ldots a_n$.

This proposition is proved by induction on the distance e:

Base case ($e = 0$): Items in this schema's item set where the distance e is 0 can be mapped to items from a standard Earley parser by the function f : $\{[A \to \alpha \bullet B\beta, i, j, 0] \in \mathcal{I}'_{Lyon}\} \to \mathcal{I}_{Earley}$ that maps $\iota = [A \to \alpha \bullet B\beta, i, j, 0]$ to $f(\iota) = [A \to \alpha \bullet B\beta, i, j]$. This mapping is trivially bijective, and it is easy to see that deductions are preserved, i.e., for example, the deduction $\iota_1 \iota_2 \vdash \iota_c$ can be made by a COMPLETER in Lyon's parser if an only if the deduction $f(\iota_1)f(\iota_2) \vdash f(\iota_c)$ can be made by a COMPLETER in Earley's parser. Since any correct item of the form $[S \to \alpha\bullet, 0, n, 0]$ in the error-repair parser is $f^{-1}(\kappa)$ for some correct final item $\kappa = [S \to \alpha\bullet, 0, n]$ in the Earley parser, and we know that the Earley parser is complete (Sikkel, 1998), it follows that all final items of the form $[S \to \alpha\bullet, 0, n, 0]$ are valid in Lyon's parser.

Induction step: Supposing that Proposition 5.1 holds for a distance value of e, we must prove that it also holds for $e + 1$.

Let $[S \to \alpha\bullet, 0, n, e + 1]$ be a correct final item for the string $a_1 \ldots a_n$. We will prove that this item is valid in the deduction system $(\mathcal{I}'_{Lyon}, \mathcal{K}(a_1 \ldots a_n), D)$.

As this item is correct for the string $a_1 \ldots a_n$, we know that it contains an approximate tree of the form $(t, e + 1)$ where t is a tree rooted at S and with $yield(t) = \underline{a}_1 \ldots \underline{a}_n$. By definition of approximate tree, we know that there must exist a tree $u \in Trees(G)$ such that $\hat{d}(t, u) = e + 1$ or, equivalently, $t \in Trans_{e+1}(u)$.

By definition of $Trans_{e+1}(u)$, this implies that there is another tree t' such that $t' \in Trans_e(u)$ and $t \in Trans_1(t')$, and this implies that there exists an approximate tree (t', e) such that $\hat{d}(t, t') = 1$.

Since $\hat{d}(t, t') = 1$, and $yield(t) = \underline{a}_1 \ldots \underline{a}_n$, we know that $yield(t')$ must be one of the following:[4]

- $\underline{a}_1 \ldots \underline{a}_{j-1} \underline{b}_j \underline{a}_{j+1} \ldots \underline{a}_n$, if $t \in Substitution(t')$,
- $\underline{a}_1 \ldots \underline{a}_{j-1} (a_{j+1}, j) \ldots (a_n, n+1)$, if $t \in Insertion(t')$,
- $\underline{a}_1 \ldots \underline{a}_{j-1} \underline{b}_j (a_j, j+1)(a_{j+1}, j+2) \ldots (a_n, n+1)$, if $t \in Deletion(t')$.

With this, we divide the proof into three cases, according to the form of $yield(t')$:

Induction step, case 1 (substitution error): In this case, $yield(t')$ $= \underline{a}_1 \ldots \underline{a}_{j-1} \underline{b}_j \underline{a}_{j+1} \ldots \underline{a}_n$. We consider the deduction system $(\mathcal{I}'_{Lyon}, \mathcal{K}(a_1 \ldots a_{j-1}\, b\, a_{j+1} \ldots a_n), D)$ obtained by applying $\$_{Lyon}$ to the grammar G and the string $a_1 \ldots a_{j-1}\, b\, a_{j+1} \ldots a_n$. Consider the item in $\mathcal{I}'$ containing the approximate tree (t', e): this item must be of the form $[S \to \alpha\bullet, 0, n, e]$, since $\hat{d}(t, t') = 1$ and $(t, e+1) \in [S \to \alpha\bullet, 0, n, e+1]$ (note that the fact that the two trees are at finite distance by the function $\hat{d}$ implies that the $S \to \alpha\bullet$ part of their corresponding items must be equal, because trees at finite distance can only differ in marked terminal and epsilon nodes in the frontier).

This item $[S \to \alpha\bullet, 0, n, e]$ is a correct final item in the deduction system $(\mathcal{I}'_{Lyon}, \mathcal{K}(a_1 \ldots a_{j-1}\, b\, a_{j+1} \ldots a_n), D)$, since t' is a marked parse tree for the input string $a_1 \ldots a_{j-1}\, b\, a_{j+1} \ldots a_n$. By the induction hypothesis, the item is also valid in this system. Thus, to prove the induction step for the substitution case, it suffices to show that the validity of this item in the system $(\mathcal{I}'_{Lyon}, \mathcal{K}(a_1 \ldots a_{j-1}\, b\, a_{j+1} \ldots a_n), D)$ implies that the item $[S \to \alpha\bullet, 0, n, e+1]$ is valid in the system $(\mathcal{I}'_{Lyon}, \mathcal{K}(a_1 \ldots a_n), D)$.

Therefore, we have reduced this case of the proof to proving the following lemma:

Lemma 5.1. *Let $(I'_{Lyon}, \mathcal{K}, D)$ be the uninstantiated parsing system obtained by applying Lyon's parsing schema to a given grammar G.*

Given a nonempty string $a_1 \ldots a_n$, and a string $a_1 \ldots a_{j-1} b a_{j+1} \ldots a_n (1 \leq j \leq n)$ obtained by substituting the jth terminal in the first string,

---

[4]Note that, as our definition of $\hat{d}$ ignores indexes associated to marked terminals, we can safely change the indexes of the marked terminals in the yield to keep them consecutive in the insertion and deletion cases.

if $[S \to \alpha\bullet, 0, n, e]$ *is a valid item in the instantiated parsing system* $(\mathcal{I}'_{Lyon},$ $\mathcal{K}(a_1 \ldots a_{j-1} \ b \ a_{j+1} \ldots a_n), \ D),$ *then* $[S \to \alpha\bullet, 0, n, e+1]$ *is valid in the instantiated parsing system* $(\mathcal{I}'_{Lyon}, \ \mathcal{K}(a_1 \ldots a_n), \ D).$

This lemma is proven by defining the following function f_1:

$$f_1 : \mathcal{I}'_{Lyon} \cup \mathcal{K}(a_1 \ldots a_{j-1} \ b \ a_{j+1} \ldots a_n) \to \mathcal{I}'_{Lyon} \cup \mathcal{K}(a_1 \ldots a_n),$$

$$f_1([A \to \alpha \bullet \beta, i, k, e]) = [A \to \alpha \bullet \beta, i, k, e] \text{ if } i > j-1 \text{ or } k < j.$$

$$f_1([A \to \alpha \bullet \beta, i, k, e]) = [A \to \alpha \bullet \beta, i, k, e+1] \text{ if } i \le j-1 \text{ and } j \le k.$$

$$f_1([b, j-1, j]) = [a_j, j-1, j].$$

$$f_1([a_i, i-1, i]) = [a_i, i-1, i], \text{ for } i \ne j.$$

and then showing that if $\iota_1, \iota_2, \ldots, \iota_a \vdash \iota_c$ in the instantiated parsing system $(\mathcal{I}'_{Lyon}, \mathcal{K}(a_1 \ldots a_{j-1} b a_{j+1} \ldots a_n), D)$, then $f_1(\iota_1), f_1(\iota_2), \ldots, f_1(\iota_a) \vdash^*$ $f_1(\iota_c)$ in the instantiated parsing system $(\mathcal{I}'_{Lyon}, \mathcal{K}(a_1 \ldots a_n), D)$. This is proven by individually considering each deduction step with which an inference $\iota_1, \iota_2, \ldots, \iota_a \vdash \iota_c$ can be performed, and checking that it is preserved in the target system.

For example, let us consider the COMPLETER step. If $\iota_1, \iota_2, \ldots, \iota_a \vdash \iota_c$ by a COMPLETER step, the number of antecedent items a must be 2 and the involved items must be of the form: $\iota_1 = [A \to \alpha \bullet B\beta, i_1, i_2, e_1]$, $\iota_2 = [B \to \gamma\bullet, i_2, i_3, e_2]$ and $\iota_c = [A \to \alpha B \bullet \beta, i_1, i_3, e_1 + e_2]$.

We compute all the possible different values of $f_1(\iota_1), f_1(\iota_2)$ and $f_1(\iota_c)$ depending on the values of the indexes:

Case 1: $j \le i_1$ or $i_3 \le j-1$: in this case,

$$f_1(\iota_1) = [A \to \alpha \bullet B\beta, i_1, i_2, e_1],$$
$$f_1(\iota_2) = [B \to \gamma\bullet, i_2, i_3, e_2],$$
$$f_1(\iota_c) = [A \to \alpha B \bullet \beta, i_1, i_3, e_1 + e_2].$$

Case 2: $i_1 \le j-1 < j \le i_2$: in this case,

$$f_1(\iota_1) = [A \to \alpha \bullet B\beta, i_1, i_2, e_1 + 1],$$
$$f_1(\iota_2) = [B \to \gamma\bullet, i_2, i_3, e_2],$$
$$f_1(\iota_c) = [A \to \alpha B \bullet \beta, i_1, i_3, e_1 + e_2 + 1].$$

Case 3: $i_2 \le j-1 < j \le i_3$: in this case,

$$f_1(\iota_1) = [A \to \alpha \bullet B\beta, i_1, i_2, e_1],$$
$$f_1(\iota_2) = [B \to \gamma\bullet, i_2, i_3, e_2 + 1],$$
$$f_1(\iota_c) = [A \to \alpha B \bullet \beta, i_1, i_3, e_1 + e_2 + 1].$$

As we can see, in any of the three cases, $f_1(\iota_1), f_1(\iota_2) \vdash f_1(\iota_c)$ in the instantiated parsing system $(\mathcal{I}'_{Lyon}, \mathcal{K}(a_1 \ldots a_n), D)$ by the application of a single COMPLETER step.

Analogous reasoning can be applied to the rest of the deduction steps in Lyon's parsing schema, concluding that if $\iota_1, \iota_2, \ldots, \iota_a \vdash \iota_c$ in the instantiated parsing system $(\mathcal{I}'_{Lyon}, \mathcal{K}(a_1 \ldots a_{j-1} b a_{j+1} \ldots a_n), D)$, then $f_1(\iota_1), f_1(\iota_2), \ldots, f_1(\iota_a) \vdash^* f_1(\iota_c)$ in the instantiated parsing system $(\mathcal{I}'_{Lyon}, \mathcal{K}(a_1 \ldots a_n), D)$. The proof for the rest of the steps will not be shown here, since a more general version of this lemma (Lemma 6.1) will be proven in detail in Section 6.3.2.2.

On the other hand, for every hypothesis $h \in \mathcal{K}(a_1 \ldots a_{j-1} b a_{j+1} \ldots a_n)$, we have that $f_1(h) \in \mathcal{K}(a_1 \ldots a_n)$ by definition of the function f_1.

Putting these two facts together, we have that:

$$\iota_1, \iota_2, \ldots, \iota_a \vdash^* \iota_c \text{ in } (\mathcal{I}'_{Lyon}, \mathcal{K}(a_1 \ldots a_{j-1} b a_{j+1} \ldots a_n), D) \Rightarrow$$
$$f(\iota_1), f(\iota_2), \ldots, f(\iota_a) \vdash^* f(\iota_c) \text{ in } (\mathcal{I}'_{Lyon}, \mathcal{K}(a_1 \ldots a_n), D).$$

If we set $a = 0$ and $\iota_c = [S \to \alpha\bullet, 0, n, e]$, this expression reduces to

$$\vdash^* [S \to \alpha\bullet, 0, n, e] \text{ in } (\mathcal{I}'_{Lyon}, \mathcal{K}(a_1 \ldots a_{j-1} b a_{j+1} \ldots a_n), D) \Rightarrow$$
$$\vdash^* [S \to \alpha\bullet, 0, n, e+1] \text{ in } (\mathcal{I}'_{Lyon}, \mathcal{K}(a_1 \ldots a_n), D)$$

which is equivalent to Lemma 5.1, and thus we have proven the substitution case of the induction step.

Induction step, cases 2 and 3 (insertion and deletion errors): The proofs for the second and third cases of the induction step are conducted analogously to the previous case. First, we consider the instantiated parsing systems obtained by applying the schema $\$_{Lyon}$ to the grammar G and $yield(t')$ and, reasoning as previously, we reduce each of the cases to the following lemmata:

Lemma 5.2. *Let* $(\mathcal{I}'_{Lyon}, \mathcal{K}, D)$ *be the uninstantiated parsing system obtained by applying Lyon's parsing schema to a given grammar G.*

Given a nonempty string $a_1 \ldots a_n$, and a string $a_1 \ldots a_{j-1} a_{j+1} \ldots a_n (1 \leq j \leq n)$ obtained by deleting the jth terminal in the first string, if $[S \to \alpha\bullet, 0, n-1, e]$ is a valid item in the instantiated parsing system $(\mathcal{I}'_{Lyon}, \mathcal{K}(a_1 \ldots a_{j-1} a_{j+1} \ldots a_n), D)$, then $[S \to \alpha\bullet, 0, n, e+1]$ is valid in the instantiated parsing system $(\mathcal{I}'_{Lyon}, \mathcal{K}(a_1 \ldots a_n), D)$.

Lemma 5.3. *Let* $(\mathcal{I}'_{Lyon}, \mathcal{K}, D)$ *be the uninstantiated parsing system obtained by applying Lyon's parsing schema to a given grammar G.*

Given a string $a_1 \ldots a_n$, and a string $a_1 \ldots a_{j-1} b a_j a_{j+1} \ldots a_n (1 \leq j \leq n+1)$ obtained by inserting a terminal b in position j of the first string, if $[S \to \alpha \bullet, 0, n+1, e]$ is a valid item in the instantiated parsing system $(\mathcal{I}'_{Lyon}, \mathcal{K}(a_1 \ldots a_{j-1} b a_j a_{j+1} \ldots a_n), D)$, then $[S \to \alpha \bullet, 0, n, e+1]$ is valid in the instantiated parsing system $(\mathcal{I}'_{Lyon}, \mathcal{K}(a_1 \ldots a_n), D)$.

To prove these lemmata, we follow an analogous procedure to that used for Lemma 5.1, but instead of the function f_1, we use the following functions f_2 and f_3, respectively:

$$f_2 : \mathcal{I}'_{Lyon} \cup \mathcal{K}(a_1 \ldots a_{j-1} a_{j+1} \ldots a_n) \to \mathcal{I}'_{Lyon} \cup \mathcal{K}(a_1 \ldots a_n),$$

$f_2([A \to \alpha \bullet \beta, i, k, e]) = [A \to \alpha \bullet \beta, i, k, e]$ if $j > k$.

$f_2([A \to \alpha \bullet \beta, i, k, e]) = [A \to \alpha \bullet \beta, i, k+1, e+1]$ if $j > i$ and $j \leq k$.

$f_2([A \to \alpha \bullet \beta, i, k, e]) = [A \to \alpha \bullet \beta, i+1, k+1, e]$ if $j \leq i$.

$f_2([x, i-1, i]) = [x, i-1, i]$, for $i < j$.

$f_2([x, i-1, i]) = [x, i, i+1]$, for $i >= j$.

$$f_3 : \mathcal{I}'_{Lyon} \cup \mathcal{K}(a_1 \ldots a_{j-1} b a_j a_{j+1} \ldots a_n) \to \mathcal{I}'_{Lyon} \cup \mathcal{K}(a_1 \ldots a_n),$$

$f_3([A \to \alpha \bullet \beta, i, k, e]) = [A \to \alpha \bullet \beta, i, k, e]$ if $j > k$.

$f_3([A \to \alpha \bullet \beta, i, k, e]) = [A \to \alpha \bullet \beta, i, k-1, e+1]$ if $j > i$ and $j \leq k$.

$f_3([A \to \alpha \bullet \beta, i, k, e]) = [A \to \alpha \bullet \beta, i-1, k-1, e]$ if $j \leq i$.

$f_3([x, i-1, i]) = [x, i-1, i]$, for $i < j$.

$f_3([b, j-1, j]) = [a_j, j-1, j]$ (if $j \leq n$), $[a_n, n-1, n]$ (otherwise)[5]

$f_3([x, i-1, i]) = [x, i-2, i-1]$, for $i \geq j$.

These two proofs, together with the one for Lemma 5.1, imply that the induction step holds for the three possible values of *yield*(t'). This concludes the proof of Proposition 5.1, and therefore, of the correctness of the parsing schema $\$_{Lyon}$.

---

[5]The particular value of $f_3([b, j-1, j])$ is not used in the proof, and therefore it is not relevant as long as it is always a valid hypothesis in $\mathcal{K}(a_1 \ldots a_n)$. Note that the system $(\mathcal{I}'_{Lyon}, \mathcal{K}(a_1 \ldots a_{j-1} b a_j a_{j+1} \ldots a_n), D)$ has one more hypothesis than the target system $(\mathcal{I}'_{Lyon}, \mathcal{K}(a_1 \ldots a_n), D)$, since the symbol b is not present in the string associated with the latter.

5.4 Obtaining minimal distance parses

In the previous section, we have proven that the error-repair parsing schema $\$_{Lyon}$, describing the algorithm by Lyon (1974), is *correct* and *complete*. This guarantees that, given a grammar and an input string, the corresponding deduction system obtained from $\$_{Lyon}$ infers all the valid approximate parses from the string and no invalid approximate parses, i.e., for every possible approximate tree (t, e) where t is a marked parse tree for the input string $a_1 \ldots a_n$, we obtain the corresponding correct final item $[S \to \alpha \bullet, 0, n, e]$.

However, when implementing a robust parser in practice, we do not want to obtain all the possible valid approximate parses (which would not be possible in finite time, since there is an infinite number of such parses). What we are interested in, as we mentioned in the definition of approximate parsing (Section 5.2.1), are the approximate parses with a minimal distance to a grammatically valid tree.

We will see that any correct error-repair parsing schema verifying a property that we will call *finite completeness* can be adapted to solve the approximate parsing problem in finite time, generating only the minimal distance parses, by adding some constraints to it. To this end, we will define some concepts that will lead us to the notion of a finitely complete schema.

Definition 5.11. Let $\$$ be an error-repair parsing schema that maps each grammar G to an uninstantiated parsing system $(\mathcal{I}', \mathcal{K}, D)$. The *bounded schema* associated to $\$$ with bound $\bar{b}$, denoted $Bound_{\bar{b}}(\$)$, is the error-repair parsing schema that maps each grammar G to the uninstantiated parsing system $Bound_{\bar{b}}(\$(G)) = Bound_{\bar{b}}(\mathcal{I}', \mathcal{K}, D) = (\mathcal{I}', \mathcal{K}, D_{\bar{b}})$, where:

$$D_{\bar{b}} = \{((X_1, X_2, \ldots, X_c), Y) \in D : dist(Y) \leq \bar{b}\}.$$

That is, a bounded parsing schema is a variant of a parsing schema that does not allow to deduce items with an associated distance greater than the bound $\bar{b}$.

For example, if we take the parsing schema $\$_{Lyon}$ as a starting point, the bounded parsing schema $Bound_{\bar{b}}(\$_{Lyon})$ is the schema that maps each grammar $G \in \mathcal{CFG}$ to the uninstantiated parsing system $(\mathcal{I}'_{Lyon}, \mathcal{K}, D_{\bar{b}})$, where $\mathcal{I}'_{Lyon}$ is the item set defined in Section 5.3, and $D_{\bar{b}}$ is the union of the sets:

$$\bar{b}\text{-INITTER:} \quad \frac{}{[S \to \bullet\gamma, 0, 0, 0]} \; S \to \gamma \in P$$

$$\bar{b}\text{-SCANNER:}\quad \frac{[A \to \alpha \bullet x\beta, i, j, e] \qquad [x, j, j+1]}{[A \to \alpha x \bullet \beta, i, j+1, e]}\ e \le \bar{b}$$

$$\bar{b}\text{-COMPLETER:}\quad \frac{[A \to \alpha \bullet B\beta, i, j, e_1] \qquad [B \to \gamma\bullet, j, k, e_2]}{[A \to \alpha B \bullet \beta, i, k, e_1 + e_2]}\ e_1 + e_2 \le \bar{b}$$

$$\bar{b}\text{-PREDICTOR:}\quad \frac{[A \to \alpha \bullet B\beta, i, j, e_1]}{[B \to \bullet\gamma, j, j, 0]}\ B \to \gamma \in P$$

$$\bar{b}\text{-SCANSUBSTITUTED:}\quad \frac{[A \to \alpha \bullet x\beta, i, j, e] \qquad [b, j, j+1]}{[A \to \alpha x \bullet \beta, i, j+1, e+1]}\ e+1 \le \bar{b}$$

$$\bar{b}\text{-SCANDELETED:}\quad \frac{[A \to \alpha \bullet x\beta, i, j, e]}{[A \to \alpha x \bullet \beta, i, j, e+1]}\ e+1 \le \bar{b}$$

$$\bar{b}\text{-SCANINSERTED:}\quad \frac{[A \to \alpha \bullet \beta, i, j, e] \qquad [b, j, j+1]}{[A \to \alpha \bullet \beta, i, j+1, e+1]}\ e+1 \le \bar{b}$$

Definition 5.12. We will say that an error-repair uninstantiated parsing system $(\mathcal{I}', \mathcal{K}, D)$ is *complete up to a distance* $\bar{b}$ if, for any input string, all the correct final items with a parsing distance not greater than $\bar{b}$ are valid.

We will say that an error-repair parsing schema $\$$ for a class of grammars $\mathcal{CG}$ is complete up to a distance $\bar{b}$ if, for every grammar $G \in \mathcal{CG}$, the uninstantiated parsing system $\$(G)$ is complete up to $\bar{b}$.

Definition 5.13. We will say that an error-repair parsing schema $\$$ is *finitely complete* if, for all $k \in (\mathbb{N} \cup \{0\})$, the bounded parsing schema $Bound_k(\$)$ is complete up to k.

Note that a finitely complete error-repair parsing schema is always complete, since we can make k arbitrarily large. On the other hand, the converse does not hold: a schema can be complete but not finitely complete if some valid final item with parsing distance k needs the presence of an item with distance greater than k to be inferred. However, it is easy to check that this is not the case with $\$_{Lyon}$:

Proposition 5.2. *The error-repair parsing schema* $\$_{Lyon}$ *is finitely complete.*

This fact can be proven in the exact same way as completeness: in the completeness proof shown in the previous section we never need to use the validity of any item with parsing distance greater than k to prove the validity of a correct final item with distance k. In particular, the proof of Proposition 5.1, that proves completeness of the instantiated parsing system $(\mathcal{I}'_{Lyon}, \mathcal{K}(a_1 \ldots a_n), D)$, can be used without changes to prove that, given a bound k, every item with distance $\leq k$ is valid in the instantiated parsing system $(\mathcal{I}'_{Lyon}, \mathcal{K}(a_1 \ldots a_n), D_k)$. This directly implies the finite completeness of $\$_{Lyon}$.

It is easy to see that, if we have a deductive engine that is able to run parsing schemata, any correct, finitely complete error-repair parsing schema $(\mathcal{I}', \mathcal{K}, D)$ can be used to build a parser that solves the approximate parsing problem in finite time, returning all valid approximate parses with minimal distance without generating any non-minimal distance parse. The simplest way to do it is the following:

```
function  RobustParser ( string  ) : item set
{
    b̄ = 0; //distance  bound  (maximum  allowed  distance)
    while ( true )
    {
        compute  validItems = v( Bound_b̄(I', K, D) , string );
        finalItems = { ι in validItems |ι is a final item
            };
        if ( finalItems ≠∅ ) return finalItems;
        b̄ = b̄ + 1; //while we do not find any approximate
            parse , we increase the allowed distance
    }
}
```

where the function v(sys,str) computes all valid items in the parsing system sys for the string str, and can be implemented as in Shieber *et al.* (1995) or by automatically generating an implementation with the compiler described in Chapter 3.

It is easy to prove that, if the approximate parsing problem has a solution for a given string (i.e., if there exists an $e \in (\mathbb{N} \cup \{0\})$ such that there is an approximate tree $(t, e) \in ApTrees(G)$ with t a marked parse tree for the sentence), then this algorithm finds it in finite time[6]. If we call E the set of natural numbers verifying that property, the loop invariant is that $\nexists\, e \in E \mid e < \bar{b}$, and the loop bound is $min(E) - \bar{b}$. The invariant, the bound and the fact that the schema is finitely complete together guarantee that the final items returned are those with minimal distance.

In practice, we can make several optimisations to this simple algorithm to improve runtime. For example, the valid items generated in each iteration can be used as hypotheses in the next one instead of inferring them again. Note that this parsing engine can execute any error-repair parsing schema (not only Lyon's) and is guaranteed to find all optimal solutions (minimal distance parses) as long as the schema is correct and finitely complete and such solutions exist. If we use the engine to execute the $\$_{Lyon}$ parsing schema as given in Section 5.3, without the DISTANCEINCREASER step (which is not needed for minimal distance parsers, as reasoned in Section 5.3.1), we obtain a parser which is roughly equivalent to the original algorithm by Lyon (1974). The only differences with respect to Lyon's algorithm in terms of items generated are those derived from the decision of not using an end-of-sentence marker and the slight modification of SCANIN-SERTED explained earlier.

5.5   Global and regional error repair

If a robust parser is able to find all the minimal-distance approximate parses for each given string, it is called a *global* error-repair parser. Therefore, all parsers which solve the approximate parsing problem as we have defined it, including the ones implemented with the technique explained in the previous section, are global error-repair parsers.

In practice, global error-repair parsers can be useful when working with small grammars or short strings, but they can get really inefficient if we need to parse long sentences or use grammars with thousands of productions, as usual in natural language processing. The main reason for this inefficiency is that this kind of parsers need to search for possible errors in every possible

---

[6]For a distance function like $\hat{d}$, a solution to the approximate parsing problem always exists. Given a grammar G and a string $a_1 \ldots a_n$, we take any marked parse tree in *Trees*(G) with yield $\underline{b}_1 \ldots \underline{b}_k$ and change it to a marked parse tree for $a_1 \ldots a_n$ by applying a finite sequence of elementary operations (for example, k deletion operations to delete the marked terminals $b_1 \ldots b_k$ followed by n insertion operations to insert $a_1 \ldots a_n$). Therefore, under that definition of distance, this algorithm always terminates in finite time.

position in the input string. For example, given an input of length n, the SCANINSERTED step of the schema $\mathbb{S}_{Lyon}$ can be executed on *any* item of the form $[A \rightarrow \alpha \bullet \beta, i, j, e]$ as long as $j < n$. This means that we will infer items based in the assumption that each of the n words in the input sentence has been generated by an insertion error. The items generated with each of these assumptions will in turn produce more items.

A more efficient alternative for error repair is that of *local* error-repair parsers (McKenzie *et al.*, 1995; Bertsch and Nederhof, 1999). These parsers work by processing the sentence without error repair until they successfully find a parse, or until they find a state where the parsing process cannot continue (which we call *detection point*). Local error-repair parsers assume that the error in the input is located at the detection point, and apply repair steps only at that point, modifying the string as necessary to continue parsing. As local error-repair parsers do not have to search the whole string for errors, they are much more efficient than global techniques. However, they do not guarantee that their results are optimal, since there are sentences where the minimal distance parses are reached by applying corrections before the detection point.

An intermediate solution is that of *regional* error repair-parsers (Vilares *et al.*, 2001, 2002, 2004). These algorithms work as non-error-repair parsers until they reach a detection point, just like local algorithms, but then they apply error-repair techniques to a *region* of states surrounding the detection point. This region may be enlarged until a satisfactory correction for the detected error is found. The particular criterion to choose, and optionally enlarge, the region can be adjusted according to the desired tradeoff between efficiency and quality of the solutions. From this standpoint, local and global error-repair parsers can be considered as extreme cases of regional algorithms where this criterion is extremely aggresive or extremely conservative, respectively.

Since parsing schemata specify a set of allowed operations on intermediate items but they abstract away from the control structures used to execute these operations, the same error-repair parsing schema can be implemented as a global, regional or local error-repair parser by using different control structures to execute it. In this section, we will see how to implement parsers with an interesting kind of regional error-repair strategy, which we will call a *minimal* regional error-repair strategy. A minimal regional error-repair parser is one that always finds at least *one* of the optimal solutions (minimal distance parses) for a given string, but does not guarantee finding *all* the optimal solutions if there are several possible minimal distance parses for the string.

Note that state-based regional error-repair parsers, like those defined by Vilares *et al.* (2001), are generally tied to a particular implementation. On the other hand, error-repair parsing schemata allow us to define more general, item-based regional parsers, where detection points and regions are sets of items instead of sets of states. Additionally, parsing schemata allow us to obtain regional parsers from the same schemata used for global parsers, in such a way that the regional parser will always return an optimal solution if the corresponding global parser is correct and finitely complete. To do this, we use the notion of a *progress function*:

Definition 5.14. Let $\mathcal{I}'$ be an approximate item set. A *progress function* for $\mathcal{I}'$ is a function $f_p : \mathcal{I}' \to \{p \in (\mathbb{N} \cup \{0\}) \mid p \le k\}$, where k is a positive integer called the *maximum progress*.

Let \$ be a correct and finitely complete error-repair parsing schema, and f_p a progress function for its item set. A minimal regional parser based on \$ can be implemented by executing the parsing systems obtained from \$ with the deductive engine in Figure 5.3, where the function v2(ded,str,min,max) computes all valid items in the deduction system ded for the input str, with the constraint that error-repair steps are only launched if at least one of their antecedents, ι, satisfies that minProgr $\le f_p(\iota) \le$ maxProgr. The set of items whose progress function is inside this interval is called the *error-repair region*, and the particular shape of this region will depend on the progress function f_c used by the parser.

Independently of this function f_c, it is guaranteed that, if \$ is correct and finitely complete, this regional parser always returns at least one minimal distance parse. To prove this, note that the value of the distance bound $\bar{b}$ is only increased in an iteration where minProgr $= 0$ and maxProgr $= max\{p \in (\mathbb{N} \cup \{0\}) \mid \exists \iota \in$ validItems $: f_p(\iota) = p\}$ and, in this situation, executing v2($Bound_{\bar{b}}(\$(G))$, string, minProgr, maxProgr) is equivalent to executing v($Bound_{\bar{b}}(\$(G))$, string), which returns all valid approximate items for the distance bound $\bar{b}$. Therefore, the whole set of valid items in the bounded parsing system $Bound_{\bar{b}}(\$(G))$ is computed before considering solutions with distance $\bar{b} + 1$. This, together with finite completeness of \$, implies that at least one minimal distance parse will be found by the algorithm before producing any non-optimal solution.

In order for the regional parser to be efficient, we should define the progress function so that it is a good approximation of how "promising" an

```
function  RegionalParser  (  string  )  :  item  set
  b̄ = 0;  //maximum  allowed  distance
  maxProgr  =  0;  //upper  region  limit
  minProgr  =  0;  //lower  region  limit
  while  (  true  )
  {
    compute  validItems  =  v2 (Bound_b̄($(G)), string ,
        minProgr , maxProgr );

    finalItems  =  {ι ∈ validItems | ι  is  a  final  item  };
    if  (  finalItems ≠ ∅  )  return  finalItems;

    newMax  =  max{p ∈ N | ∃i ∈  validItems  : f_p(i) = p}

    if  (  newMax > maxProgr  )  {
        maxProgr  =  newMax;  minProgr  =  newMax;
    }
    else  if  (  minProgr > 0  )  minProgr  =  minProgr −1;
    else  b̄ = b̄+1;
  }
```

Fig. 5.3 Pseudocode of a deductive parsing engine that implements a minimal regional error-repair strategy.

item is towards reaching a final item. The criteria to choose a good progress function are similar to those that characterise a good heuristic function in an informed search problem. Thus, the ideal progress function would be one such that $f(\iota) = 0$ if ι is not necessary to infer a final item, and $f(\iota) > f(\kappa)$ if ι can be used to infer a final item in less steps than κ. Obviously this function cannot be used (until the deduction process is finished, we do not know if a given item can lead to a final item or not); but functions that provide a good approximation of this ideal heuristic will produce efficient parsers. In the degenerate case where $f_p(\iota) = 0$ for any item ι, the progress function does not provide any information and the regional error-repair parser is equivalent to the global algorithm seen previously.

A simple yet adequate function in the case of the schema $\$_{Lyon}$ is $f_{p_j}([A \rightarrow \alpha \bullet \beta, i, j, e]) = j$, which simply evaluates an item according to its index j. Another alternative is $f_{p_{j-i}}([A \rightarrow \alpha \bullet \beta, i, j, e]) = j - i$. Both

Table 5.1   Performance results for the global and regional error-repair parsers when parsing sentences from the ATIS test set. Each row corresponds to a value of the minimal parsing distance (or error count), and shows the amount of sentences in the set with that minimal parsing distance, their average length and the average number of items generated by both algorithms when parsing these sentences. The last column represents the relative improvement of the regional parser over the global parser in terms of the amount of items generated.

Min. Dist.	Num. of Sentences	Avg. Len.	Avg. Items (Global)	Avg. Items (Regional)	Improvement (%)
0	70	11.04	37,558	37,558	0.00%
1	24	11.63	194,249	63,751	65.33%
2	2	18.50	739,705	574,534	22.33%
3	2	14.50	1,117,123	965,137	13.61%
>3	none	n/a	n/a	n/a	n/a

functions prioritise the items that have progressed further to the right in the input string, and take maximum values for final items.

5.5.1   *Performance of global and regional parsers*

In order to test our parsers and study their performance, we have used the system described in Chapter 3 to execute Lyon's parsing schema both as a global error-repair parser, as described in Section 5.4, and as a minimal regional error-repair parser, as in Section 5.5. The progress function used for the regional parser is the f_{p_j} function as defined above.

The grammar and sentences used for testing are from the DARPA ATIS3 system. Particularly, we have used the same test sentences that were used by Moore (2000). This test set is suitable for our purpose, since it comes from a real-life application and contains ungrammatical sentences. In particular, 28 of the 98 sentences in the set are ungrammatical. By running our error-repair parsers, we find that the minimal edit distance to a grammatical sentence is 1 for 24 of them (i.e., these 24 sentences have a possible repair with a single error), 2 for two of them and 3 for the remaining two.

Table 5.1 shows the average number of items generated by our parsers with respect to the minimal parsing distance of the inputs. As we can see, regional parsing reduces item generation by a factor of three in sentences with a single error. In sentences with more than one error the improvements are smaller: this is because, before returning any solution with distance $e + 1$, the regional parser generates all valid items with distance e (i.e., all the items a global parser would generate up to this distance). However, we should note that parsing time grows faster than the number of items generated, so these relative improvements in items translate to larger relative improvements in runtime. Moreover, in practical settings we can expect sentences with several errors to be less frequent than sentences with a single error, as in this case. Thus, the faster runtimes make item-based regional error-repair parsers a good practical alternative to global algorithms.

5.6 Discussion

In this chapter we have introduced error-repair parsing schemata, a formal framework that extends Sikkel's theory of parsing schemata, and can be used to easily define, analyse and compare error-repair parsers. With this new theoretical tool, all the advantages of parsing schemata that we have seen in the previous chapters are extended to error-repair parsers, including the possibility of implementing them with the system described in Chapter 3. Furthermore, as parsing schemata capture the logic of the algorithms while abstracting away from control structures, the same error-repair parsing schema can be implemented with different repair strategies (global, regional or local) depending on the control structures that we use to handle the execution of its deduction steps.

As an example, we have used error-repair parsing schemata to describe the Earley-based error-repair algorithm first described by Lyon (1974), to prove its correctness, to generate a deductive implementation of the original algorithm, and to obtain a faster, regional error-repair parser based on the same parsing schema. We have also performed an empirical comparison to measure the efficiency gain obtained by applying a regional error-repair strategy with respect to global repair.

The methods that we have used for obtaining these results are generic and can be applied to other parsers. In the next chapter, we will present a transformation that can be used to convert standard parsing schemata satisfying certain conditions to correct error-repair parsing schemata. With this transformation, we can automatically obtain correct global and regional error-repair parsers from standard parsing schemata such as those for the CYK or Left-Corner parsers that we have used in Chapter 4.

Chapter 6

Transforming standard parsers into error-repair parsers

In the last chapter, we defined the formalism of error-repair parsing schemata and used it to describe a particular parsing algorithm with error-repair capabilities, prove its correctness, and obtain implementations of it with regional and global repair strategies.

In this chapter, we use this formalism to define a general transformation technique to automatically obtain robust, error-repair parsers from standard non-robust parsers (Gómez-Rodríguez *et al.*, 2010a, 2009a). If our method is applied to a correct parsing schema satisfying certain conditions, the resulting error-repair parsing schema is guaranteed to be correct. The required conditions are weak enough to be fulfilled by a wide variety of popular parsers used in natural language processing, such as CYK, Earley and Left-Corner.

The transformation is defined as a function that maps correct parsing schemata to correct error-repair parsing schemata that can successfully obtain approximate parses for input sentences minimising the Levenshtein distance to a grammatical sentence, by using the extended pseudometric $\hat{d}$ defined in Section 5.2.2 as tree distance function.

We first provide an informal description of the transformation and how it is applied, and then we define it formally and prove its correctness. Finally, we discuss some optimisations and simplifications that can be applied as post-processing, and will be useful when the transformation is used in practice.

6.1 From standard parsers to error-repair parsers

Most standard, non-robust parsers work by using grammar rules to build trees and link them together to form larger trees, until a complete parse can be found. Our transformation is based on generalising parser deduction steps to enable them to link approximate trees and still obtain correct results, and adding some standard steps that introduce error hypotheses into the item set, which will be gracefully integrated into parse trees by the generalised steps.

The particular strategy used by parsers to build and link trees obviously varies between algorithms but, in spite of this, we can usually find two kinds of deduction steps in parsing schemata: those which introduce a new tree into the parse from scratch, and those which link a set of trees to form a larger tree. We will call the former *predictive steps* and the latter *yield union steps*.

Predictive steps can be identified because the yield of the trees in their consequent item does not contain any marked terminal symbol, i.e., they generate trees which are not linked to the input string. Examples of predictive steps are the Earley INITTER and PREDICTOR steps. Yield union steps can be identified because the sequence of marked terminals in the yield of the trees of their consequent item (which we call the *marked yield* of these items)[1] is the concatenation of the marked yields of one or more of their antecedents,[2] and the trees in the consequent item are formed by linking trees in antecedent items. Examples of yield union steps are Earley COMPLETER and SCANNER (see Figure 2.6 on page 22), and all the steps in the CYK parsing schema (Figure 2.5 on page 22).

If all the steps in a parsing schema are predictive steps or yield union steps, we will call it a *prediction-completion parsing schema*. Most of the parsing schemata which can be found in the literature for widely-used parsers are prediction-completion parsing schemata, which allows us to obtain error-repair parsers from them in a systematic way.

6.1.1 *Outline of the transformation*

The *error-repair transformation* of a prediction-completion parsing system $\mathbb{P}$ is the error-repair parsing system $\mathcal{R}(\mathbb{P})$ obtained by applying the following changes to it:

---

[1] In the sequel, we will use the notation $yield_m(t)$ to refer to the marked yield of a tree t, and $yield_m(\iota)$ to refer to the common marked yield of the trees in an item ι, which we will call the marked yield of the item.

[2] Actually, predictive steps can also be seen as yield union steps where the marked yield of the consequent item is the concatenation of the marked yield of *zero* of their antecedents. From this perspective it is not necessary to define predictive steps, but the concept has been introduced for clarity.

(1) Transform the item set into the corresponding approximate item set by extending each item with a field which will store its parsing distance.

(2) Add the following steps to the schema:

(a) SUBSTITUTIONHYPOTHESIS = $\{[a, i, i+1] \vdash [b, i, i+1, 1] \mid b \in \Sigma\}$.[3]
The consequent of this step contains the tree $b \to \underline{a}_{i+1}$, for each symbol a_{i+1} in the input string (input symbol) and each $b \in \Sigma$ (expected symbol). Generating this item corresponds to the error hypothesis that the symbol a_{i+1} that we find in the input string is the product of a substitution error, and should be b instead.

(b) DELETIONHYPOTHESIS = $\{\vdash [b, i, i, 1] \mid b \in \Sigma\}$.
The consequent item contains the tree $b \to \epsilon$, for each position i in the input string. This corresponds to the error hypothesis that the symbol b, which should be the $i+1$th symbol in the input, has been deleted. The item $[b, i, i, 1]$ allows us to use this symbol during parsing even if it does not appear in the input sentence.

(c) INSERTIONHYPOTHESIS = $\{[a, i, i+1] \vdash [\epsilon, i, i+1, 1]\}$.
The consequent of this step contains the tree $\epsilon \to \underline{a}_{i+1}$, for each input symbol a_{i+1} in the input string, which corresponds to the hypothesis that the symbol a_{i+1} in the input is the product of an insertion error, and therefore should not be taken into account in the parse.

(d) BEGINNINGINSERTIONCOMBINER =

$$\{[\epsilon, 0, j, e_1], [(a|\epsilon), j, k, e_2] \vdash [(a|\epsilon), 0, k, e_2]\}.$$

OTHERINSERTIONCOMBINER =

$$\{[(a|\epsilon), i, j, e_1], [\epsilon, j, k, e_2] \vdash [(a|\epsilon), i, k, e_1 + e_2]\}.$$

These steps produce trees of the form $a_2(\epsilon(\underline{a}_1)a_2(\underline{a}_2))$ and $a_{i+1}(\underline{a}_{i+1}\epsilon(\underline{a}_{i+2}))$, respectively, when they are used to combine a single insertion hypothesis. Subsequent applications of the steps will produce larger trees. If the first symbol in the input is an *inserted* character, the insertion hypothesis is combined with the hypothesis immediately to its right. Insertion hypotheses corresponding to symbols other than the first one are combined with the hypothesis immediately to their left.

This is done because any correct parsing schemata must have steps to handle subtrees rooted at terminals that can be straightforwardly

---

[3] We remind the reader that, due to the extensive use of expressions of sets of deduction steps in the explanations and proofs throughout this chapter, we will use this compact notation (explained in Section 2.3.2) to refer to sets of steps, rather than the inference rule notation employed in the rest of the chapters of this book.

transformed to handle these extended insertion hypotheses, while some (such as CYK) do not possess steps to handle subtrees rooted at ϵ, so their conversion would be more complex without these INSERTIONCOMBINER steps.

(e) CORRECTHYPOTHESIS $= \{[a, i, i+1] \vdash [a, i, i+1, 0]\}$.

The consequent of this item contains the tree $a \rightarrow \underline{a}_{i+1}$, for each symbol a_{i+1} in the input string. Therefore, it is equivalent to the hypothesis $[a, i, i+1]$. This item corresponds to the hypothesis that there is no error in the input symbol a_{i+1}, hence the distance value 0.

(3) For every predictive step in the schema (steps producing an item with an empty yield), change the step to its generalisation obtained (in practice) by setting the distance associated with each antecedent item A_i to an unbound variable e_i, and set the distance for the consequent item to zero. For example, the Earley step:

$$\text{PREDICTOR} = \{[A \rightarrow \alpha \bullet B\beta, i, j] \vdash [B \rightarrow \bullet\gamma, j, j] \mid B \rightarrow \gamma \in P\}$$

produces the step

$$\text{PREDICTOR'} = \{[A \rightarrow \alpha \bullet B\beta, i, j, e] \vdash [B \rightarrow \bullet\gamma, j, j, 0] \mid B \rightarrow \gamma \in P\}.$$

(4) For every yield union step in the schema (steps using items with yield limits (i_0, i_1), (i_1, i_2), ..., (i_{a-1}, i_a) to produce an item with yield $(i_0 \ldots i_a)$):

- If the step requires a hypothesis $[a, i, i+1]$, then change all appearances of the index $i+1$ to a new unbound index j.[4]
- Set the distance for each antecedent item A_k with yield (i_{k-1}, i_k) to an unbound variable e_k, and set the distance for the consequent to the sum of these variables, $e_1 + e_2 + \ldots + e_a$.
- Set the distance for the rest of antecedent items, if there is any, to unbound variables e'_j.

Example 6.1. The Earley step

$$\text{COMPLETER} = \{[A \rightarrow \alpha \bullet B\beta, i, j], [B \rightarrow \gamma\bullet, j, k]$$
$$\vdash [A \rightarrow \alpha B \bullet \beta, i, k]\}$$

---

[4]This is done because steps including hypotheses as antecedents are not strictly yield union steps according to the formal definition of yield union step that we will see later in Section 6.2.2. However, these steps can always be easily transformed to yield union steps by applying this transformation. Note that this change does not alter any of the significant properties of the original (standard) parsing schema, since items $[a, i, j]$ with $j \neq i+1$ can never appear in the deduction process.

produces the step

$$\text{COMPLETER'} = \{[A \to \alpha \bullet B\beta, i, j, e_1], [B \to \gamma\bullet, j, k, e_2]$$
$$\vdash [A \to \alpha B \bullet \beta, i, k, e_1 + e_2]\}.$$

The Earley step

$$\text{SCANNER} = \{[A \to \alpha \bullet a\beta, i, j], [a, j, j+1]$$
$$\vdash [A \to \alpha a \bullet \beta, i, j+1]\}$$

produces the step

$$\text{SCANNER'} = \{[A \to \alpha \bullet a\beta, i, j, e_1], [a, j, k, e_2]$$
$$\vdash [A \to \alpha a \bullet \beta, i, k, e_1 + e_2]\}.$$

The CYK step

$$\text{CYKUNARY} = \{[a, i, i+1] \vdash [A, i, i+1] \mid A \to a \in P\}$$

produces

$$\text{CYKUNARY'} = \{[a, i, j, e] \vdash [A, i, j, e] \mid A \to a \in P\}.$$

6.2 Formal description of the error-repair transformation

By applying these four simple transformation rules to a prediction-completion parsing schema, we obtain an error-repair parsing schema which shares its underlying semantics. As the transformation rules are totally systematic, they can be applied automatically, so that a system based on parsing schemata, such as the one described in Chapter 3, can generate implementations of error-repair parsers from non-error-repair parsing schemata. However, in order for the transformation to be useful we need to ensure that the error-repair parsers obtained from it are correct.

In order to do this, we first need to define some concepts that will take us to a formal definition of the transformation that we have informally described in the previous section.

6.2.1 *Some properties of trees and items*

Let $t \in \textit{Trees}(G)$ be a constituency parse tree. We will say that t is an *anchored tree* if there is at least one marked terminal $\underline{a}_i$ in $\textit{yield}(t)$. If t does not contain any marked terminal, then we will call it a *non-anchored tree*.

Note that the presence of marked terminals binds anchored trees to particular positions in the input string, while non-anchored trees are not bound to positions.

Definition 6.1. We say that an anchored tree t is *substring-anchored* if its yield is of the form $\alpha \underline{a}_{l+1} \underline{a}_{l+2} \cdots \underline{a}_r \beta$, where α and β contain no marked terminals, for some $l, r \in (\mathbb{N} \cup \{0\})$ such that $l < r$. The values l and r are called the *leftmost yield limit* and the *rightmost yield limit* of t, respectively, and we will denote them $left(t)$ and $right(t)$.

Definition 6.2. We say that a tree t is a *contiguous yield tree* if it is either substring-anchored or non-anchored.

We define the *marked yield* of a contiguous yield tree t, denoted $yield_m(t)$, as:

- The empty string ϵ, if t is non-anchored,
- The string $\underline{a}_{l+1} \underline{a}_{l+2} \cdots \underline{a}_r$, if t is substring-anchored with yield limits $left(t) = l$, $right(t) = r$.

Definition 6.3. Let $\mathcal{I}$ be an item set.

- We will say that an item $\iota \in \mathcal{I}$ is a *homogeneously anchored item* if there exist l and $r \in (\mathbb{N} \cup \{0\})$ such that, for every tree $t \in \iota$, t is substring-anchored and verifies that $left(t) = l$ and $right(t) = r$. In this case, we will call l the *leftmost yield limit* of the item ι, denoted $left(\iota)$, and r the *rightmost yield limit* of ι, denoted $right(\iota)$.
- We will call $\iota \in \mathcal{I}$ a *non-anchored item* if, for every tree $t \in \iota$, t is non-anchored.
- We will call any item $\iota \in \mathcal{I}$ which is in neither of these two cases a *heterogeneously anchored item*.

We will say that an item set $\mathcal{I}$ is *homogeneous* if it contains no heterogenously anchored items.

Note that all trees contained in items in a homogeneous item set are contiguous yield trees.

Example 6.2. The Earley, CYK and Left-Corner parsing schemata defined by Sikkel (1997) (and shown on pages 22 and 67 of this book) have, by construction, homogeneous item sets. Earley and Left-Corner items of the form $\iota = [A \to \alpha \bullet \beta, i, j]$ where $i < j$ are homogeneously anchored items, where $left(\iota) = i$ and $right(\iota) = j$. Items where $i = j$ are non-anchored items. In the case of CYK, items of the form $\iota = [A, i, j]$ where $i < j$ are homogeneously anchored, with $\mathit{left}(\iota) = i$ and $\mathit{right}(\iota) = j$.

Definition 6.4. Let $\mathcal{I}$ be a homogeneous item set, $\mathcal{H}$ a set of possible hypotheses for a terminal alphabet Σ.[5] An *item representation set* for $\mathcal{I}$ is a set $R = \{(q, i, j) \in E \times (\mathbb{N} \cup \{0\}) \times (\mathbb{N} \cup \{0\}) \mid i \le j\}$, where E is any set such that $\Sigma \subseteq E$ and there exists a function $r_R : R \to \mathcal{I} \cup \mathcal{H}$ (which we will call an *item representation function*) satisfying that it is surjective (every item has at least one inverse image) and, for all $(q, i, j) \in R$, the following conditions hold:

- if $i < j$ and $\iota = r_R(q, i, j)$ is nonempty, then ι is a homogeneously anchored item with $\mathit{left}(\iota) = i$ and $\mathit{right}(\iota) = j$.
- if $i = j$ and $\iota = r_R(q, i, j)$ is nonempty, then ι is a non-anchored item.
- if $q \in \Sigma$ and $j = i + 1$, $\iota = r_R(q, i, j)$ is the hypothesis $[q, i, i + 1] = \{q((q, i + 1))\} \in \mathcal{H}$.
- if $q \in \Sigma$ and $j \ne i + 1$, $\iota = r_R(q, i, j)$ is the empty item $\varnothing$.

Note that a final item for a string of length n will always be of the form $r_R(q, 0, n)$ for some q.

Example 6.3. In the case of the Earley parser for a CFG $G = (N, \Sigma, P, S)$, we consider the representation set $R_{Earley} = \{(q, i, j) \in (D(P) \cup \Sigma) \times (\mathbb{N} \cup \{0\}) \times (\mathbb{N} \cup \{0\}) \mid i \le j\}$, where the set of dotted productions $D(P)$ is defined as $\{(A \to \alpha, k) \mid A \to \alpha \in P \wedge k \in (\mathbb{N} \cup \{0\}) \wedge 0 \le k \le |\alpha|)\}$. This allows us to define the obvious representation function for the Earley item set, $r_{R_{Earley}} : ((A \to \gamma, k), i, j) \to [A \to \alpha \bullet \beta, i, j]$, where α is the substring $\gamma_1 \ldots \gamma_k$ of γ and β is the rest of γ; and $r_{R_{Earley}} : (a, i, j) \to [a, i, j]$.

6.2.2 *Some properties of deduction steps*

The item-related concepts defined in the previous section can be used to formally characterise yield union and predictive step sets, which were informally introduced in Section 6.1.1, and are a prerequisite for the error-repair transformation.

Definition 6.5. Let $\mathcal{I}$ be a homogeneous item set, and $R \subseteq E \times (\mathbb{N} \cup \{0\}) \times (\mathbb{N} \cup \{0\})$ an item representation set for $\mathcal{I}$, with representation function

---

[5]Note that, in this definition, $\mathcal{H}$ represents the set of all the possible hypotheses of the form $\{a((a, i))\}$ with $a \in \Sigma^*$ and $i \in \mathbb{N}$, and not only the hypotheses associated to a particular input string.

r_R. If we use the notation $[a, b, c]$ as shorthand for $r_R(a, b, c)$, then a *yield union step set* is a set of deduction steps of the form:

$$\{[q_1, i_0, i_1], [q_2, i_1, i_2], \ldots, [q_m, i_{m-1}, i_m],$$
$$[c_1, j_1, k_1], [c_2, j_2, k_2], \ldots, [c_n, j_n, k_n] \vdash$$
$$[q_c, i_0, i_m] \mid$$
$$i_0 \le i_1 \le \ldots \le i_m \in (\mathbb{N} \cup \{0\}) \wedge j_1, \ldots, j_n, k_1, \ldots, k_n \in (\mathbb{N} \cup \{0\}) \wedge$$
$$j_i \le k_i \wedge P(q_1, q_2, \ldots, q_m, c_1, c_2, \ldots, c_n, q_c) = 1\}$$

where P is a boolean function, $P : E^{m+n+1} \to \{0, 1\}$.

Therefore, a yield union step set is a step set in which some of the antecedent items have contiguous yields whose union is the consequent's yield. If we represent the antecedent and consequent items as $[q, l, r]$, the only constraints allowed on the left and right positions l and r are that l should always be less than or equal to r for all items, and that the (l, r) intervals of some antecedents must be contiguous and their union be the interval corresponding to the consequent. Any constraint is allowed on the entities q and c, as denoted by P.

Example 6.4. The set of Earley COMPLETER steps is a yield union step set with the representation function $r_{R_{Earley}}$ defined above, because it can be written as:

$$\{[q_1, i_0, i_1], [q_2, i_1, i_2] \vdash [q_c, i_0, i_2] \mid$$
$$i_0 \le i_1 \le i_2 \in (\mathbb{N} \cup \{0\}) \wedge P(q_1, q_2, q_c) = 1\}$$

with $P(x, y, z) = (\exists A, B, \alpha, \beta, \gamma \mid x = A \to \alpha \bullet B\beta, y = B \to \gamma \bullet, z = A \to \alpha B \bullet \beta)$.

Definition 6.6. Let $\mathcal{I}$ be a homogeneous item set, and $R \subseteq E \times (\mathbb{N} \cup \{0\}) \times (\mathbb{N} \cup \{0\})$ an item representation set for $\mathcal{I}$, with representation function r_R. If we write $[a, b, c]$ as shorthand for $r_R(a, b, c)$, a *predictive step set* is a set of deduction steps of the form:

$$\{[q_1, j_1, k_1], [q_2, j_2, k_2], \ldots, [q_n, j_n, k_n] \vdash$$
$$[q_c, f(j_1, k_1, j_2, k_2, \ldots, j_n, k_n), f(j_1, k_1, j_2, k_2, \ldots, j_n, k_n)] \mid$$
$$j_1, \ldots, j_n, k_1, \ldots, k_n \in (\mathbb{N} \cup \{0\}) \wedge j_i \le k_i \wedge P(q_1, q_2, \ldots, q_n, q_c) = 1\},$$

where P is a boolean function, $P : E^{n+1} \to \{0, 1\}$, and f is a nonnegative integer function, $f : (\mathbb{N} \cup \{0\})^{2n} \to (\mathbb{N} \cup \{0\})$.

Therefore, a predictive step set is a step set in which the consequent is a non-anchored item. If we represent the antecedent and consequent items as $[q,l,r]$, the only constraints allowed on the left and right positions l and r are that l should always be less than or equal to r for all items, and that the (l,r) indexes of the consequent must be equal and a function of the (l,r) indexes of the antecedents. Any constraint is allowed on the entities q, as denoted by P.

Example 6.5. The set of Earley PREDICTOR steps is a predictive step set, because it can be written as:

$$\{[q_1,j_1,k_1]\} \vdash [q_c, f(j_1,k_1), f(j_1,k_1)] \mid$$
$$j_1,k_1 \in (\mathbb{N} \cup \{0\}) \wedge j_1 \le k_1 \wedge P(q_1,q_c) = 1\}$$

where $f(x,y) = y$, and $P(x,y) = (\exists A,B,\alpha,\beta,\gamma \mid x = A \to \alpha \bullet B\beta, y = B \to \bullet\gamma)$ with $B \to \bullet\gamma$ a valid production in the grammar.

Definition 6.7. An uninstantiated parsing system $(\mathcal{I},\mathcal{K},D)$ is a *prediction-completion parsing system* if there exists a representation function r_R such that D can be written as union of sets $D_1 \cup D_2 \cup \ldots \cup D_n$, where each D_i is either a predictive step set or a yield union step set with respect to that representation function.

A parsing schema $\mathbb{S}$ is said to be a *prediction-completion parsing schema* if it maps each grammar G in a class $\mathcal{CG}$ to a prediction-completion parsing system.

Example 6.6. It is easy to check that the *Earley*, *CYK* and *Left-Corner* parsing schemata are prediction-completion parsing schemata, as their sets of deduction steps can be rewritten as the union of predictive step sets and yield union step sets. For example, in the *Earley* parsing schema, the standard INITTER and PREDICTOR are predictive step sets, while COMPLETER and SCANNER are yield union step sets. In the case of the SCANNER step, we can see that it is a yield union step set by rewriting it as SCANNER $= \{[A \to \alpha \bullet x\beta, i, j], [x,j,k] \vdash [A \to \alpha x \bullet \beta, i, k]\}$ (see footnote on page 134).

6.2.3 The error-repair transformation

Let $\mathbb{S} = (\mathcal{I},\mathcal{K},D)$ be a prediction-completion parsing system.

Let $D = D_1 \cup D_2 \cup \ldots \cup D_n$ be an expression of D where each D_i is either a predictive step set or a yield union step set with respect to a representation function r_R associated to a representation set $R = \{(q, i, j) \in E \times (\mathbb{N} \cup \{0\}) \times (\mathbb{N} \cup \{0\}) \mid i \leq j\}$. This expression must exist, by definition of the prediction-completion parsing system. As before, we will denote $r_R(e, i, j)$ by $[e, i, j]$.

The *error-repair transformation* of $, denoted $\mathcal{R}(\$)$, is an error-repair parsing system $(\mathcal{I}', \mathcal{K}, D')$ under the distance function $\hat{d}$, where $\mathcal{I}'$ and D' are defined as follows.

6.2.3.1 *Items of the error-repair transformation*

$\mathcal{I}' = \mathcal{I}'_1 \cup \mathcal{I}'_2$, with

$$\mathcal{I}'_1 = \{ \ \{(t, x) \in ApTrees(G) \mid t \text{ is substring-anchored} \wedge$$
$$left(t) = i \wedge right(t) = j \wedge$$
$$\exists i', j' \in (\mathbb{N} \cup \{0\}), t' \in [q, i', j'] \cup \{\epsilon(\epsilon)\} : \hat{d}(t, t') = x\} \ \mid$$
$$q \in E \cup \{\epsilon\}, \ i, j, x \in (\mathbb{N} \cup \{0\}) \ \}$$

and

$$\mathcal{I}'_2 = \{ \ \{(t, x) \in ApTrees(G) \mid t \text{ is non-anchored} \wedge$$
$$\exists i', j' \in \mathbb{N}, t' \in [q, i', j'] \cup \{\epsilon(\epsilon)\} : \hat{d}(t, t') = x\} \ \mid$$
$$q \in E \cup \{\epsilon\}, \ x \in (\mathbb{N} \cup \{0\}) \ \}.$$

Note that $\mathcal{I}'$ satisfies the definition of an approximate item set if, and only if, $\hat{d}(t_1, t_2) = \infty$ for every $t_1 \in [q_1, i_1, j_1], t_2 \in [q_2, i_2, j_2]$ such that $q_1 \neq q_2$ (this can be easily proved by the triangle inequality, and it can be seen that if this condition does not hold, there will be trees that appear in more than one item in $\mathcal{I}'$, thus violating the definition). Known item sets such as the Earley, CYK or Left-Corner item sets meet this condition when using the distance function $\hat{d}$, since if two items have $q_1 \neq q_2$, their respective trees differ in non-frontier nodes and therefore the distance between them is always ∞.

6.2.3.2 *Deduction steps of the error-repair transformation*

We define a set $R' = \{(q, i, j, e) \in (E \cup \epsilon) \times (\mathbb{N} \cup \{0\}) \times (\mathbb{N} \cup \{0\}) \times (\mathbb{N} \cup \{0\}) \mid i \leq j\}$ for $\mathcal{I}'$, and call it a *robust representation set* for $\mathcal{I}'$.

We define $r'_R : R' \rightarrow (\mathcal{I}' \cup \mathcal{H})$ as the function that maps each tuple (q, i, j, x) to the item:

- $\{(t, x) \in ApTrees(G) \mid t \text{ is substring-anchored} \ \wedge \ left(t) = i \ \wedge \ right(t) = j \wedge \exists i', j' \in (\mathbb{N} \cup \{0\}), t' \in [q, i', j'] \cup \{\epsilon(\epsilon)\} : d(t, t') = x\} \in \mathcal{I}'_1$, if $i \neq j$.

- $\{(t,x) \in ApTrees(G) \mid t$ is non-anchored $\wedge \exists i',j' \in (\mathbb{N} \cup \{0\}), t' \in [q,i',j'] \cup \{\epsilon(\epsilon)\} : d(t,t') = x\} \in \mathcal{I}_2'$, if $i = j$.

We call r_R' a *robust representation function* for $\mathcal{I}'$, and we will denote $r_R'(q,i,j,d)$ by $[\![q,i,j,d]\!]$. Note that the function r_R' is trivially surjective by construction: the images for each of the two cases of its definition are $\mathcal{I}_1'$ and $\mathcal{I}_2'$, respectively, and each hypothesis $[a,i,i+1] \in \mathcal{H}$ is the image of $(a,i,i+1,0)$.

The set of deduction steps of the error-repair transformation is defined as $D' =$ CorrectHyp $\cup$ SubstHyp $\cup$ DelHyp $\cup$ InsHyp $\cup$ BegInsComb $\cup$ OthInsComb $\cup$ DistIncr $\cup$ D_1' $\cup$ D_2' $\cup$ ... $\cup$ D_n', where[6]

CorrectHyp $= \{[a,i,j] \vdash [\![a,i,j,0]\!]\}$

SubstHyp $= \{[a,i,j] \vdash [\![b,i,j,1]\!] \mid b \in \Sigma\}$

DelHyp $= \{\vdash [\![b,i,i,1]\!] \mid b \in \Sigma\}$

InsHyp $= \{[a,i,j] \vdash [\![\epsilon,i,j,1]\!] \mid b \in \Sigma\}$

BegInsComb $= \{[\![\epsilon,0,j,e_1]\!], [\![x,j,k,e_2]\!] \vdash [\![x,0,k,e_1+e_2]\!] \mid x \in \Sigma \cup \{\epsilon\}\}$

OthInsComb $= \{[\![x,i,j,e_1]\!], [\![\epsilon,j,k,e_2]\!] \vdash [\![x,i,k,e_1+e_2]\!] \mid x \in \Sigma \cup \{\epsilon\}\}$

DistIncr $= \{[\![x,i,j,e]\!] \vdash [\![x,i,j,e+1]\!] \mid x \in E \cup \{\epsilon\}\}$

For each yield union step set D_i of the form:

$$D_i = \{[q_1,i_0,i_1],[q_2,i_1,i_2],\ldots,[q_m,i_{m-1},i_m],$$
$$[c_1,j_1,k_1],[c_2,j_2,k_2],\ldots,[c_n,j_n,k_n] \vdash$$
$$[q_c,i_0,i_m] \mid i_0 \leq i_1 \leq \ldots \leq i_m \in (\mathbb{N} \cup \{0\})$$
$$\wedge j_1,\ldots,j_n,k_1,\ldots,k_n \in (\mathbb{N} \cup \{0\}) \wedge j_i \leq k_i \wedge$$
$$P(q_1,q_2,\ldots,q_m,c_1,c_2,\ldots,c_n,q_c) = 1\}$$

we obtain:

$$D_i' = \{[\![q_1,i_0,i_1,e_1]\!],[\![q_2,i_1,i_2,e_2]\!],\ldots,[\![q_m,i_{m-1},i_m,e_m]\!],$$
$$[\![c_1,j_1,k_1,e_1']\!],[\![c_2,j_2,k_2,e_2']\!],\ldots,[\![c_n,j_n,k_n,e_n']\!] \vdash$$
$$[\![q_c,i_0,i_m,e_1+\ldots+e_m]\!] \mid i_0 \leq i_1 \leq \ldots \leq i_m \in (\mathbb{N} \cup \{0\})$$
$$\wedge j_1,\ldots,j_n,k_1,\ldots,k_n,e_1',\ldots,e_n',e_1,\ldots,e_m \in (\mathbb{N} \cup \{0\}) \wedge j_i \leq k_i \wedge$$
$$P(q_1,q_2,\ldots,q_m,c_1,c_2,\ldots,c_n,q_c) = 1\}$$

---

[6]The names of deduction steps have been shortened with respect to those given in Section 6.1.1 for economy of space.

and for each predictive step set D_i of the form:

$$\{[q_1, j_1, k_1], [q_2, j_2, k_2], \ldots, [q_n, j_n, k_n] \vdash$$
$$[q_c, f(j_1, k_1, j_2, k_2, \ldots, j_n, k_n), f(j_1, k_1, j_2, k_2, \ldots, j_n, k_n)] \mid$$
$$j_1, \ldots, j_n, k_1, \ldots, k_n \in (\mathbb{N} \cup \{0\}) \wedge j_i \leq k_i \wedge$$
$$P(q_1, q_2, \ldots, q_n, q_c) = 1\},$$

we obtain:

$$D'_i = \{[\![q_1, j_1, k_1, e_1]\!], [\![q_2, j_2, k_2, e_2]\!], \ldots, [\![q_n, j_n, k_n, e_n]\!] \vdash$$
$$[\![q_c, f(j_1, k_1, j_2, k_2, \ldots, j_n, k_n), f(j_1, k_1, j_2, k_2, \ldots, j_n, k_n), 0]\!] \mid$$
$$j_1, \ldots, j_n, k_1, \ldots, k_n, e_1, \ldots, e_n \in (\mathbb{N} \cup \{0\})$$
$$\wedge j_i \leq k_i \wedge P(q_1, q_2, \ldots, q_n, q_c) = 1\}.$$

Note that we have included a step in the transformation, DISTINCR, that is used to increase the parsing distance of an item. This is a general version of the DISTANCEINCREASER step explained for Lyon's algorithm in Section 5.3.1. As in that case, this step is not necessary in practical implementations whose goal is to find minimal distance items, but it is needed to guarantee strict completeness.

Example 6.7. Consider the Earley parsing schema, with the SCANNER step rewritten in order to be a yield union step set, as explained in Example 6.6. Its error-repair transformation is given by $(\mathcal{I}', \mathcal{K}, D')$, where:

$$\mathcal{I}' = \mathcal{I}'_{11} \cup \mathcal{I}'_{12} \cup \mathcal{I}'_{13} \cup \mathcal{I}'_{21} \cup \mathcal{I}'_{22},$$

$\mathcal{I}'_{11} = [\![A \to \alpha \bullet \beta, i, j, e]\!]$ with $i < j$, representing the set of substring-anchored approximate trees (t', e) such that $left(t') = i$, $right(t') = j$, and $\hat{d}(t', t) = e$ for some t in an Earley item of the form $[A \to \alpha \bullet \beta, i', j']$ for some $i', j' \in (\mathbb{N} \cup \{0\})$,

$\mathcal{I}'_{12} = [\![a, i, j, e]\!]$ with $i \neq j$, representing the set of substring-anchored approximate trees (t', e) such that $left(t') = i$, $right(t') = j$, and $\hat{d}(t', t) = e$ for some t in a hypothesis of the form $[a, i', j']$ for some $i', j' \in (\mathbb{N} \cup \{0\})$,

$\mathcal{I}'_{13} = [\![\epsilon, i, j, e]\!]$ with $i \neq j$, representing the set of substring-anchored approximate trees (t', e) such that $left(t') = i$, $right(t') = j$, and $\hat{d}(t', t) = e$ for the tree $t = \epsilon(\epsilon)$,

$\mathcal{I}'_{21} = [\![A \to \alpha \bullet \beta, i, i, e]\!]$, representing the set of non-anchored approximate trees (t', e) such that $\hat{d}(t', t) = e$ for some t in an Earley item of the form $[A \to \alpha \bullet \beta, i', j']$ for some i', j',

$\mathcal{I}'_{22} = [\![\epsilon, i, i, e]\!]$, representing the set of non-anchored approximate trees (t', e) such that $\hat{d}(t', t) = e$ for $t = \epsilon(\epsilon)$,

$r'_R(x, i, j, e) = [\![x, i, j, e]\!]$, for all $x \in D(P) \cup \Sigma \cup \{\epsilon\}$,

D' = CORRECTHYP $\cup$ SUBSTHYP $\cup$ DELHYP $\cup$ INSHYP $\cup$ BEGINSCOMB $\cup$ OTHINSCOMB $\cup$ DISTINCR $\cup$ DISTINCR2 $\cup$ DISTINCR3 $\cup$ INITTER' $\cup$ SCANNER' $\cup$ COMPLETER' $\cup$ PREDICTOR', where

CORRECTHYP = $\{[a, i, j] \vdash [\![a, i, j, 0]\!]\}$,

SUBSTHYP = $\{[a, i, j] \vdash [\![b, i, j, 1]\!] \mid b \in \Sigma\}$,

DELHYP = $\{\vdash [\![b, i, i, 1]\!] \mid b \in \Sigma\}$,

INSHYP = $\{[a, i, j] \vdash [\![\epsilon, i, j, 1]\!]\}$,

BEGINSCOMB = $\{[\![\epsilon, 0, j, e_1]\!], [\![x, j, k, e_2]\!] \vdash [\![x, 0, k, e_1 + e_2]\!] \mid x \in \Sigma \cup \{\epsilon\}\}$,

OTHINSCOMB = $\{[\![x, i, j, e_1]\!], [\![\epsilon, j, k, e_2]\!] \vdash [\![x, i, k, e_1 + e_2]\!] \mid x \in \Sigma \cup \{\epsilon\}\}$,

DISTINCR = $\{[\![x, i, j, e]\!] \vdash [\![x, i, j, e + 1]\!]\}$,

DISTINCR2 = $\{[\![A \to \alpha \bullet \beta, i, j, e]\!] \vdash [\![A \to \alpha \bullet \beta, i, j, e + 1]\!]\}$,

DISTINCR3 = $\{[\![\epsilon, i, j, e]\!] \vdash [\![\epsilon, i, j, e + 1]\!]\}$,

INITTER' = $\{\vdash [\![S \to \bullet\gamma, 0, 0, 0]\!]\}$,

SCANNER' = $\{[\![A \to \alpha \bullet x\beta, i, j, e_1]\!], [\![x, j, k, e_2]\!]$
$\vdash [\![A \to \alpha x \bullet \beta, i, k, e_1 + e_2]\!]\}$,

COMPLETER' = $\{[\![A \to \alpha \bullet B\beta, i, j, e_1]\!], [\![B \to \gamma\bullet, j, k, e_2]\!] \vdash [\![A \to \alpha B \bullet \beta, i, k, e_1 + e_2]\!]\}$,

PREDICTOR' = $\{[\![A \to \alpha \bullet B\beta, i, j, e_1]\!] \vdash [\![B \to \bullet\gamma, j, j, 0]\!]\}$.

6.3 Proof of correctness of the error-repair transformation

The error-repair transformation function $\mathcal{R}$ maps prediction-completion parsing systems to error-repair parsing systems. However, in order for this transformation to be useful, we need it to guarantee that the robust parsers generated will be correct under certain conditions. This will be done in the following two theorems.

Let $\$ = (\mathcal{I}, \mathcal{K}, D)$ be a prediction-completion parsing system with representation function $r_R(q, i, j) = [q, i, j]$, and with $D = D_1 \cup D_2 \cup \ldots \cup D_n$ an expression of D where each D_i is either a predictive step set or a yield union step set.

Theorem 6.1. *(preservation of soundness of the transformation)*

If $(\mathcal{I}, \mathcal{K}, D)$ is sound, every deduction step δ in a predictive step set $D_i \subseteq D$ has a nonempty consequent, and for every deduction step δ in a yield union step set $D_i \subseteq D$ of the form

$$D_i = \{ \, [q_1, i_0, i_1], [q_2, i_1, i_2], \ldots, [q_m, i_{m-1}, i_m],$$
$$[c_1, j_1, k_1], [c_2, j_2, k_2], \ldots, [c_n, j_n, k_n] \vdash$$
$$[q_c, i_0, i_m] \mid i_0 \leq i_1 \leq \ldots \leq i_m \in (\mathbb{N} \cup \{0\})$$
$$\wedge j_1, \ldots, j_n, k_1, \ldots, k_n \in (\mathbb{N} \cup \{0\}) \wedge j_i \leq k_i \wedge$$
$$P(q_1, q_2, \ldots, q_m, c_1, c_2, \ldots, c_n, q_c) = 1 \}$$

there exists a function $C_\delta : Trees'(G)^m \to Trees'(G)$ (tree combination function) such that:

- *If $(t_1, \ldots, t_m)$ is a tuple of trees in $Trees(G)$ such that $t_w \in [q_w, i_{w-1}, i_w]$ $(1 \leq w \leq m)$, then $C_\delta(t_1, \ldots, t_m) \in [q_c, i_0, i_m]$.*
- *If $(t_1, \ldots, t_m)$ is a tuple of trees in $Trees(G)$ such that $t_w \in [q_w, i_{w-1}, i_w]$ $(1 \leq w \leq m)$, and $(t'_1, \ldots, t'_m)$ is a tuple of contiguous yield trees such that $\hat{d}(t'_w, t_w) = e_w (1 \leq i \leq m)$, then $\hat{d}(C_\delta(t_1, \ldots, t_m), C_\delta(t'_1, \ldots, t'_m)) = \Sigma^m_{w=1} e_w$, and $C_\delta(t'_1, \ldots, t'_m)$ is a contiguous yield tree with $yield_m(C_\delta(t'_1, \ldots, t'_m)) = yield_m(t'_1) yield_m(t'_2) \ldots yield_m(t'_m)$.*

Then, $\mathcal{R}(\mathcal{I}, \mathcal{K}, D)$ is sound.

Theorem 6.2. *(preservation of completeness of the transformation)*

If $(\mathcal{I}, \mathcal{K}, D)$ is sound and complete, then $\mathcal{R}(\mathcal{I}, \mathcal{K}, D)$ is complete.

Note that the condition regarding the existence of tree combination functions in Theorem 6.1 is usually straightforward to verify. A yield union step set normally combines two partial parse trees in $Trees(G)$ in some way, producing a new partial parse tree in $Trees(G)$ covering a bigger portion of the input string. In practice, the existence of a tree combination function simply means that we can also combine in the same way trees that are not in $Trees(G)$, and that the obtained tree's minimal distance to a tree in $Trees(G)$ is the sum of those of the original trees (i.e. the combined tree contains the errors or discrepancies from all the antecedent trees). For example, in the case of the Earley COMPLETER step, it is easy to see that the function that maps a pair of trees of the form $A(\alpha(...)B\beta)$ and $B(\gamma(...))$ to the combined tree $A(\alpha(...)B(\gamma(...))\beta)$ obtained by adding the children of B in the second tree as children of B in the first tree, is a valid combination function. Combination functions for the remaining yield union steps in CYK, Earley and Left-Corner parsers are equally obvious.

6.3.1 *Proof of Theorem 6.1*

Let $\$ = (\mathcal{I}, \mathcal{K}, D)$ be a prediction-completion parsing system satisfying the conditions of Theorem 6.1, and $\mathcal{R}(\$) = (\mathcal{I}', \mathcal{K}, D')$ the error-repair transformation of $\$$.

We define a *correct item* in the error-repair parsing system $\mathcal{R}(\$)$ for a particular input string $a_1 \ldots a_n$ as an approximate item $r'_R(q, i, j, e) = [\![q, i, j, e]\!]$ containing an approximate tree (t, e) such that t is a contiguous yield tree with $yield_m(t) = \underline{a}_{i+1} \ldots \underline{a}_j$ (we call such an approximate tree a *correct approximate tree* for that item and string). Note that a final item containing such an approximate tree verifies the definition of a correct final item that we gave earlier.

We will prove that $\mathcal{R}(\$)$ is sound (all valid final items are correct) by proving the stronger claim that *all valid items are correct*.

To prove this, we take into account that a valid item is either a hypothesis or the consequent of a deduction step with valid antecedents. Therefore, in order to prove that valid items are correct, it suffices to show that:

(i) hypotheses are correct, and that
(ii) if the antecedents of a deduction step are correct, then the consequent is correct.

Proving (i) is trivial, since each hypothesis $[a, i-1, i]$ obtained from the function $\mathcal{K}$ contains a single tree with yield $\underline{a}_i$.

To prove (ii), we will show that it holds for all the deduction step sets in D'. Let $D = D_1 \cup D_2 \cup \ldots \cup D_n$ be an expression of D where each D_i is either a predictive step set or a yield union step set (this expression must exist, since $\$$ is a prediction-completion parsing system). Then the set of deduction steps D', used in the error-repair parsing system $\mathcal{R}(\$)$, can be written as $D' = $ CORRECTHYP $\cup$ SUBSTHYP $\cup$ DELHYP $\cup$ INSHYP $\cup$

BEGINSCOMB $\cup$ OTHINSCOMB $\cup$ DISTINCR $\cup$ D_1' $\cup$ D_2' $\cup$ ... $\cup$ D_n', as defined above. We will show that (ii) holds for each of the deduction step sets D_i, by proving it separately for each step set:

- For the deduction step sets D_i', by considering two possible cases:
  (1) D_i' comes from a yield union step set D_i.
  (2) D_i' comes from a predictive step set D_i.
- For the fixed deduction step sets CORRECTHYP, SUBSTHYP, etc., by considering each set separately.

6.3.1.1 *Proof for case (1)*

Let us consider the first case, where D_i' comes from a yield union step set D_i. Then, by definition of the error-repair transformation, D_i can be written as:

$$D_i = \{ \ [q_1, i_0, i_1], [q_2, i_1, i_2], \ldots, [q_m, i_{m-1}, i_m],$$
$$[c_1, j_1, k_1], [c_2, j_2, k_2], \ldots, [c_n, j_n, k_n] \vdash$$
$$[q_c, i_0, i_m] \mid i_0 \leq i_1 \leq \ldots \leq i_m \in (\mathbb{N} \cup \{0\})$$
$$\wedge j_1, \ldots, j_n, k_1, \ldots, k_n \in (\mathbb{N} \cup \{0\}) \wedge j_i \leq k_i \wedge$$
$$P(q_1, q_2, \ldots, q_m, c_1, c_2, \ldots, c_n, q_c) = 1\},$$

and D_i' can be written as:

$$D_i' = \{ [\![q_1, i_0, i_1, e_1]\!], [\![q_2, i_1, i_2, e_2]\!], \ldots, [\![q_m, i_{m-1}, i_m, e_m]\!],$$
$$[\![c_1, j_1, k_1, e_1']\!], [\![c_2, j_2, k_2, e_2']\!], \ldots, [\![c_n, j_n, k_n, e_n']\!] \vdash$$
$$[\![q_c, i_0, i_m, e_1 + \ldots + e_m]\!] \mid i_0 \leq i_1 \leq \ldots \leq i_m \in (\mathbb{N} \cup \{0\})$$
$$\wedge j_1, \ldots, j_n, k_1, \ldots, k_n, e_1', \ldots, e_n', e_1, \ldots, e_m \in (\mathbb{N} \cup \{0\}) \wedge j_i \leq k_i \wedge$$
$$P(q_1, q_2, \ldots, q_m, c_1, c_2, \ldots, c_n, q_c) = 1\}.$$

Let $\delta' \in D_i'$ be a particular deduction step in this set. We will prove that, if the antecedents of δ' are correct, then the consequent is also correct.

Let $\delta \in D_i$ be the deduction step in D_i with the same values of $q_1, \ldots, q_m$, $i_0, \ldots, i_m$, $c_1, \ldots, c_n$, $j_1, \ldots, j_n$, $k_1, \ldots, k_n$ as δ'. Let C_δ be a combination function for this step δ, which must exist by the hypotheses of the theorem.

If the antecedents of δ' are correct, then there exist m approximate trees $(t_w', e_w) \in [\![q_w, i_{w-1}, i_w, e_w]\!] (1 \leq w \leq m)$. By definition of r_R', we know that for each t_w' there exists a tree $t_w \in [q_w, i_w', i_w'']$ such that $\hat{d}(t_w', t_w) = e_w$. Taking into account that indexes associated to marked terminals do not affect our distance $\hat{d}$, we can assume, without loss of generality, that $t_w \in [q_w, i_{w-1}, i_w]$.

By the first condition that C_δ must verify, we know that $C_\delta(t_1, \ldots, t_n) \in [q_c, i_0, i_m]$.

By the second condition, we know that $\hat{d}(C_\delta(t'_1, \ldots, t'_n), C_\delta(t_1, \ldots, t_n)) = \Sigma_{w=1}^m e_w$.

These two facts imply that $(C_\delta(t'_1, \ldots, t'_n), \Sigma_{w=1}^m e_w)$ is a member of an item $[\![q_c, k_1, k_2, \Sigma_{w=1}^m e_w]\!] \in \mathcal{I}'$ for some $k_1, k_2 \in \mathbb{N}$.

By hypothesis, the antecedents of δ' are correct, so we know that $yield(t'_w) = \underline{a}_{i_{w-1}+1} \cdots \underline{a}_{i_w}$. Therefore, by the second condition of a combination function, $C_\delta(t'_1, \ldots, t'_n)$ is a contiguous yield tree with yield $\underline{a}_{i_0} \cdots \underline{a}_{i_m}$. Hence, we know that $k_1 = i_0$, $k_2 = i_m$, and $(C_\delta(t'_1, \ldots, t'_n), \Sigma_{w=1}^m e_w)$ is a correct approximate tree for the consequent item of δ', $[\![q_c, i_0, i_m, \Sigma_{w=1}^m e_w]\!]$. This proves that the consequent of δ' is correct.

6.3.1.2 *Proof for case (2)*

Let us consider the second case, where D'_i comes from a predictive step set D_i. In this case, the consequent of any deduction step $\delta' \in D'_i$ is of the form $[\![q_c, v, v, 0]\!]$ for some v. By construction of r'_R, this means that the consequent is the set of non-anchored approximate trees $(t, 0)$ with $t \in [q_c, k_1, k_2]$ for any $k_1, k_2 \in (\mathbb{N} \cup \{0\})$.

Let $\delta \in D_i$ be the deduction step in D_i with the same values of $q_1, \ldots, q_n$, $j_1, \ldots, j_n$, $k_1, \ldots, k_n$ as δ'. The consequent of this step is $[q_c, v, v] \in \mathcal{I}$. By definition of representation function, $[q_c, v, v]$ must be a non-anchored item. Therefore, any tree $t \in [q_c, v, v]$ is non-anchored. By hypothesis, since $[q_c, v, v]$ is a consequent of a deduction step from a predictive step set $D_i \subseteq D$, we know that $[q_c, v, v]$ is nonempty, so there exists at least one non-anchored tree $t \in [q_c, v, v]$. The tree $(t, 0)$ is a correct approximate tree in $[\![q_c, v, v, 0]\!]$. Therefore, the consequent of δ' is correct.

6.3.1.3 *Proof for fixed deduction step sets*

We consider each deduction step set separately:

- A CORRECTHYP step is of the form $[a, i, j] \vdash [\![a, i, j, 0]\!]$. The antecedent of this step can only be correct in $ if $j = i + 1$, since otherwise it equals the empty item. If the antecedent is correct, then there exists a hypothesis $[a, j - 1, j]$, containing a tree $a((a, j)) \in Trees(G)$. In this case, since $j = i + 1$, the consequent is $[\![a, j - 1, j, 0]\!]$.

  By definition of r'_R, the consequent item $[\![a, j - 1, j, 0]\!]$ is the set of substring-anchored approximate trees $(t, 0) \in ApTrees(G)$ such that

$left(t) = j-1, right(t) = j$, and $\hat{d}(t, u) = 0$ for some $u \in [a, k_1, k_2](k_1, k_2 \in (\mathbb{N} \cup \{0\}))$. One such tree is $(a((a, j)), 0) \in ApTrees(G)$, which is trivially a correct tree for this item. Therefore, the consequent item of CorrectHyp is correct.

- The consequent item of a step in SubstHyp, $[\![b, j-1, j, 1]\!]$, is the set of substring-anchored approximate trees $(t, 1) \in ApTrees(G)$ such that $left(t) = j-1, right(t) = j$, and $\hat{d}(t, u) = 1$ for some $u \in [b, k_1, k_2]$. One such tree is $(b((a, j)), 1) \in ApTrees(G)$, where $b((a, j))$ is at distance 1 from the tree $b((b, j)) \in [b, j-1, j]$ by a substitution operation. This is a correct tree for the consequent, therefore the consequent of SubstHyp is correct. Note that the antecedent is not used in the proof, so the transformation would still be sound with a step $\vdash [\![b, j-1, j, 1]\!]$. We only use the antecedent to restrict the range of j.

- In the case of DelHyp, a correct tree for the consequent is $(b(\epsilon), 1)$, where $b(\epsilon)$ is at distance 1 from any $b((b, j)) \in [b, j-1, j]$.

- In the case of InsHyp, a correct tree for the consequent is $(\epsilon((a, j)), 1)$, in which $\epsilon((a, j))$ is at distance 1 from $\epsilon(\epsilon)$.

- A correct tree for the consequent of steps in BegInsComb is obtained by appending a correct tree in the antecedent $[\![\epsilon, 0, j, e_1]\!]$ as the leftmost child of a correct tree in the antecedent $[\![x, j, k, e_2]\!]$.

- A correct tree for the consequent of steps in OthInsComb is obtained by appending a correct tree in the antecedent $[\![\epsilon, j, k, e_2]\!]$ as the rightmost child of a correct tree in the antecedent $[\![x, i, j, e_1]\!]$.

- A correct tree for the consequent of steps in DistIncr is $(t, e+1)$, for any approximate tree (t, e) in the antecedent $[\![x, i, j, e]\!]$.

As a result, we have proven that, under the theorem's hypotheses, (ii) holds for every deduction step. This implies that all valid items are correct and, therefore, that $\mathcal{R}(\$)$ is sound, as we wanted to prove.

6.3.2   *Proof of Theorem 6.2*

Let $\$ = (\mathcal{I}, \mathcal{K}, D)$ be a sound and complete prediction-completion parsing system, and $\mathcal{R}(\$) = (\mathcal{I}', \mathcal{K}, D')$ the error-repair transformation of $\$$. We will prove that $\mathcal{R}(\$)$ is complete. Proving completeness for this deduction system is proving that, given an input string $a_1 \ldots a_n$, all correct final items are valid. Therefore, given a string $a_1 \ldots a_n$, we have to prove that every item containing an approximate tree (t, e) such that t is a marked parse tree for $a_1 \ldots a_n$ can be inferred from the hypotheses.

Since the robust representation function for $\mathcal{R}(\$)$, r'_R, is surjective, every final item in this deduction system can be written as $[\![q,i,j,e]\!]$. Thus, proving completeness is equivalent to proving the following proposition:

Proposition 6.1. *Given any string* $a_1 \ldots a_n$, *every correct final item of the form* $[\![q,i,j,e]\!]$ *is valid in the instantiated parsing system* $\mathcal{R}(\$)$ $(a_1 \ldots a_n) = (\mathcal{I}', \mathcal{K}(a_1 \ldots a_n), D')$.

We will prove this proposition by induction on the parsing distance e.

6.3.2.1 *Base case (e=0)*

Items in the item set $\mathcal{I}'$ where the distance e is 0 can be mapped to items from the item set $\mathcal{I}$ (corresponding to the original non-error-repair parser) by the function $f : \{[\![q,i,j,0]\!] \in \mathcal{I}'\} \to \mathcal{I}$ that maps $\iota = [\![q,i,j,0]\!]$ to $f(\iota) = [q,i,j]$. This mapping is trivially bijective, and it is easy to see that deductions are preserved. The deduction $\iota_1 \iota_2 \vdash \iota_c$ can be made by a step from D'_i if and only if the deduction $f(\iota_1)f(\iota_2) \vdash f(\iota_c)$ can be made by a step from D_i. Moreover, an item $f(\iota)$ contains a tree t if and only if ι contains the approximate tree $(t,0)$, so $f(\iota)$ is a final item in the standard parser if and only if ι is a final item in the error-repair parser. Since any correct final item of the form $[\![q,i,j,0]\!]$ in the error-repair parser is $f^{-1}(\kappa)$ for some correct final item $\kappa = [q,i,j]$ in the standard parser, and we know by hypothesis that the standard parser is complete, it follows that all final items with distance 0 are valid in our error-repair parser.

6.3.2.2 *Induction step*

Supposing that the proposition holds for a distance value e, we must prove that it also holds for $e+1$.

Let $[\![q,0,n,e+1]\!]$ be a correct final item for the string $a_1 \ldots a_n$. We will prove that this item is valid in the deduction system $(\mathcal{I}', \mathcal{K}(a_1 \ldots a_n), D')$.

As this item is correct for the string $a_1 \ldots a_n$, we know that it contains an approximate tree $(t, e+1)$ where t is a tree rooted at S with $yield(t) = \underline{a}_1 \ldots \underline{a}_n$. By definition of approximate tree, we know that there exists a tree $u \in Trees(G)$ such that $\hat{d}(t,u) = e+1$ or, equivalently, $t \in Trans_{e+1}(u)$.[7]

---

[7]Strictly speaking, the definition of approximate tree only guarantees us that $\hat{d}(t,u) \leq e+1$, and not strict equality. However, this is irrelevant for the proof. In the case where $d(t,u) < e+1$, we would have that $[\![q,0,n,d(t,u)]\!]$ is a correct final item, and therefore valid by the induction hypothesis, so we conclude that $[q,0,n,e+1]$ is valid by applying $D^{DistIncr}$ steps.

By definition of $Trans_{e+1}(u)$, this implies that there is another tree t' such that $t' \in Trans_e(u)$ and $t \in Trans_1(t')$, and this implies that there exists an approximate tree (t', e) such that $\hat{d}(t, t') = 1$.

Since $\hat{d}(t, t') = 1$, and $yield(t) = \underline{a}_1 \ldots \underline{a}_n$, we know that $t \in Substitution(t') \cup Insertion(t') \cup Deletion(t')$, and therefore $yield(t')$ must be one of the following:

(1) $\underline{a}_1 \ldots \underline{a}_{j-1} (b, j) \underline{a}_{j+1} \ldots \underline{a}_n$, if $t \in Substitution(t')$,[8]
(2) $\underline{a}_1 \ldots \underline{a}_{j-1} (a_{j+1}, j) \ldots (a_n, n-1)$, if $t \in Insertion(t')$,
(3) $\underline{a}_1 \ldots \underline{a}_{j-1} \underline{b}_j (a_j, j+1) (a_{j+1}, j+2) \ldots (a_n, n+1)$, if $t \in Deletion(t')$.

We divide the proof into three cases according to the form of $yield(t')$:

Induction step, case (1) (substitution error)   Suppose that $yield(t')$ is of the form $a_1 \ldots \underline{a}_{j-1} (b, j) \underline{a}_{j+1} \ldots \underline{a}_n$. Consider the deduction system $(\mathcal{I}', \mathcal{K}(a_1 \ldots a_{j-1} b a_{j+1} \ldots a_n), D')$ obtained by applying our uninstantiated parsing system to the string $a_1 \ldots a_{j-1} b a_{j+1} \ldots a_n$. Consider the item in $\mathcal{I}'$ containing the approximate tree (t', e): this item must be of the form $[\![q, 0, n, e]\!]$, since $\hat{d}(t, t') = 1$ and $(t, e+1) \in [\![q, 0, n, e+1]\!]$ (under the distance function $\hat{d}$, if trees in two items $[\![q_1, i_1, j_1, e_1]\!]$ and $[\![q_2, i_2, j_2, e_2]\!]$ are at finite distance, then q_1 must equal q_2).

This item $[\![q, 0, n, e]\!]$ is a correct final item in this system, since t' is a marked parse tree for the input string $a_1 \ldots a_{j-1} b a_{j+1} \ldots a_n$. By the induction hypothesis, this item is also valid in this system. If we prove that the validity of this item in the system $(\mathcal{I}', \mathcal{K}(a_1 \ldots a_{j-1} b a_{j+1} \ldots a_n), D')$ implies that the item $[\![q, 0, n, e+1]\!]$ is valid in the system $(\mathcal{I}', \mathcal{K}(a_1 \ldots a_n), D')$, the induction step will be proved for the substitution case.

Therefore, we have reduced the substitution case of the proof to proving the following lemma:

Lemma 6.1. *Let $\mathcal{R}(\$) = (\mathcal{I}', \mathcal{K}, D')$ be the uninstantiated parsing system obtained by applying the error-repair transformation to a sound and complete parsing system $\$$.*

Given a nonempty string $a_1 \ldots a_n$, and a string $a_1 \ldots a_{j-1} b a_{j+1} \ldots a_n$ $(1 \le j \le n)$ obtained by substituting the jth terminal in the first string.

If $[\![q, 0, n, e]\!]$ is a valid item in the instantiated parsing system $\mathcal{R}(\$)$ $(a_1 \ldots a_{j-1} b a_{j+1} \ldots a_n) = (\mathcal{I}', \mathcal{K}(a_1 \ldots a_{j-1} b a_{j+1} \ldots a_n), D')$, then

---

[8] As our definition of $\hat{d}$ ignores indexes associated to marked terminals, we can safely assume that the marked terminal inserted in the frontier has the index j. In the other cases, we follow the same principle to reindex the marked terminals.

$[\![q, 0, n, e + 1]\!]$ *is valid in the instantiated parsing system* $\mathcal{R}(\$)(a_1 \ldots a_n)$ $= (\mathcal{I}', \mathcal{K}(a_1 \ldots a_n), D')$.

In order to prove this lemma, we define a function $f_1 : \mathcal{I}' \to \mathcal{I}'$ as follows:

$f_1([\![q, i, k, e]\!]) = [\![q, i, k, e]\!]$ if $i > j - 1$ or $k < j$

$f_1([\![q, i, k, e]\!]) = [\![q, i, k, e + 1]\!]$ if $i \leq j - 1$ and $j \leq k$

We will prove that if $\iota_1, \iota_2, \ldots \iota_a \vdash \iota_c$ in the instantiated parsing system $(\mathcal{I}', \mathcal{K}(a_1 \ldots a_{j-1} \ b \ a_{j+1} \ldots a_n), D')$, then $\mathcal{K}(a_1 \ldots a_n) \cup \{f_1(\iota_1), f_1(\iota_2), \ldots f_1(\iota_a)\} \vdash^* f_1(\iota_c)$ in the instantiated parsing system $(\mathcal{I}', \mathcal{K}(a_1 \ldots a_n), D')$.

We say that $\iota_1, \iota_2, \ldots \iota_a \vdash \iota_c$ in some instantiated parsing system if ι_c can be obtained from $\iota_1, \iota_2, \ldots \iota_a$ by application of a single deduction step. Therefore, we will prove the implication by considering all the possible deduction steps with which we can perform such a deduction:

- CORRECTHYP:

  If $\iota_1, \iota_2, \ldots \iota_a \vdash \iota_c$ by a CORRECTHYP step, then $a = 2, \iota_1 = [\![a, x-1, x, 0]\!]$ and $\iota_c = [\![a, x - 1, x, 0]\!]$. If we compute $f_1(\iota_1)$ and $f_1(\iota_c)$ depending on the values of the indexes i, j, we obtain that:

  if $x \neq j$, $f_1(\iota_1) = [\![a, x - 1, x, 0]\!]$ and $f_1(\iota_c) = [\![a, x - 1, x, 0]\!]$

  if $x = j$, $f_1(\iota_1) = [\![a, x - 1, x, 1]\!]$ and $f_1(\iota_c) = [\![a, x - 1, x, 1]\!]$

  In both cases we have that $\mathcal{K}(a_1 \ldots a_n) \cup \{f_1(\iota_1)\} \vdash^* f_1(\iota_c)$, because $f_1(\iota_1) = f_1(\iota_c)$.

- SUBSTHYP:

  By reasoning analogously to the previous case, we obtain:

  if $x \neq j$, $f_1(\iota_1) = [\![a, x - 1, x, 0]\!]$ and $f_1(\iota_c) = [\![b, x - 1, x, 1]\!]$

  if $x = j$, $f_1(\iota_1) = [\![a, x - 1, x, 1]\!]$ and $f_1(\iota_c) = [\![b, x - 1, x, 2]\!]$

  In the first case, we have that we can infer $f_1(\iota_c)$ from $f_1(\iota_1)$ by a SUBSTHYP step. In the second case, we can infer $f_1(\iota_c)$ from $\mathcal{K}(a_1 \ldots a_n)$: if we take the hypothesis $[\![a_x, x - 1, x, 0]\!] = [\![a_x, x - 1, x]\!] \in \mathcal{K}(a_1 \ldots a_n)$, we can infer $\iota_t = [\![b, x-1, x, 1]\!]$ from it by using a SUBSTHYP step, and then infer $f(\iota_c) = [\![b, x - 1, x, 2]\!]$ from ι_t by using a DISTINCR step.

- DELHYP:

  In this case, we always have that $\iota_c = [\![b, x, x, 1]\!]$ and $f_1(\iota_c) = [\![b, x, x, 1]\!]$, and therefore $f_1(\iota_c)$ can be inferred directly from the empty set by a DELHYP step.

- INSHYP:

  In this case, we have:

if $x \neq j$, $f_1(\iota_1) = [\![a, x - 1, x, 0]\!]$ and $f_1(\iota_c) = [\![\epsilon, x - 1, x, 1]\!]$

if $x = j$, $f_1(\iota_1) = [\![a, x - 1, x, 1]\!]$ and $f_1(\iota_c) = [\![\epsilon, x - 1, x, 2]\!]$

In the first case, we can infer $f_1(\iota_c)$ from $f_1(\iota_1)$ by a INSHYP step. In the second case, we can infer $f_1(\iota_c)$ from $\mathcal{K}(a_1 \ldots a_n)$: if we take the hypothesis $[\![a_x, x - 1, x, 0]\!] = [\![a_x, x - 1, x]\!] \in \mathcal{K}(a_1 \ldots a_n)$, we can infer $\iota_t = [\![\epsilon, x - 1, x, 1]\!]$ from it by using a INSHYP step, and then infer $f(\iota_c) = [\![\epsilon, x - 1, x, 2]\!]$ from ι_t by using a DISTINCR step.

- BEGINSCOMB:

  In the case of BEGINSCOMB, we have:

  (1) if $0 < j \leq i_1$, $f_1(\iota_1) = [\![\epsilon, 0, i_1, e_1 + 1]\!]$, $f_1(\iota_2) = [\![x, i_1, i_2, e_2]\!]$ and $f_1(\iota_c) = [\![x, 0, i_2, e_1 + e_2 + 1]\!]$.

  (2) if $i_2 < j \leq k$, $f_1(\iota_1) = [\![\epsilon, 0, i_1, e_1]\!]$, $f_1(\iota_2) = [\![x, i_1, i_2, e_2 + 1]\!]$, and $f_1(\iota_c) = [\![x, 0, i_2, e_1 + e_2 + 1]\!]$.

  (3) otherwise, $f_1(\iota_1) = [\![\epsilon, 0, i_1, e_1]\!]$, $f_1(\iota_2) = [\![x, i_1, i_2, e_2]\!]$ and $f_1(\iota_c) = [\![x, 0, i_2, e_1 + e_2]\!]$.

  In any of the three cases, $f_1(\iota_c)$ can be inferred from $f_1(\iota_1)$ and $f_1(\iota_2)$ by a BEGINSCOMB step.

- OTHINSCOMB:

  This case is analogous to the BEGINSCOMB case.

- DISTINCR:

  Reasoning as in the previous cases, we obtain that either $\iota_1 = [\![x, i, j, e]\!]$ and $\iota_c = [\![x, i, j, e+1]\!]$, or $\iota_1 = [\![x, i, j, e+1]\!]$ and $\iota_c = [\![x, i, j, e+2]\!]$. In both cases, the resulting deduction can be performed by a DISTINCR step.

- D_i' coming from a predictive step set D_i:

  Let us consider the case of a step D_i' which comes from a predictive step set D_i. Then D_i' can be written as

  $$D_i' = \{[\![q_1, j_1, k_1, e_1]\!], [\![q_2, j_2, k_2, e_2]\!], \ldots, [\![q_n, j_n, k_n, e_n]\!] \vdash$$

  $$[\![q_c, f(j_1, k_1, j_2, k_2, \ldots, j_n, k_n), f(j_1, k_1, j_2, k_2, \ldots, j_n, k_n), 0]\!] \mid$$

  $$j_1, \ldots, j_n, k_1, \ldots, k_n, e_1, \ldots, e_n \in (\mathbb{N} \cup \{0\})$$

  $$\wedge j_i \leq k_i \wedge P(q_1, q_2, \ldots, q_n, q_c) = 1\}.$$

  In this case, we have that:

  $$f_1(\iota_1) = [\![q_1, j_1, k_1, e_1 + b_1]\!]$$

  $$f_1(\iota_2) = [\![q_2, j_2, k_2, e_2 + b_2]\!]$$

  $$\vdots$$

  $$f_1(\iota_n) = [\![q_n, j_n, k_n, e_n + b_n]\!]$$

  where b_i can be either 0 or 1, and

$$f_1(\iota_c) = [\![q_c, f(j_1, k_1, j_2, k_2, \ldots, j_n, k_n), f(j_1, k_1, j_2, k_2, \ldots, j_n, k_n), 0]\!].$$

Clearly, $f_1(\iota_c)$ can be inferred from $f_1(\iota_1) \ldots f_1(\iota_n)$ by a $D'i$ step.

- D'_i coming from a yield union step set D_i:

  In the case of a step D'_i coming from a yield union step set D_i in the non-error-repair schema, we can write D'_i as

$$D'_i = \{ [\![q_1, i_0, i_1, e_1]\!], [\![q_2, i_1, i_2, e_2]\!], \ldots, [\![q_m, i_{m-1}, i_m, e_m]\!],$$
$$[\![c_1, j_1, k_1, e'_1]\!], [\![c_2, j_2, k_2, e'_2]\!], \ldots, [\![c_n, j_n, k_n, e'_n]\!] \vdash$$
$$[\![q_c, i_0, i_m, e_1 + \ldots + e_m]\!] \mid i_0 \le i_1 \le \ldots \le i_m \in (\mathbb{N} \cup \{0\})$$
$$\wedge j_1, \ldots, j_n, k_1, \ldots, k_n, e'_1, \ldots, e'_n, e_1, \ldots, e_m \in (\mathbb{N} \cup \{0\})$$
$$\wedge j_i \le k_i \wedge P(q_1, q_2, \ldots, q_m, c_1, c_2, \ldots, c_n, q_c) = 1 \}$$

In this case, we have

$$f(\iota_1) = [\![q_1, i_0, i_1, e_1 + b_j(i_0, i_1)]\!]$$
$$f(\iota_2) = [\![q_2, i_1, i_2, e_2 + b_j(i_1, i_2)]\!]$$
$$\vdots$$
$$f(\iota_m) = [\![q_m, i_{m-1}, i_m, e_m + b_j(i_{m-1}, i_m)]\!]$$
$$f(\iota_{m+1}) = [\![c_1, j_1, k_1, e'_1 + b_j(j_1, k_1)]\!]$$
$$\vdots$$
$$f(\iota_{m+n}) = [\![c_n, j_n, k_n, e'_n + b_j(j_n, k_n)]\!],$$

where $b_j(n_1, n_2)$ is the function returning 1 if $n_1 < j \le n_2$ and 0 otherwise.

For the consequent, we have that:

$$f(\iota_c) = [\![q_c, i_0, i_m, e_1 + \ldots + e_m + b_j(i_0, i_m)]\!].$$

We know that $b_j(i_0, i_m) = b_j(i_0, i_1) + \ldots + b_j(i_{m-1}, i_m)$, since position j can belong at most to one of the intervals $(i_{w-1}, i_w]$. If it does belong to one of the intervals, it also belongs to $(i_0, i_m]$, so both members of the expression equal one. On the other hand, if it does not belong to any of the intervals $(i_{w-1}, i_w]$, nor can it belong to $(i_0, i_m]$, so both members equal zero.

Therefore, $f(\iota_c)$ can be deduced from $f(\iota_1) \ldots f(\iota_{m+n})$ directly by applying the D'_i step.

With this we have proven that, for any deduction $\iota_1, \iota_2, \ldots \iota_a \vdash \iota_c$ made in the instantiated parsing system $(\mathcal{I}', \mathcal{K}(a_1 \ldots a_{j-1} b a_{j+1} \ldots a_n), D')$, we have $\mathcal{K}(a_1 \ldots a_n) \cup \{f_1(\iota_1), f_1(\iota_2), \ldots f_1(\iota_a)\} \vdash^* f_1(\iota_c)$ in the instantiated parsing system $(\mathcal{I}', \mathcal{K}(a_1 \ldots a_n), D')$.

This implies that, if $\mathcal{K}(a_1 \ldots a_{j-1}\, b\, a_{j+1} \ldots a_n) \cup \{\iota_1, \iota_2, \ldots \iota_a\} \vdash^* \iota_c$ in $(\mathcal{I}', \mathcal{K}(a_1 \ldots a_{j-1}\, b\, a_{j+1} \ldots a_n), D')$, then $\mathcal{K}(a_1 \ldots a_n) \cup \{f_1(\iota_1), f_1(\iota_2), \ldots, f_1(\iota_a)\} \vdash^* f_1(\iota_c)$ in $(\mathcal{I}', \mathcal{K}(a_1 \ldots a_n), D')$. In the particular case where $a = 0$ and $\iota_c = [\![q, 0, n, e]\!]$, we have that $f_1(\iota_c) = [\![q, 0, n, e + 1]\!]$ is valid in $(\mathcal{I}', \mathcal{K}(a_1 \ldots a_n), D')$, and therefore this proposition for that particular case is equivalent to Lemma 6.1. Thus, we have proven the substitution case of the induction step.

Induction step, case (2) (insertion error) In this case, we have that $yield(t') = \underline{a}_1 \ldots \underline{a}_{j-1}(a_{j+1}, j) \ldots (a_n, n - 1)$. Following a similar reasoning to that in the previous case, we can reduce this to proving the following lemma:

Lemma 6.2. *Let* $\mathcal{R}(\$) = (\mathcal{I}', \mathcal{K}, D')$ *be the uninstantiated parsing system obtained by applying the error-repair transformation to a sound and complete parsing system* $\$$.

Given a nonempty string $a_1 \ldots a_n$, *and a string* $a_1 \ldots a_{j-1} a_{j+1} \ldots a_n$ ($1 \le j \le n$) *obtained by deleting the jth terminal in the first string.*

If $[\![q, 0, n - 1, e]\!]$ *is a valid item in the instantiated parsing system* $(\mathcal{I}', \mathcal{K}(a_1 \ldots a_{j-1} a_{j+1} \ldots a_n), D')$, *then* $[\![q, 0, n, e + 1]\!]$ *is valid in the instantiated parsing system* $(\mathcal{I}', \mathcal{K}(a_1 \ldots a_n), D')$.

The proof, which we shall not detail, is also analogous to that of the previous case. In this case, the function that we use to map items and deductions in $(\mathcal{I}', \mathcal{K}(a_1 \ldots a_{j-1} a_{j+1} \ldots a_n), D')$ to those in $(\mathcal{I}', \mathcal{K}(a_1 \ldots a_n), D')$ is the function f_2 defined by:

$$f_2([\![q, i, k, e]\!]) = [\![q, i, k, e]\!] \text{ if } j > k$$
$$f_2([\![q, i, k, e]\!]) = [\![q, i, k + 1, e + 1]\!] \text{ if } j > i \text{ and } j \le k$$
$$f_2([\![q, i, k, e]\!]) = [\![q, i + 1, k + 1, e]\!] \text{ if } j \le i$$

Induction step, case (3) (deletion error) Reasoning as in the previous cases, we can reduce this case to the following lemma:

Lemma 6.3. *Let* $\mathcal{R}(\$) = (\mathcal{I}', \mathcal{K}, D')$ *be the uninstantiated parsing system obtained by applying the error-repair transformation to a sound and complete parsing system* $\$$.

Given a string $a_1 \ldots a_n$, *and a string* $a_1 \ldots a_{j-1}\, b\, a_j a_{j+1} \ldots a_n$ ($1 \le j \le n$) *obtained by inserting a terminal b in position j of the first string.*

If $[\![q, 0, n+1, e]\!]$ is a valid item in the instantiated parsing system $(\mathcal{I}',$ $\mathcal{K}(a_1 \ldots a_{j-1}\, b\, a_j a_{j+1} \ldots a_n),\, D')$, then $[\![q, 0, n, e+1]\!]$ is valid in the instantiated parsing system $(\mathcal{I}',\, \mathcal{K}(a_1 \ldots a_n),\, D')$.

This lemma can be proved by using the same principles as in the previous ones, and the following function f_3:

$$f_3([\![q, i, k, e]\!]) = [\![q, i, k, e]\!] \text{ if } j > k$$
$$f_3([\![q, i, k, e]\!]) = [\![q, i, k-1, e+1]\!] \text{ if } j > i \text{ and } j \le k$$
$$f_3([\![q, i, k, e]\!]) = [\![q, i-1, k-1, e]\!] \text{ if } j \le i$$

6.3.2.3 End of the proof of Theorem 6.2

This concludes the proof of the induction step for Proposition 6.1 and, therefore, it is proved that our error-repair transformation preserves completeness (Theorem 6.2).

6.4 Optimising the results of the transformation

The error-repair transformation that we have defined allows us to obtain error-repair parsers from non-error-repair ones. We also have formally shown that the error-repair parsers obtained by the transformation are always correct if the starting parser satisfies certain conditions, which are easy to verify for widely known parsers such as CYK, Earley or Left-Corner.

However, as we can see in the Example 6.7 obtained by transforming the Earley parser, the extra steps generated by our transformation make the semantics of the resulting parser somewhat hard to understand. Furthermore, the SUBSTHYP and DELHYP steps would negatively affect performance if implemented directly in a deductive engine, as they generate a number of hypotheses proportional to the size of the terminal alphabet Σ. Once we have used our transformation to obtain a correct error-repair parser, we can apply some simplifications to it in order to obtain a simpler, more efficient one which will generate the same items except for the modified hypotheses. That is, we can bypass items of the form $[a, i, j, e]$. In order to do this:

- We remove the steps that generate items of this kind.
- For each step requiring an item of the form $[a, i, j, e]$ as an antecedent, we change this requirement to the set of hypotheses of the form $[b, i1, i2]$ needed to generate such an item from the error hypothesis steps.

Example 6.8. Given the SCANNER' step obtained by transforming an Earley SCANNER step,

$$\text{SCANNER'} = \{[A \to \alpha \bullet a\beta, i, j, e_1], [a, j, k, e_2] \vdash [A \to \alpha a \bullet \beta, i, k, e_1 + e_2]\}$$

we can make the following observations:

- The item $[a, j, k, e_2]$ can only be generated from error hypothesis steps if $e_2 = k - j$, $e_2 = k - j - 1$ or $e_2 = k - j + 1$. It is trivial to see that the hypothesis steps added by the transformation always preserve this property. Therefore, we can separately consider each of these three cases.
- The item $[a, j, k, k - j]$ is valid if and only if $k > j$. This item can be obtained by combining a substitution hypothesis $[b, j, j + 1, 1]$ with $k - j - 1$ insertion hypotheses $[\epsilon, j + 1, j + 2, 1], \ldots, [\epsilon, j + (k - j - 1), j + (k - j), 1]$ via OTHERINSERTIONCOMBINER steps.
- The item $[a, j, k, k - j + 1]$ is valid if and only if $k \geq j$. This item can be obtained by combining a deletion hypothesis $[b, j, j, 1]$ with $k - j$ insertion hypotheses $[\epsilon, j, j + 1, 1], \ldots, [\epsilon, j + (k - j - 1), j + (k - j), 1]$ via OTHERINSERTIONCOMBINER steps.
- The item $[a, j, k, k - j - 1]$ is valid if and only if one of the following holds:

(1) $j = 0$ (therefore our item is $[a, 0, k, k - 1]$, and thus $k > 0$), and we have the hypothesis $[a, w - 1, w]$ for $w \leq k$. In this case, the item $[a, 0, k, k-1]$ can be obtained by applying the COMBINER steps to a correct hypothesis and $k - 1$ insertion hypotheses: $[\epsilon, 0, 1, 1]$, $[\epsilon, 1, 2, 1], \ldots, [a, w - 1, w, 0], [\epsilon, w, w + 1, 1], \ldots, [\epsilon, k - 1, k]$.

(2) $j > 0$ and we have the hypothesis $[a, j, j + 1]$. In this case, the item $[a, j, k, k - j - 1]$ (k must be $\geq j + 1$) can be obtained by applying the COMBINER steps to a correct hypothesis and $k - 1$ insertion hypotheses: $[a, j, j + 1, 0], [\epsilon, j + 1, j + 2, 1], \ldots, [\epsilon, k - 1, k]$.

Therefore, we can change the SCANNER step to the following set of steps:

- For $e_2 = k - j$:

$$\text{GENERALSUBSSCAN} = \{[A \to \alpha \bullet a\beta, i, j, e]$$
$$\vdash [A \to \alpha a \bullet \beta, i, k, e + k - j] \mid k \geq j + 1\}$$

- For $e_2 = k - j + 1$:

$$\text{GENERALDELESCAN} = \{[A \to \alpha \bullet a\beta, i, j, e]$$
$$\vdash [A \to \alpha a \bullet \beta, i, k, e + k - j + 1] \mid k \geq j\}$$

- For $e_2 = k - j - 1$ and $j = 0$:

$$\text{GENERALSCAN1} = \{[A \to \alpha \bullet a\beta, 0, 0, e][a, w - 1, w]$$
$$\vdash [A \to \alpha a \bullet \beta, 0, k, e + k - 1] \mid 0 < w \leq k\}$$

- For $e_2 = k - j - 1$ and $j > 0$:

$$\text{GENERALSCAN2} = \{[A \to \alpha \bullet a\beta, i, j, e], [a, j, j + 1]$$
$$\vdash [A \to \alpha a \bullet \beta, i, k, e + k + j - 1] \mid k \geq j + 1\}.$$

Note that GENERALSUBSSCAN is equivalent to the SCANSUBSTITUTED step in Lyon's parser (Section 5.3) in the particular case that $k = j + 1$. Similarly, GENERALDELESCAN is equivalent to Lyon's SCANDELETED when $k = j$, and the GENERALSCANs are equivalent to Lyon's SCANNER when $k = 1$ and $k = j + 1$ respectively.

Insertions are repaired for greater values of k. For example, if $k = j + 3$ in GENERALSUBSSCAN, we are supposing that we scan over a substituted symbol and two inserted symbols. The order of these is irrelevant, since the same consequent item would be obtained in any of the possible cases.

In the case of the last two steps, we are scanning over a correct symbol and $k - (j + 1)$ inserted symbols. In this case order matters, so we get two different steps: GENERALSCAN1 is used to scan any symbols inserted before the first expected symbol, followed by the first symbol, and then any symbols inserted between the first and the second expected symbols of the string; and GENERALSCAN2 is used to scan any expected symbol in the input string and the symbols inserted between it and the next one.

Additionally, the DISTINCR steps can be removed from the transformation in practice. This step is needed if we are interested in completeness with respect to the full set of correct final items, but, since it increases the distance measure without modifying any tree, it is unnecessary if we are only interested in minimal-distance parses, as is usually the case in practice. A similar reasoning can be applied to constrain GENERALDELESCAN to the case where $k = j$.

Example 6.9. With these simplifications, the parser obtained from transforming the *Earley* parsing schema has the following deduction steps:

$$\text{INITTER'} = \{\vdash [S \to \bullet\gamma, 0, 0, 0] \mid S \to \gamma \in P\}$$

COMPLETER' $= \{[A \to \alpha \bullet B\beta, i, j, e_1], [B \to \gamma\bullet, j, k, e_2]$
$\vdash [A \to \alpha B \bullet \beta, i, k, e_1 + e_2]\}$

PREDICTOR' $= \{[A \to \alpha \bullet B\beta, i, j, e] \vdash [B \to \bullet\gamma, j, j, 0] \mid B \to \gamma \in P\}$

GENERALSUBSSCAN $= \{[A \to \alpha \bullet a\beta, i, j, e]$
$\vdash [A \to \alpha a \bullet \beta, i, k, e + k - j] \mid k \geq j + 1\}$

GENERALDELESCAN $= \{[A \to \alpha \bullet a\beta, i, j, e] \vdash [A \to \alpha a \bullet \beta, i, j, e + 1]\}$

GENERALSCAN1 $= \{[A \to \alpha \bullet a\beta, 0, 0, e][a, w - 1, w]$
$\vdash [A \to \alpha a \bullet \beta, 0, k, e + k - 1] \mid 0 < w \leq k\}$

GENERALSCAN2 $= \{[A \to \alpha \bullet a\beta, i, j, e], [a, j, j + 1]$
$\vdash [A \to \alpha a \bullet \beta, i, k, e + k + j - 1] \mid k \geq j + 1\}.$

This algorithm is a variant of Lyon's parser that generates the same set of valid items, although inference sequences are contracted because a single GENERALSCAN step can deal with several inserted characters.

Example 6.10. If we apply the same ideas to a CYK bottom-up parser, we obtain an error-repair parser with the following deduction steps:

BINARY $= \{[B, i, j, e_1], [C, j, k, e_2] \vdash [A, i, k, e_1 + e_2] \mid A \to BC \in P\}$

SUBSUNARY $= \{\vdash [A, j, k, k - j] \mid A \to a \in P \wedge k \geq j + 1\}$

DELEUNARY $= \{\vdash [A, j, j, 1] \mid A \to a \in P\}$

GENUNARY1 $= \{[a, w - 1, w] \vdash [A, 0, k, k - 1] \mid A \to a \in P \wedge 0 < w \leq k\}$

GENUNARY2 $= \{[a, j, j + 1] \vdash [A, j, k, k - j - 1] \mid A \to a \in P \wedge k \geq j + 1\}.$

6.5 Discussion

In this chapter, we have used the error-repair parsing schemata introduced in Chapter 5 to define a transformation that can be applied to standard parsers in order to obtain robust, error-repair parsers. We have formally proven that the parsing algorithms obtained are correct if the original algorithm satisfies certain conditions. These conditions are weak enough to hold for well-known parsing schemata such as those for Earley, CYK or Left-Corner parsers.

The transformation is completely systematic, enabling it to be applied automatically by a parsing schema compiler (like the one described in

Chapter 3). This means that, by providing such a system with a description of a standard parsing schema, we can automatically obtain a working implementation of an error-repair parser. This implementation can be made to use a global or regional error-repair strategy, depending on which of the deductive engine variants presented in Chapter 5 we configure the compiler to use.

This chapter concludes Part 3 of this monograph, in which we have defined an extension of parsing schemata for the description of error-repair parsers. This new formalism provides not only a theoretical framework for these parsers, but also a practical tool for parser developers, since the compiler presented in Chapter 3 can be used with these extended schemata to generate practical implementations of error-repair parsers. Additionally, the transformation presented in the current chapter can be used to obtain these implementations directly from non-error-repair parsing schemata.

In the following part, we define another extension of parsing schemata to provide support for dependency-based parsers, and use it both to provide a uniform formal description of several existing dependency parsers, and to define novel algorithms for parsing several sets of mildly non-projective dependency structures.

PART 4

Parsing Schemata for Dependency Parsers

Chapter 7

Dependency parsing schemata

All the parsing algorithms that we have seen until now correspond to constituency-based parsers, since the framework of parsing schemata (Sikkel, 1997) is based on constituency trees. In this chapter we define a new formalism, based on parsing schemata, that can be used to describe, analyse and compare dependency-based parsing algorithms. This formalism, called *dependency parsing schemata*, was first introduced in Gómez-Rodríguez *et al.* (2008).

We use this abstraction to describe several well-known projective and non-projective dependency parsers from the literature, and show how it can be used to prove the correctness of some of these parsers and establish formal relations between them.

Additionally, we show how a variant of these dependency parsing schemata can be used to describe parsers for the Link Grammar formalism, and existing projective dependency parsers can be adapted to work with Link Grammar.

7.1 Motivation

Dependency parsing consists of finding the structure of a sentence as expressed by a set of directed links (called *dependencies*) between individual words. This is an alternative to constituency parsing, which tries to find a division of the sentence into meaningful segments called *constituents*, which are then broken up into smaller constituents.

Although most research on computational linguistics has traditionally focused on constituency parsing, dependency formalisms have received wide interest in recent years, while being successfully applied to tasks such as machine translation (Ding and Palmer, 2005; Shen *et al.*, 2008), textual entailment recognition (Herrera *et al.*, 2005), relation extraction (Culotta and Sorensen, 2004; Fundel *et al.*, 2006) and question answering (Cui *et al.*, 2005). Dependency structures directly show head-modifier and head-complement relationships which form the basis of predicate argument structure, but are not represented explicitly in constituency trees, while providing a conceptually simpler representation in which no non-lexical nodes have to be postulated by the parser. In addition to this, some dependency parsers (McDonald *et al.*, 2005b) are able to represent so-called *non-projective structures*, where the set of words dominated by each node are not required to be continuous substrings of the input. This feature becomes especially important when parsing variable word order languages in which discontinuous constituents are common.

The formalism of parsing schemata, introduced by Sikkel (1997) and described in Chapter 2 of this book, is a useful tool for the study of constituency parsers as it provides formal, high-level descriptions of parsing algorithms that can be used to prove their formal properties (such as correctness), establish relations between them, derive new parsers from existing ones and obtain efficient implementations automatically (Chapter 3). The formalism was initially defined for CFGs and later applied to other constituency-based formalisms, such as TAGs (see Section 4.3). However, since parsing schemata are defined as deduction systems over sets of constituency trees, they cannot be used to describe dependency parsers.

In this chapter, we define an analogous formalism that can be used to define, analyse and compare dependency parsers (Gómez-Rodríguez *et al.*, 2008, 2010b). We use this framework to provide uniform, high-level descriptions for a wide range of well-known algorithms described in the literature, including both projective and non-projective parsers. We also show how some of these algorithms formally relate to each other and how we can use these relations and the formalism itself to prove their correctness. Finally, we adapt the framework to the dependency-related grammatical formalism of Link Grammar, which uses undirected links to represent syntactic structure (Sleator and Temperley, 1991, 1993), and show how parsers for this formalism can be obtained by adapting the schemata for existing dependency parsers.

Apart from describing and studying existing parsing algorithms, dependency parsing schemata also provide a useful framework for the development of new parsers. An example of this is given in Chapter 8, where we define novel parsing algorithms for several classes of structures that allow restricted but practical degrees of non-projectivity, called mildly non-projective dependency structures.

7.2 The formalism of dependency parsing schemata

In the original formulation of parsing schemata that we have seen in Chapter 2, schemata are deduction systems whose domain is a set of items, and items are defined as sets of partial parse trees, members of some partition of a set *Trees(G)* that contains all the constituency trees licensed by a given grammar *G*. Although parsing schemata were initially defined for context-free parsers, they can be adapted to different constituency-based grammar formalisms, by finding a suitable definition of *Trees(G)* for each particular formalism and a way to define deduction steps from its rules. However, since the concept of *Trees(G)* and the subsequent definitions are based on constituency trees, parsing schemata are not directly applicable to dependency parsing.

In spite of this problem, many of the dependency parsers described in the literature have the property of being constructive, in the sense that they proceed by combining smaller structures to form larger ones until they find a complete parse for the input sentence. Therefore, it is possible to define a variant of parsing schemata, where these structures can be defined as items and the strategies used for combining them can be expressed as inference rules. However, in order to define such a formalism we first have to tackle some issues specific to dependency parsers:

- Traditional parsing schemata are used to define grammar-based parsers, in which the parsing process is guided by some set of rules which are used to license deduction steps. For example, an Earley PREDICTOR step is tied to a particular grammar rule, and can only be executed if such a rule exists. Some dependency parsers are also grammar-based, such as those described by Lombardo and Lesmo (1996), Barbero *et al.* (1998) and Kahane *et al.* (1998), which are tied to the formalisations of dependency grammar using context-free like rules described by Hays (1964) and Gaifman (1965). However, many of the most widely used algorithms (Eisner, 1996; Yamada and Matsumoto, 2003) do not use a formal grammar at all. In these, decisions about which dependencies to create are taken individually, using probabilistic models (Eisner, 1996) or classifiers (Yamada and Matsumoto, 2003). To represent these algorithms as deduction systems, we use the notion of *D-rules* (Covington, 1990). D-rules are simple rules of the form $a \to b$, which express that word b can have a as a dependent. Deduction steps in non-grammar-based parsers can be tied to the D-rules associated with the links they create. In this way, we obtain a representation of the semantics of these parsing strategies that is independent of the particular model used to take the decisions associated with each D-rule.

- The fundamental structures in dependency parsing are *dependency graphs*. Therefore, as items for constituency parsers are defined as sets of partial constituency trees, it is tempting to define items for dependency parsers as sets of partial dependency graphs. However, predictive grammar-based algorithms such as those of Lombardo and Lesmo (1996) and Kahane *et al.* (1998) have operations which postulate rules and cannot be defined in terms of dependency graphs, since they do not do any modifications to the graph. In order to make the formalism general enough to include these parsers, we define items in terms of sets of partial dependency *trees* as shown in Figure 7.1. Note that a dependency graph can always be extracted from such a tree, as we will see shortly.

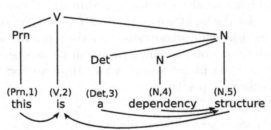

Fig. 7.1   Representation of a dependency structure with a tree. The arrows below the words correspond to its associated dependency graph.

- Some of the most popular dependency parsing algorithms, like that of Eisner (1996), work by connecting *spans* which can represent *disconnected* dependency graphs. Such spans cannot be represented by a single dependency tree. Therefore, our formalism allows items to be sets of *forests* of partial dependency trees, instead of sets of trees.

Taking these considerations into account, we define the concepts that we need to describe item sets for dependency parsers:

Let Σ be an alphabet of terminal symbols.

Definition 7.1. We define the set of *partial dependency trees* (denoted *D-trees*), as the set of finite trees where children of each node have a left-to-right ordering, each node is labelled with an element of $\Sigma \cup (\Sigma \times \mathbb{N})$ and the following conditions hold:

- All nodes labelled with marked terminals $\underline{a}_i \in (\Sigma \times \mathbb{N})$ are leaves,
- Nodes labelled with terminals $a \in \Sigma$ do not have more than one daughter labelled with a marked terminal, and if they have such a daughter node, it is labelled $\underline{a}_i$ for some $i \in \mathbb{N}$,
- Left siblings of nodes labelled with $\underline{a}_k$ or a_k do not have any daughter labelled $\underline{a}_j$ with $j \geq k$. Right siblings of nodes labelled $\underline{a}_k$ or a_k do not have any daughter labelled $\underline{a}_j$ with $j \leq k$.

We denote the root node of a partial dependency tree T as $root(T)$. If $root(T)$ has a daughter node labelled with a marked terminal $\underline{a}_h$, we will say that $\underline{a}_h$ is the *head* of the tree T, denoted by $head(T)$. If all nodes labelled with terminals in T have a daughter labelled with a marked terminal, we will say that T is *grounded*.[1]

Figure 7.1 shows a dependency tree for a sentence, together with its associated dependency graph. The dependency graph corresponding to a given tree can be obtained as follows:

Definition 7.2. Let $T \in$ *D-trees* be a partial dependency tree. Its *associated dependency graph*, $g(T)$, is a graph (V, E) such that:

- $V = \{\underline{a}_i \in (\Sigma \times \mathbb{N}) \mid \underline{a}_i$ is the label of a node in $T\}$,
- $E = \{(\underline{a}_i, \underline{a}_j) \in (\Sigma \times \mathbb{N})^2 \mid$ there exist nodes C, D in T such that D is a daughter of C, $\underline{a}_j$ is a daughter of C and $\underline{a}_i$ is a daughter of $D\}$.

Note that the mapping from *grounded* dependency trees to graphs is bijective: for every dependency graph $\hat{G}$, there is an unique grounded partial dependency tree T such that $g(T) = \hat{G}$. This tree can be built by creating a terminal node a that will be the parent of each marked terminal node $\underline{a}_i$ in the graph, and then making the terminal node b the parent of the terminal node a for each dependency link going from $\underline{a}_i$ to $\underline{b}_j$ in the graph. On the other hand, if we allow non-grounded dependency trees, then different trees can be associated with the same graph, since nodes labelled with a terminal

---

[1] For simplicity of notation, we will often omit the word "partial" when referring to partial dependency trees, since parsing schemata are always defined on sets of partial dependency trees.

that lack a daughter labelled with a marked terminal convey information that is not found in the dependency graph.

We will write an edge $(\underline{a}_i, \underline{a}_j)$ of a dependency graph as $\underline{a}_i \to \underline{a}_j$. Each of these edges is called a *dependency link*, meaning that the word a_i is a syntactic *dependent* (or *child*) of a_j or, conversely, that a_j is the *parent*, *governor* or *head* of a_i.

An important notion when defining dependency parsers is that of *projectivity*. Projective dependency graphs are those where each node dominates a contiguous substring of the input string. The relevance of projectivity comes from the fact that projective dependency structures can be parsed efficiently, in cubic time with respect to input length, while the recognition problem for general non-projective structures is NP-complete (Neuhaus and Bröker, 1997). For this reason, many of the parsers whose schemata we will see in this chapter are projective parsers, meaning that they can only analyse projective dependency structures.

When we translate the concept of projectivity from dependency graphs to the trees in *D-trees*, we obtain the following definition:

Definition 7.3. A partial dependency tree $T \in D\text{-}trees$ is said to be *projective* if $yield(T)$ cannot be written as $\ldots \underline{a}_i \ldots \underline{a}_j \ldots$ where $i \geq j$, i.e., if the marked terminals in $yield(T)$ are ordered by their indexes.

It is easy to verify that the dependency graph $g(T)$ is projective with respect to the linear order of marked terminals $\underline{a}_i$, according to the usual definition of projectivity found in the literature (Nivre, 2006a), if and only if the tree T is projective. A tree with an ordered yield trivially satisfies the condition that the marked terminals in the yield of each of its terminal nodes form a contiguous substring of the input sentence and the third constraint in Definition 7.1 guarantees that trees corresponding to projective graphs must *always* have their yield ordered.

Definition 7.4. A partial dependency tree $T \in D\text{-}trees$ is a *parse tree* for a given string $a_1 \ldots a_n$ if its yield is a permutation of $\underline{a}_1 \ldots \underline{a}_n$. If its yield is exactly $\underline{a}_1 \ldots \underline{a}_n$, we will say it is a *projective parse tree* for the string.

Definition 7.5. Let $\delta \subseteq D\text{-}trees$ be the set of dependency trees which are acceptable according to a given grammar G (which may be a grammar of D-rules or of CFG-like rules, as explained above). We define an *item set* for dependency parsing as a set $\mathcal{I} \subseteq \Pi$, where Π is a partition of $\wp(\delta)$.

Once we have this definition of an item set for dependency parsing, the remaining definitions are analogous to those given in Section 2.3.2 for constituency parsing, so we will not detail them here. A *dependency parsing system* is a deduction system $(\mathcal{I}, \mathcal{H}, D)$ where $\mathcal{I}$ is a dependency item set as defined above, $\mathcal{H}$ is a set containing *initial items* or *hypotheses* and $D \subseteq (\wp(\mathcal{H} \cup \mathcal{I}) \times \mathcal{I})$ is a set of *deduction steps* defining an inference relation $\vdash$.

Final items in this formalism will be those containing some forest F containing a parse tree for some arbitrary string. An item containing such a tree for a particular string $a_1 \ldots a_n$ will be called a *correct final item* for that string in the case of non-projective parsers. When defining projective parsers, correct final items will be those containing *projective* parse trees for $a_1 \ldots a_n$. This distinction is relevant because the concepts of soundness and correctness of parsing schemata are based on correct final items (cf. Section 2.3.3), and we expect correct projective parsers to produce only projective structures, while non-projective parsers should find all possible structures including non-projective ones.

7.3 Parsing schemata for projective dependency parsers

In this section, we will show how dependency parsing schemata can be used to describe several well-known projective dependency parsers in the literature.

7.3.1 *Collins (1996)*

One of the most straightforward projective dependency parsing strategies is the one described by Collins (1996), which is directly based on the CYK constituency parsing algorithm. This parser works with dependency trees which are linked to each other by creating dependency links between their heads. The schema for Collins' parser maps every set of D-rules G and string $a_1 \ldots a_n$ to an instantiated dependency parsing system $(\mathcal{I}_{Col96}, \mathcal{H}, D_{Col96})$ such that:

- The item set is defined as

$$\mathcal{I}_{Col96} = \{[i, j, h] \mid 1 \leq i \leq h \leq j \leq n\},$$

where an item $[i, j, h]$ is defined as the set of forests containing a single projective dependency tree T such that T is grounded, $yield(T) = \underline{a}_i \ldots \underline{a}_j$ and $head(T) = \underline{a}_h$.[2]

- For an input string $a_1 \ldots a_n$, the set of hypotheses is:

$$\mathcal{H} = \{[i, i, i] \mid 0 \leq i \leq n + 1\},$$

i.e., the set of forests containing a single dependency tree of the form $a_i(\underline{a}_i)$. This same set of hypotheses can be used for all the parsers and expressed as a standard function $\mathcal{K}$, as in the constituency case, so we will not make it explicit for subsequent schemata. Note that the words a_0 and a_{n+1} used in the definition do not appear in the input. These are dummy terminals that we will call beginning of sentence (BOS) and end of sentence (EOS) marker, respectively, and will be needed by some parsers.

- The set of final items is $\{[1, n, h] \mid 1 \leq h \leq n\}$: these items trivially represent parse trees for the input sentence, where a_h is the sentence's head.

- The set of deduction steps, D_{Col96}, is the union of the following:

$$\text{R-Link:} \quad \frac{[i, j, h_1] \qquad [j + 1, k, h_2]}{[i, k, h_2]} \quad a_{h_1} \rightarrow a_{h_2}$$

$$\text{L-Link:} \quad \frac{[i, j, h_1] \qquad [j + 1, k, h_2]}{[i, k, h_1]} \quad a_{h_2} \rightarrow a_{h_1}$$

allowing us to join two contiguous trees by linking their heads with a rightward or leftward link, respectively.

As we can see, we use D-rules as side conditions for the parser's deduction steps, since this parsing strategy is not grammar-based. Conceptually, the parsing schema we have just defined describes a recogniser: given a set of D-rules and an input string $a_i \ldots a_n$, the sentence can be parsed (projectively) under those D-rules if and only if this deduction system can infer a correct final item. However, when executing this schema with a deductive

---

[2]Note that our convention for indexes in items in dependency parsing schemata is not the same that we have used for constituency parsers. Here we use indexes i, j for items which trees whose yield spans a substring $\underline{a}_i \ldots \underline{a}_j$ of the input, following previous notation in the dependency parsing literature (see for example Eisner and Satta (1999); Paskin (2001)), while in schemata for constituency-based parsers we used i, j for items with yields spanning substrings $\underline{a}_{i+1} \ldots \underline{a}_j$, as usual when describing constituency parsers (Sikkel, 1997; Shieber *et al.*, 1995).

engine, we can recover the parse forest by following back pointers in the same way as it is done with constituency parsers (Billot and Lang, 1989).

Of course, boolean D-rules are of limited interest in practice. However, this schema provides a formalisation of a parsing strategy which is independent of the way linking decisions are taken in a particular implementation. In practice, statistical models can be used to decide whether a step linking words a and b (i.e., having $a \rightarrow b$ as a side condition) is executed or not, and probabilities can be attached to items in order to assign different weights to different analyses of the sentence. In this context, the side conditions specifying D-rules provide an explicit representation of the choice points where probabilistic decisions have to be made by the control structures executing the schema. The same principle applies to the rest of D-rule-based parsers described in this chapter.

7.3.2 *Eisner (1996)*

By counting the number of free variables used in each deduction step of Collins' parser, we can conclude that it has a time complexity of $O(n^5)$. This complexity arises from the fact that a parentless word (head) may appear in any position in the partial results generated by the parser and the complexity can be reduced to $O(n^3)$ by ensuring that parentless words can only appear at the first or last position of an item. This is the principle behind the parser defined by Eisner (1996), which is still in wide use today (Corston-Oliver *et al.*, 2006; McDonald *et al.*, 2005a). The parsing schema for this algorithm is defined as follows:

The item set is:

$$\mathcal{I}_{Eis96} = \{[i, j, True, False] \mid 0 \leq i \leq j \leq n\}$$
$$\cup \{[i, j, False, True] \mid 0 \leq i \leq j \leq n\}$$
$$\cup \{[i, j, False, False] \mid 0 \leq i \leq j \leq n\},$$

where each item $[i, j, True, False]$ is the same set as the item $[i, j, j] \in \mathcal{I}_{Col96}$, each item $[i, j, False, True]$ corresponds to the item $[i, j, i] \in \mathcal{I}_{Col96}$ and each item $[i, j, False, False]$ is defined as the set of forests of the form $\{T_1, T_2\}$ such that T_1 and T_2 are grounded, $head(T_1) = \underline{a}_i$, $head(T_2) = \underline{a}_j$, and $\exists k \in \mathbb{N}(i \leq k < j) \mid yield(T_1) = \underline{a}_i \cdots \underline{a}_k \ \wedge \ yield(T_2) = \underline{a}_{k+1} \cdots \underline{a}_j$.

Note that the flags b, c in an item $[i, j, b, c]$ indicate whether the words in positions i and j, respectively, have a parent in the item or not. Items with one of the flags set to *True* represent dependency trees where the word in position i or j is the head, while items with both flags set to *False* represent pairs of trees headed at positions i and j which jointly dominate the substring $\underline{a}_i \ldots \underline{a}_j$. Items of this kind correspond to disconnected dependency graphs.

The set of deduction steps is as follows:[3]

$$\text{INITTER: } \frac{[i,i,i] \quad [i+1,i+1,i+1]}{[i,i+1,\textit{False},\textit{False}]}$$

$$\text{R-LINK: } \frac{[i,j,\textit{False},\textit{False}]}{[i,j,\textit{True},\textit{False}]} \; a_i \rightarrow a_j$$

$$\text{L-LINK: } \frac{[i,j,\textit{False},\textit{False}]}{[i,j,\textit{False},\textit{True}]} \; a_j \rightarrow a_i$$

$$\text{COMBINESPANS: } \frac{[i,j,b,c] \quad [j,k,\textit{not}(c),d]}{[i,k,b,d]}$$

where the R-LINK and L-LINK steps establish a dependency link between the heads of an item containing two trees (i.e., having both flags set to *False*), producing a new item containing a single tree. The COMBINESPANS step is used to join two items that overlap at a single word, which must have a parent in only one of the items, so that the result of joining trees coming from both items (without creating any dependency link) is a well-formed dependency tree.

The set of final items is $\{[0,n,\textit{False},\textit{True}]\}$. Note that these items represent dependency trees rooted at the BOS marker a_0, which acts as a "dummy head" for the sentence. In order for the algorithm to parse sentences correctly, we will need to define D-rules to allow a_0 to be linked to the real sentence head.

7.3.3 *Eisner and Satta (1999)*

Eisner and Satta (1999) define an $O(n^3)$ parser for split head automaton grammars that can be used for dependency parsing. This algorithm is conceptually simpler than that of (Eisner, 1996), since it only uses items representing single dependency trees, avoiding items of the form $[i,j,\textit{False},\textit{False}]$.

---

[3]Alternatively, we could consider items of the form $[i,i+1,\textit{False},\textit{False}]$ to be hypotheses for this parsing schema, so we would not need an *Initter* step. However, we have chosen to use a standard set of hypotheses valid for all parsers because this allows for more straightforward proofs of relations between schemata.

Its item set is

$$\mathcal{I}_{ES99} = \{[i,j,i] \mid 0 \le i \le j \le n\} \cup \{[i,j,j] \mid 0 \le i \le j \le n\},$$

where items are defined as in Collins' parsing schema.

The deduction steps for this parser are the following:

$$\text{R-LINK:} \quad \frac{[i,j,i] \qquad [j+1,k,k]}{[i,k,k]} \ a_i \rightarrow a_k$$

$$\text{L-LINK:} \quad \frac{[i,j,i] \qquad [j+1,k,k]}{[i,k,i]} \ a_k \rightarrow a_i$$

$$\text{R-COMBINER:} \quad \frac{[i,j,i] \qquad [j,k,j]}{[i,k,i]}$$

$$\text{L-COMBINER:} \quad \frac{[i,j,j] \qquad [j,k,k]}{[i,k,k]}$$

where LINK steps create a dependency link between two dependency trees spanning adjacent segments of the input, and COMBINER steps join two overlapping trees by a graph union operation that does not create new links, similarly to the previous parser.

The set of final items is $\{[0,n,0]\}$: by convention, parse trees have a_0 (the BOS marker) as their head, as in the previous algorithm.

Note that, when described for head automaton grammars as in Eisner and Satta (1999), this algorithm seems more complex to understand and implement than the previous one, as it requires four different kinds of items in order to keep track of the state of the automata used by the grammars. However, this abstract representation of its underlying semantics as a dependency parsing schema shows that this parsing strategy is in fact conceptually simpler for dependency parsing.

7.3.4 *Yamada and Matsumoto (2003)*

Yamada and Matsumoto (2003) define a deterministic, shift-reduce dependency parser guided by support vector machines, which achieves over 90% dependency accuracy on section 23 of the Penn treebank. Parsing schemata are not suitable for directly describing deterministic parsers, since they work at a high abstraction level where a set of operations are defined without imposing order constraints on them. However, many deterministic parsers can be viewed as particular optimisations of more general, nondeterministic algorithms. In this case, if we represent the actions of the parser as deduction steps while abstracting from the deterministic implementation details, we obtain an interesting nondeterministic parser.

Actions in Yamada and Matsumoto's parser create links between two target nodes, which act as heads of neighbouring dependency trees. One of the actions creates a link where the left target node becomes a child of the right one, and the head of a tree located directly to the left of the target nodes becomes the new left target node. The other action is symmetric, performing the same operation with a right-to-left link. An $O(n^3)$ nondeterministic parser generalising this behaviour can be defined by using an item set:

$$\mathcal{I}_{YM03} = \{[i,j] \mid 0 \leq i \leq j \leq n+1\},$$

where each item $[i,j]$ is defined as the item $[i,j,\textit{False},\textit{False}]$ in $\mathcal{I}_{Eis96}$; and the deduction steps are as follows:

$$\text{INITTER: } \frac{[i,i,i] \qquad [i+1,i+1,i+1]}{[i,i+1]}$$

$$\text{R-LINK: } \frac{[i,j] \qquad [j,k]}{[i,k]} \ a_j \to a_k$$

$$\text{L-LINK: } \frac{[i,j] \qquad [j,k]}{[i,k]} \ a_j \to a_i$$

The set of final items is $\{[0,n+1]\}$. In order for this set to be well-defined, the grammar must have no D-rules of the form $a_i \to a_{n+1}$, i.e., it must not allow the EOS marker to govern any words. If this is the case, it is trivial to see that every forest in an item of the form $[0,n+1]$ must contain a parse tree rooted at the BOS marker and with yield $\underline{a}_0 \cdots \underline{a}_n$.

As can be seen from the schema, this algorithm requires less bookkeeping than any other of the parsers described here.

7.3.5 *Lombardo and Lesmo (1996) and other Earley-based parsers*

The algorithms in the above examples are based on taking individual decisions about dependency links, represented by D-rules. Other parsers, such as that of Lombardo and Lesmo (1996), use grammars with context-free like rules which encode the preferred order of dependents for each given governor, as defined by Gaifman (1965). For example, a rule of the form $N(Det * PP)$ is used to allow N to have Det as left dependent and PP as right dependent.

The algorithm by Lombardo and Lesmo (1996) is a version of Earley's CFG parser (Earley, 1970) using Gaifman's dependency grammar, and can be written by using an item set:

$$\mathcal{I}_{LomLes} = \{[A(\alpha \bullet \beta), i, j] \mid A(\alpha\beta) \in P \wedge 1 \leq i \leq j \leq n\}$$

where each item $[A(\alpha\bullet\beta), i, j]$ represents the set of partial dependency trees rooted at A, where the direct children of A are $\alpha\beta$, and the subtrees rooted at α have yield $\underline{a}_i \ldots \underline{a}_j$. Note that, while the trees appearing in items in the previous algorithms are always grounded trees, Lombardo and Lesmo's parser uses both grounded (in items $[A(\alpha\bullet), i, j]$) and non-grounded (in items $[A(\alpha \bullet \beta), i, j]$, where β is nonempty) trees.

The deduction steps for this parsing schema are the following:

$$\text{INITTER: } \frac{}{[(\bullet S), 1, 0]} *(S) \in P$$

$$\text{PREDICTOR: } \frac{[A(\alpha \bullet B\beta), i, j]}{[B(\bullet\gamma), j+1, j]} B(\gamma) \in P$$

$$\text{SCANNER: } \frac{[A(\alpha \bullet \star\beta), i, h-1] \qquad [h, h, h]}{[A(\alpha \star \bullet\beta), i, h]} a_h \text{ IS } A$$

$$\text{COMPLETER: } \frac{[A(\alpha \bullet B\beta), i, j] \qquad [B(\gamma\bullet), j+1, k]}{[A(\alpha B \bullet \beta), i, k]}$$

The final item set is $\{[(S\bullet), 1, n]\}$.

As we can see, the schema for Lombardo and Lesmo's parser resembles the Earley constituency parser in Figure 2.6 (page 22), with some changes to adapt it to dependency grammar (for example, the SCANNER always moves the dot over the head symbol $*$).

Analogously, other dependency parsing schemata based on CFG-like rules can be obtained by modifying CFG parsing schemata of Sikkel (1997) in a similar way. The algorithm by Barbero *et al.* (1998) can be obtained from the Left-Corner parser, and the one by Courtin and Genthial (1998) is a variant of the head-corner parser.

7.3.6   *Nivre (2003)*

Nivre (2003) describes a shift-reduce algorithm for projective dependency parsing, later extended by Nivre *et al.* (2004). With linear-time performance and competitive parsing accuracy (Nivre *et al.*, 2006; Nivre and McDonald, 2008), it is one of the parsers included in the MaltParser system (Nivre *et al.*, 2007b), in wide use today (Nivre *et al.*, 2007a; Surdeanu *et al.*, 2008).

The parser works by reading the sentence from left to right, using a stack and four different kinds of transitions between configurations. The transition system defined by all the possible configurations and transitions is nondeterministic, but machine learning techniques are used to train a mechanism that selects a single transition to undertake at each state, so that the parser becomes deterministic.

By encoding configurations into entities and transitions into deduction steps, we can define a simple deduction system for Nivre's parser as follows (where $a :: B$ represents the stack which is the result of pushing element a onto stack B, and $\langle \rangle$ represents the empty stack):

$$Initter \ \frac{}{(0, \langle \rangle, \varnothing)}$$

$$Shift \ \frac{(f, S, V)}{(f + 1, f :: S, V)}$$

$$L\text{-}Link \ \frac{(f, l :: S, V)}{(f + 1, f :: l :: S, V \cup \{a_f \to a_l\})} \ a_f \to a_l \ | \nexists \ a_f \to a_k \in V$$

$$R\text{-}Link \ \frac{(f, l :: S, V)}{(f, S, V \cup \{a_l \to a_f\})} \ a_l \to a_f \ | \nexists \ a_l \to a_k \in V$$

$$Reduce \ \frac{(f, l :: S, V)}{(f, S, V)} \ \exists a_l \to a_k \in V$$

Parser configurations are tuples (f, S, V) where f is a position of the input string, S is a stack and V is a set of dependency links, which will contain a parse for the input when the system reads the complete sentence.

Note that this is a deduction system that literally describes the transitions of the parser as defined in Nivre *et al.* (2004), but it is not a parsing schema by the definitions given in this chapter, because the entities it works with are not items.[4] The antecedents and consequents in this deduction system are parser configurations, but these configurations do not correspond to disjoint sets of partial dependency structures (several configurations may correspond to the same partial dependency structures), and therefore do not conform to the definition of an item set. However, we can obtain a parsing schema for Nivre's parser by abstracting away the rules in this system that are implementing control structures, and keeping only the parser's tree building logic.

First of all, note that parser configurations (f, S, V) include the full set of dependency links (V) that the algorithm has constructed up to a point. However, the parser does not need all this information in order to make decisions about dependency links (side conditions). The only information that the algorithm needs in order to make these decisions is whether elements in the stack have been assigned a head or not. If we represent this by using a stack of pairs (l, b), where l is the position of a word in the string and b is a flag equalling 1 if the word has been assigned a head or 0 if it has not, we obtain the following simplified deduction system:

$$\textit{Initter } \frac{}{(0, \langle \rangle)}$$

$$\textit{Shift } \frac{(f, S)}{(f + 1, (f, 0) :: S)}$$

$$\textit{L-Link } \frac{(f, (l, h) :: S)}{(f + 1, (f, 1) :: (l, h) :: S)} \ a_f \to a_l$$

$$\textit{R-Link } \frac{(f, (l, 0) :: S)}{(f, S)} \ a_l \to a_f$$

$$\textit{Reduce } \frac{(f, (l, 1) :: S)}{(f, S)}$$

This is a simple representation of the algorithm but it is still not strictly a parsing schema, since there are entities that correspond to the same dependency structures. For example, a *Reduce* configuration never makes any change to the dependency graph it is working with, it merely removes a

---

[4]This is the reason why we have represented the entities within round brackets instead of square brackets, as we reserve the latter notation for items.

node from the stack, meaning that we are not going to add more dependents to it. Therefore, $(f, (l, 1) :: S)$ and (f, S) cannot be distinct items in a schema as defined in this chapter.

In order to obtain a schema, we need to abstract from the control structures used to parse the sentence (shift and reduce) and keep only what the parser actually does, i.e., the way in which it joins dependency structures and builds links between them. In this case, the *Reduce* step is just a mechanism to select which of a set of possible "linkable words" is going to be linked to the word we are currently reading. Two different configurations corresponding to the same partial dependency structure may have different lists of words in the stack depending on which *Reduce* steps have been executed. In the parsing schema for Nivre's parser, these configurations will have to correspond to the same item. In order to define an item set for this parser, we have to observe which words *might* be in the stack at each configuration.

Let T be a partial dependency structure. We say that a word in T is *right-linkable* if it is not a dependent of any word situated to its right, and it is not covered by any dependency link (a_j is covered by the link $a_i \rightarrow a_k$ if $i < j < k$ or $i > j > k$).

It is easy to check that we cannot create a link between a non-right-linkable word and any word to the right of T without violating the projectivity property in our dependency structure. When Nivre's parser is reading a particular word a_f, we can say the following about all words to the left of a_f ($a_0 \ldots a_{f-1}$):

- If the word a_i is not right-linkable, then it cannot be on the stack.
- If the word a_i does not have a head, then it must be on the stack (note that words that do not have a head assigned are always right-linkable).
- If the word a_i has a head and it is right-linkable, then it may be on the stack or not (it depends on the particular transitions that we have executed).

Therefore, we can obtain a dependency parsing schema for Nivre's parser by representing items with a list (instead of a stack) containing all the words found so far which are right-linkable, and a flag associated to each word telling us if it has been assigned a head or not. Instead of using *Reduce* steps to decide which word to choose as a head of the currently-read word, we allow any word in the list that does not have a headless word to its right to be the head (note that this is equivalent to performing several *Reduce* transitions followed by an *L-link* transition).

By applying these ideas, we obtain the parsing schema where:

The item set is:

$$\mathcal{I}_{Niv} = \{[i, \langle (i_1, b_1), \ldots, (i_k, b_k) \rangle]$$
$$\mid 0 \leq i \leq n+1 \wedge 0 \leq i_1 \leq \ldots \leq i_k \leq n \wedge b_j \in \{0,1\}\}$$

where an item $[i, L]$ represents the set of forests of the form $F = (T_1, \ldots, T_w)$ $(w > 0)$ satisfying the following:

- The concatenation of the yields of $T_1, \ldots, T_w$ is $\underline{a}_0 \cdots \underline{a}_i$,
- The heads of the trees $T_1, \ldots, T_{w-1}$ are the words $\underline{a}_j \mid (j, 0) \in L$,
- The head of the tree T_w is the word $\underline{a}_i$,
- The right-linkable words in the partial dependency graph corresponding to F are the words $\underline{a}_j \mid (j, b) \in L$, with $b \in \{0,1\}$.

The set of final items is $\{[n+1, \langle (0,0), (v_1, 1), \ldots, (v_k, 1) \rangle] \mid 1 \leq v_j \leq n\}$, the set of items containing a forest with a single dependency tree T headed at the dummy symbol $\underline{a}_0$, whose yield is the whole input string, and which contains any set of right-linkable words.

The deduction steps are as follows:

$$\text{INITTER: } \frac{}{[0, \langle \rangle]}$$

$$\text{ADVANCE: } \frac{[i, \langle (i_1, b_1), \ldots, (i_k, b_k) \rangle]}{[i+1, \langle (i_1, b_1), \ldots, (i_k, b_k), (i, 0) \rangle]}$$

$$\text{L-LINK: } \frac{[i, \langle (i_1, b_1), \ldots, (i_k, b_k), (l, b), (v_1, 1), \ldots, (v_r, 1) \rangle]}{[i+1, \langle (i_1, b_1), \ldots, (i_k, b_k), (l, b), (i, 1) \rangle]} \quad a_i \to a_l$$

$$\text{R-LINK: } \frac{[i, \langle (i_1, b_1), \ldots, (i_k, b_k), (h, 0), (v_1, 1), \ldots, (v_r, 1) \rangle]}{[i, \langle (i_1, b_1), \ldots, (i_k, b_k) \rangle]} \quad a_h \to a_i$$

Which is a correct parsing schema describing Nivre's parser.

Note that a nondeterministic implementation of this schema in a generic deductive engine would have exponential complexity. The linear complexity in Nivre's algorithm is achieved by using control structures that deterministically select a single transition at each state, which are abstracted away in this schema representation.

7.3.7   *Covington's projective parser (Covington, 2001)*

Covington (2001) defines a non-projective dependency parser, and then gives a projective variant of it, called Algorithm LSUP (for List-based Search with Uniqueness and Projectivity). Unfortunately, this algorithm is not complete as it is given in the paper, since it is not able to parse every possible projective dependency structure. The reason is that, when creating leftward links, it assumes that the head of a word a_i must be a reflexive-transitive head of the word a_{i-1}, which is not always necessarily the case. For example, the structure shown in Figure 7.2 cannot be parsed with Covington's projective parser, because the constraints imposed by the algorithm prevent it from being able to find the head of a_4.

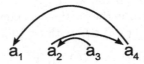

Fig. 7.2   Projective dependency structure that cannot be parsed with Covington's LSUP algorithm.

The MaltParser system (Nivre *et al.*, 2007b) includes an implementation of a variant of Covington's LSUP parser where these constraints have been relaxed, so that it is complete. This implementation has the same tree-building logic as the parser by Nivre (2003), differing from it in the control structures. Thus, it can be considered as a different implementation of the schema provided in Section 7.3.6.

7.4   Relations between dependency parsers

The framework of parsing schemata can be used to establish relations between different parsing algorithms. These relations are useful in understanding and comparing different parsers and their particular features. They can also be used to obtain new algorithms from existing ones or to derive formal properties of a parser (such as soundness or correctness) from the properties of related algorithms.

Sikkel (1994) defines several kinds of relations between schemata, which have been outlined in Section 2.3.4. Most of the parsers described in Section 7.3 can be related via generalisation and filtering, as shown in Figure 7.3.

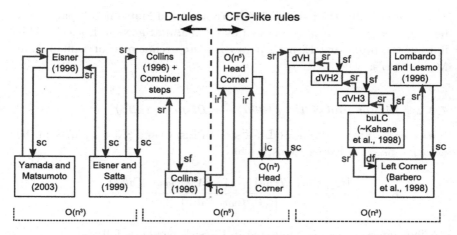

Fig. 7.3 Formal relations between several well-known dependency parsers. Arrows going upwards correspond to generalisation relations, while those going downwards correspond to filtering. The specific subtype of relation is shown in each arrow's label, following the notation introduced in Section 2.3.4.

We do not show full formal proofs of all the relations shown in the figure, but we outline the proofs for some of the most interesting cases:

7.4.1 *Yamada and Matsumoto (2003)* $\xrightarrow{sr}$ *Eisner (1996)*

It is easy to see from the schema definitions that $\mathcal{I}_{YM03} \subseteq \mathcal{I}_{Eis96}$. In order to prove the relation between these parsers, we need to verify that every deduction step in the schema for the algorithm by Yamada and Matsumoto (2003) can be emulated by a sequence of inferences in the one obtained from the parser by Eisner (1996). In the case of the INITTER step this is trivial, since the INITTERs of both parsers are equivalent. If we write the R-LINK step of Yamada and Matsumoto's parser in the notation we have used for Eisner items, we have:

$$R\text{-}Link \frac{[i,j,False,False] \qquad [j,k,False,False]}{[i,k,False,False]} \; a_j \rightarrow a_k$$

This can be emulated in Eisner's parser by an R-LINK step followed by a COMBINESPANS step:

$$[j,k,False,False] \vdash [j,k,True,False] \text{ (by R-LINK)},$$
$$[j,k,True,False],[i,j,False,False] \vdash [i,k,False,False]$$
$$\text{(by COMBINESPANS)}.$$

Symmetrically, the L-LINK step in Yamada and Matsumoto's parser can be emulated by an L-LINK followed by a COMBINESPANS in Eisner's. This finishes the proof that Eisner's parser is a step refinement of Yamada and Matsumoto's.

7.4.2   *Eisner and Satta (1999)* $\xrightarrow{sr}$ *Eisner (1996)*

In this case, if we write the R-LINK step in Eisner and Satta's parser in the notation used for Eisner items, we have:

$$\text{R-LINK:} \quad \frac{[i,j,False,True] \qquad [j+1,k,True,False]}{[i,k,True,False]} \quad a_i \to a_k$$

This inference can be emulated in Eisner's parser as follows:

$$\vdash [j,j+1,False,False] \text{ (by INITTER)},$$
$$[i,j,False,True],[j,j+1,False,False] \vdash [i,j+1,False,False]$$
$$\text{(by COMBINESPANS)},$$
$$[i,j+1,False,False],[j+1,k,True,False] \vdash [i,k,False,False]$$
$$\text{(by COMBINESPANS)},$$
$$[i,k,False,False] \vdash [i,k,True,False] \text{ (by R-LINK)}.$$

The proof corresponding to the L-LINK step is symmetric. As for the *R-Combiner* and *L-Combiner* steps in Eisner and Satta's parser, it is easy to see that they are particular cases of the COMBINESPANS step in Eisner's, and therefore can be emulated by a single application of COMBINESPANS.

Note that, in practice, the relations in Sections 7.4.1 and 7.4.2 mean that the parsers by Eisner and Satta (1999) and Yamada and Matsumoto (2003) are more efficient than that of Eisner (1996), since they generate fewer items and need fewer steps to perform the same deductions. These two parsers also have the interesting property that they use disjoint item sets (one uses items representing trees while the other uses items representing pairs of trees), and the union of these disjoint sets is the item set used by Eisner's parser. Also note that the optimisation in Yamada and Matsumoto's parser comes from contracting deductions in Eisner's parser so that linking operations are immediately followed by combining operations. In contrast, Eisner and Satta's parser does the opposite, forcing combining operations to be followed by linking operations.

7.4.3 Other relations

If we generalise the linking steps in Eisner and Satta's parser so that the head of each item can be in any position, we obtain a correct $O(n^5)$ parser which can be filtered to the parser by Collins (1996) just by eliminating the COMBINER steps.

From Collins' parser, we can obtain an $O(n^5)$ head-corner parser[5] based on CFG-like rules by an item refinement in which each Collins item $[i, j, h]$ is split into a set of items $[A(\alpha \bullet \beta \bullet \gamma), i, j, h]$. Of course, the formal refinement relation between these parsers only holds if the D-rules used for Collins' parser correspond to the CFG rules used for the head-corner parser. For every D-rule $B \to A$ there must be a corresponding CFG-like rule $A \to \dots B \dots$ in the grammar used by the head-corner parser.

Although this parser uses three indices i, j, h, using CFG-like rules to guide linking decisions makes the h indices unnecessary, so they can be removed. This simplification is an item contraction which results in an $O(n^3)$ head-corner parser. From here, we can follow the procedure in Sikkel (1994) to relate this head-corner algorithm to parsers analogous to other algorithms for CFGs. In this way, we can refine the head-corner parser to a variant of the algorithm by de Vreught and Honig (1989) (Sikkel, 1997),[6] and by successive filters we reach a left-corner parser which is equivalent to the one described by Barbero *et al.* (1998), and a step contraction of the Earley-based dependency parser by Lombardo and Lesmo (1996). The proofs for these relations are the same as those described in Sikkel (1994), except that the dependency variants of each algorithm are simpler (due to the absence of epsilon rules and the fact that the rules are lexicalised).[7]

---

[5] A head-corner parser (van Noord, 1997) is an algorithm that starts the process of parsing the right-hand side of each CFG rule (corresponding to each dependency subtree, in dependency parsing, or each constituent, in constituency-based parsing) by its syntactic head. Once a head has been located, the parser proceeds bidirectionally to scan its left and right dependents.

[6] The algorithm by de Vreught and Honig for CFGs is a bidirectional bottom-up parser intended for parallel processing. In this algorithm the recognition of the right-hand side of each rule can start by any of its symbols (not necessarily the head, as in a head-corner parser), and then expands from left to right to cover the whole rule.

[7] The names of the schemata $dVH1, dVH2, dVH3$ and $buLC$ shown in Figure 7.3 come from Sikkel (1994, 1997). Each of these dependency parsing schemata is a version of the homonymous schema described by Sikkel, adapted for dependency parsing.

7.5   Proving the correctness of dependency parsers

Another useful feature of the parsing schemata framework is that it provides
a formal way to define the correctness of a parser (see Section 2.3.3) which
we can use to prove that our parsers are correct. Furthermore, relations
between schemata can be used to derive the correctness of a schema from
that of related ones. In this section, we will show how we can prove that
the algorithms by Yamada and Matsumoto (2003) and Eisner and Satta
(1999) are correct, and use that fact to prove the correctness of the one by
Eisner (1996).

7.5.1   *Eisner and Satta (1999) is correct*

In order to prove the correctness of a parser, we must prove its soundness
and completeness (see Section 2.3.3). Soundness is easy to verify in this
case, since we only need to check that every individual deduction step in the
parser infers a correct consequent item when applied to correct antecedents
(i.e., in this case, that steps always generate non-empty items that conform
to the definition in Section 7.3.3). This is shown by checking that, given
two antecedents of a deduction step that contain a tree licensed by a set of
D-rules G, the consequent of the step also contains such a tree. This can be
seen by building the tree for the consequent from the trees corresponding
to the antecedents, which is done by a graph union operation (in the case of
COMBINER steps) or by linking the heads of both trees with a dependency
relation licensed by G (in the case of LINK steps).

The difficulty is proving completeness, for which we need to prove that
all correct final items are valid (i.e., can be inferred by the schema). To
show this, we will prove the stronger result that all correct items are valid.

We will show this by strong induction on the *length* of items, where the
length of an item $\iota = [i, k, h]$ is defined as $length(\iota) = k - i + 1$. Correct
items of length 1 are the hypotheses of the schema (of the form $[i, i, i]$)
which are trivially valid. We will prove that, if all correct items of length
m are valid for all $1 \leq m < l$, then items of length l are also valid.

Let $[i, k, i]$ be an item of length l in $\mathcal{I}_{ES99}$ (thus, $l = k - i + 1$). If this
item is correct, then it contains a grounded dependency tree T such that
$yield(T) = \underline{a}_i \ldots \underline{a}_k$ and $head(t) = \underline{a}_i$.

By construction, the root of T is labelled a_i. Let a_j be the rightmost
daughter of a_i in T. Since T is projective, we know that the yield of a_j
must be of the form $\underline{a}_l \ldots \underline{a}_k$, where $i < l \leq j \leq k$. If $l < j$, then a_l is the

leftmost transitive dependent of a_j in T, and if $k > j$, then we know that a_k is the rightmost transitive dependent of a_j in T.

Let T_j be the subtree of T rooted at a_j. Let T_1 be the tree obtained from removing T_j from T. Let T_2 be the tree obtained by removing all the children to the right of $\underline{a}_j$ from T_j, and T_3 be the tree obtained by removing all the children to the left of $\underline{a}_j$ from T_j. By construction, T_1 belongs to a correct item $[i, l-1, i]$, T_2 belongs to a correct item $[l, j, j]$ and T_3 belongs to a correct item $[j, k, j]$. Since these three items have a length strictly less than l, by the inductive hypothesis, they are valid. This allows us to prove that the item $[i, k, i]$ is also valid, since it can be obtained from these valid items by the following inferences:

$[i, l-1, i], [l, j, j] \vdash [i, j, i]$ (by the *L-Link* step),

$[i, j, i], [j, k, j] \vdash [i, k, i]$ (by the *L-Combiner* step).

This proves that all correct items of length l which are of the form $[i, k, i]$ are correct under the induction hypothesis. The same can be proved for items of the form $[i, k, k]$ by symmetric reasoning, thus proving that the parsing schema for Eisner and Satta's parser is correct.

7.5.2 *Yamada and Matsumoto (2003) is correct*

In order to prove correctness of this parser, we follow the same procedure as above. Soundness is again trivial to verify, by building forests for the consequents of steps from those corresponding to the antecedents. To prove completeness, we use strong induction on the length of items, where the length of an item $[i, j]$ is defined as $j - i + 1$.

The induction step is proven by considering any correct item $[i, k]$ of length $l > 2$ ($l = 2$ is the base case here since items of length 2 are generated by the *Initter* step) and proving that it can be inferred from valid antecedents of length less than l, so it is valid. To show this, we note that, if $l > 2$, either a_i has at least one right dependent or a_k has at least one left dependent in the item. Supposing that a_i has a right dependent, if T_1 and T_2 are the trees rooted at a_i and a_k in a forest in $[i, k]$, we call a_j the rightmost daughter of a_i and consider the following trees:

- V = the subtree of T_1 rooted at a_j,
- U_1 = the tree obtained by removing V from T_1,
- U_2 = the tree obtained by removing all children to the right of $\underline{a}_j$ from V,

- U_3 = the tree obtained by removing all children to the left of $\underline{a}_j$ from V.

We observe that the forest $\{U_1, U_2\}$ belongs to the correct item $[i, j]$, while $\{U_3, T_2\}$ belongs to the correct item $[j, k]$. From these two items, we can obtain $[i, k]$ by using the L-LINK step. Symmetric reasoning can be applied if a_i has no right dependents but a_k has at least one left dependent, and analogously to the case of the previous parser, we conclude that the schema for the parser by Yamada and Matsumoto is correct.

7.5.3 *Eisner (1996) is correct*

By using the previous proofs and the relationships between schemata that we explained earlier, it is easy to prove that the parser by Eisner (1996) is correct. Soundness is, as always, straightforward, and completeness can be proven by using the properties of other algorithms. Since the set of final items in Eisner (1996) and Eisner and Satta (1999) are the same, and the former is a step refinement of the latter, the completeness of Eisner and Satta's parser directly implies the completeness of Eisner's parser.

  Alternatively, we can use Yamada and Matsumoto's parser to prove the correctness of Eisner's parser if we redefine the set of final items in the latter to be items of the form $[0, n + 1, False, False]$, which are equally valid as final items since they always contain parse trees. This idea can be applied to transfer proofs of completeness across any refinement relation.

7.6 Parsing schemata for non-projective dependency parsers

The parsing schemata that we have seen up to now in this chapter correspond to parsers that are restricted to projective dependency structures, i.e., structures in which the set of reflexive-transitive dependents of each given node forms a contiguous substring of the input. However, the dependency parsing schema formalism is general enough to handle non-projective parsers as well. In this section, we see how several non-projective parsing algorithms in the literature can be described as parsing schemata. More non-projective parsers are described in the next chapter, where we introduce novel algorithms for parsing mildly non-projective dependency structures.

7.6.1 *Pseudo-projectivity*

Pseudo-projective parsers can generate non-projective analyses in polynomial time by using a projective parsing strategy and then postprocessing the results to establish non-projective links. The projective parsing strategy can be represented by a projective dependency parsing schema like the ones seen in Section 7.3. For example, the algorithm by Kahane *et al.* (1998) uses a strategy like that of Lombardo and Lesmo (1996), but using the following initialiser step instead of the INITTER and PREDICTOR:[8]

$$\text{INITTER: } \frac{}{[A(\bullet\alpha), i, i-1]} \; A(\alpha) \in P \wedge 1 \le i \le n$$

7.6.2 *Attardi (2006) and the MH_k parser*

The non-projective parser by Attardi (2006) is an extension of the algorithm by Yamada and Matsumoto (2003) that adds additional shift and reduce actions to handle non-projective dependency structures. The extra actions allow the parser to link to nodes that are several positions deep in the stack, which causes the creation of non-projective links. In particular, Attardi (2006) uses six non-projective actions: two actions to link to nodes that are 2 positions deep; another two actions for nodes that are 3 positions deep; and a third pair of actions that generalises the previous ones to n positions deep for any n. Thus, the maximum depth in the stack to which links can be created can be configured according to the actions that we allow to use. Here we will call Att_d the variant of the algorithm that allows links only up to depth d, and Att_∞ the original, unrestricted algorithm with the unlimited depth actions.

Similarly as is the case of Yamada and Matsumoto's parser, a nondeterministic version of the algorithm Att_d can be described by a parsing schema whose item set is:

$$\mathcal{I}_{Att} = \{[h_1, h_2, \ldots, h_m] \mid 0 \le h_1 < \ldots < h_m \le n+1\}$$

where $[h_1, h_2, \ldots, h_m]$ is the set of dependency forests of the form $\{T_1, T_2, \ldots, T_m\}$ such that:

---

[8]The initialisation step as reported in Kahane's paper is different from this one, as it directly consumes a nonterminal from the input. However, using this step results in an incomplete algorithm. The problem can be fixed either by using the step shown here instead (bottom-up Earley strategy) or by adding an additional step, turning it into a bottom-up Left-Corner parser.

- $T_1, T_2, \ldots, T_m$ are grounded,
- $head(T_i) = \underline{a}_{h_i}$ for each $i \in \mathbb{N} \mid 1 \leq i \leq m$,
- If we define the *projection* of a node to be the set of nodes in its yield, then the projections of the nodes $h_1, h_2, \ldots, h_m$ are pairwise disjoint, and their union is $\{\underline{a}_{h_1}, \underline{a}_{h_1+1}, \ldots, \underline{a}_{h_m-1}, \underline{a}_{h_m}\}$.

The set of deduction steps for Att_d is the following:

$$\text{INITTER:} \quad \frac{[i,i,i] \qquad [i+1,i+1,i+1]}{[i,i+1]}$$

$$\text{COMBINE:} \quad \frac{[h_1, h_2, \ldots, h_m] \qquad [h_m, h_{m+1}, \ldots, h_p]}{[h_1, h_2, \ldots, h_p]}$$

$$\text{LINK:} \quad \frac{[h_1, h_2, \ldots, h_m]}{[h_1, h_2, \ldots, h_{i-1}, h_{i+1}, \ldots, h_m]} \quad a_{h_i} \to a_{h_j}$$

such that $1 < i < m, 1 \leq j \leq m, j \neq i, |j - i| \leq d$.

As expected, deduction steps for Att_∞ are obtained by removing the constraint $|j - i| \leq d$ from this set, since this restriction corresponds to the maximum stack depth to which dependency links can be created in the algorithm.

The set of final items is $\{[0, n+1]\}$. Note that, although this set is analogous to the final item set for Yamada and Matsumoto's parser, they are not the same set, since an Attardi item of the form $[0, n+1]$ may contain forests with non-projective dependency trees.

As can be seen by the number of indexes handled by the steps in the schema, a nondeterministic implementation of Att_d has exponential complexity with respect to input length. Of course, this problem does not exist in the implementation by Attardi (2006), since he uses control structures to deterministically decide the transition to take at each state.

It is easy to prove that the algorithm Att_∞ is a correct non-projective parser. Soundness is proven as in the previous algorithms seen in this chapter, and completeness can be shown by reasoning that every correct final item $[0, n+1]$ can be obtained by first performing $n+1$ INITTER steps to obtain items $[i, i+1]$ for each $0 \leq i \leq n$, then using n COMBINERs to join all of these items into $[0, 1, \ldots, n, n+1]$, and then performing the LINK steps corresponding to the links in a tree contained in $[0, n+1]$ to obtain this final item. The algorithm Att_d where d is finite is not correct with respect to the set of non-projective dependency structures, since it only parses a restricted subset of them (Attardi, 2006). Note that the algorithm Att_d is a static filter (see Section 2.3.4) of Att_{d+1} for every natural number d, since the set of deduction steps of Att_d is a subset of that of Att_{d+1}.

It is possible to define a variant of this parser such that its nondeterministic implementation has polynomial complexity, instead of being exponential. This can be done by limiting the number of trees in each forest contained in an item, rather than limiting stack depth. This produces a parsing schema describing a parser that we will call MH_k (for multi-headed with at most k heads per item) whose item set is:

$$\mathcal{I}_{MH_k} = \{[h_1, h_2, \ldots, h_m] \mid 0 \le h_1 < \ldots < h_m \le n + 1 \wedge 2 \le m \le k\}$$

where $[h_1, h_2, \ldots, h_m]$ is defined as in $\mathcal{I}_{Att}$, and the deduction steps are the following:

$$\text{INITTER:} \quad \frac{[i, i, i] \qquad [i+1, i+1, i+1]}{[i, i+1]}$$

$$\text{COMBINE:} \quad \frac{[h_1, h_2, \ldots, h_m] \qquad [h_m, h_{m+1}, \ldots, h_p]}{[h_1, h_2, \ldots, h_p]}$$

such that $p \le k$

$$\text{LINK:} \quad \frac{[h_1, h_2, \ldots, h_m]}{[h_1, h_2, \ldots, h_{i-1}, h_{i+1}, \ldots, h_m]} \, a_{h_i} \rightarrow a_{h_j}$$

such that $1 < i < m, 1 \le j \le m, j \ne i$.

Like the Att_d parser, MH_k parses a restricted subset of non-projective dependency structures, such that the set of structures parsed by MH_k is always a subset of those parsed by MH_{k+1}. The MH_∞ parser, obtained by assuming that the number of trees per forest is unbounded, is equivalent to Att_∞, and therefore correct with respect to the set of non-projective dependency structures.

For finite values of k, it can easily be checked that MH_{d+2} is a static filter of Att_d, since its sets of items and deduction steps are subsets of those of Att_d. Therefore, the set of structures parsed by MH_{d+2} is also a subset of those parsed by Att_d.

The computational complexity of the MH_k parser is $O(n^k)$. Note that, in the case where $k = 3$, MH_3 is a step refinement of the parser by Yamada and Matsumoto (2003) that parses projective structures only, but by modifying the bound k we can build polynomial-time algorithms that parse larger sets of non-projective dependency structures. The MH_k parser has the property of being able to parse any possible dependency structure as long as we make k large enough.

7.6.3   MST parser (McDonald et al., 2005b)

McDonald *et al.* (2005b) present a parser which is able to find the best non-projective analysis for a given sentence in $O(n^2)$ time under a strong independency assumption called an *edge-factored model*, i.e., a model where each dependency decision is assumed to be independent from all the others (McDonald and Satta, 2007). Despite the limitations of this model, this MST (maximum spanning tree) parser provides state-of-the-art performance for projective and non-projective structures, and it is widely used today (Che *et al.*, 2008; Surdeanu *et al.*, 2008; Nivre and McDonald, 2008).

The parser works by considering the weighted graph formed by all the possible dependencies between pairs of input words, and applying a maximum spanning tree algorithm to find a dependency tree covering all the words in the sentence and maximising the sum of weights.

The efficient maximum spanning tree algorithm for directed graphs suggested by McDonald *et al.* (2005b) is not constructive, in the sense that it does not work by building structures and combining them into large structures until it finds the solution. Instead, the algorithm works by using a greedy strategy to select a candidate set of edges for the spanning tree, which may contain cycles and therefore not form a legal dependency tree. A cycle elimination procedure is then iteratively applied to this graph until cycles are eliminated and a legal dependency tree is obtained.

The formalism of parsing schemata specifies parsers in a constructive way, by describing how partial solutions can be linked to form larger partial solutions. This means that the cycle elimination procedure in McDonald's parser cannot be described by a schema. In other words, parsing schemata describe the logic of parsers while abstracting from control structures. In other parsers that we have described, the correctness of the algorithm can be guaranteed by describing the possible ways of combining intermediate results (items), and any control structure will do as long as it executes all the steps, and thus generates all the possible valid items. On the other hand, in this algorithm, specific control structures are needed to eliminate cycles in the generated graph, and therefore to guarantee correctness.

However, this does not mean that we cannot write a parsing schema for McDonald's parser. Even if control structures are essential for this algorithm to work correctly, there is still some logic behind these control structures which can be represented by a schema, whose item set is:

$$\mathcal{I}_{MD05} = \{[i \rightarrow j] \mid 0 \leq i \leq n \wedge 0 \leq j \leq n \wedge i \neq j\} \cup \{[0,k] \mid 0 \leq k \leq n\},$$

where an item of the form $[i \rightarrow j]$ is defined as the set of forests containing a single dependency tree t such that t is grounded, $yield(t) = \underline{a}_i\underline{a}_j$ or $\underline{a}_j\underline{a}_i$, and $head(t) = \underline{a}_j$ (this is the tree corresponding to the partial dependency graph containing a single dependency link $i \rightarrow j$); and an item of the form $[0,k]$ is defined as the set of forests containing a single dependency tree t such that t is grounded, $yield(t)$ is a permutation of $\underline{a}_0 \ldots \underline{a}_k$ and $head(t) = \underline{a}_0$.

The set of final items is $\{[0,n]\}$, as this item contains a non-projective parse for the whole input, rooted at the dummy head symbol a_0. The deduction steps are as follows:

$$\text{INITTER:} \quad \frac{[i,i,i] \qquad [j,j,j]}{[i \rightarrow j]} \; a_i \rightarrow a_j$$

$$\text{GRAPHBUILDER:} \quad \frac{[1 \rightarrow h_1] \qquad [2 \rightarrow h_2] \qquad \ldots \qquad [k \rightarrow h_k]}{[0,k]}$$

This schema is not correct by our definition of correctness because if we use a generic control structure to execute it by generating every possible inference, we would obtain some incorrect items, due to the necessity of eliminating cycles. For example, under the set of D-rules $\{a_1 \rightarrow a_2, a_2 \rightarrow a_1\}$, if we apply the *GraphBuilder* step to infer:

$$\text{GRAPHBUILDER} \quad \frac{[1 \rightarrow 2] \qquad [2 \rightarrow 1]}{[0,2]}$$

we find that the generated item $[0,2]$ is not correct, since it does not contain valid dependency structures under this set of rules. Obviously, the reason for this is that we have built it by combining items that form a cycle in the dependency graph. In order to build a working implementation of a parser from this schema, we need control structures to disallow cycles, like those defined in McDonald *et al.* (2005b), so that incorrect items are not generated and the soundness property is satisfied.

However, this representation of the parser's logic as a schema is interesting because it allows us to see the information that the parser is using to build dependency structures, and this is directly related to the assumptions that must be made when using it with a statistical model. In particular, we can see that a final item representing a full dependency graph can only be inferred from the items representing its individual dependencies, which are generated independently of each other. This illustrates the fact that this parser can only use edge-factored models, i.e., models where dependency links are considered independently of each other.

Weight information can easily be incorporated to the schema's items as follows:

$$\text{INITTER:} \quad \frac{[i,i,i] \qquad [j,j,j]}{[i \rightarrow j; (w_{ij})]} \quad a_i \rightarrow a_j(w_{ij})$$

$$\text{GRAPHBUILDER:} \quad \frac{[1 \rightarrow h_1; (w_1)]}{[0,k; (w_1 + w_2 + \ldots + w_k)]} \quad \ldots \quad [k \rightarrow h_k; (w_k)]$$

where w_{ij} is the weight assigned by the model to a dependency $a_i \rightarrow a_j$.

7.6.4 *Covington's non-projective parser (Covington, 1990;2001)*

Covington's non-projective parsing algorithm, described briefly in Covington (1990) and with more detail in Covington (2001) as algorithm LSU (for List-based Search with Uniqueness), is a straightforward parser that works by reading the input sentence from left to right, word by word, and establishing dependency links between the currently read word and previous words in the input. In order to do this, the parser keeps two lists: one with all the words encountered so far, and one with those that do not yet have a head assigned. A new word can be linked as a dependent of any of the words in the first list, and as a head of any of the words in the second list.

The parsing schema corresponding to this algorithm has an item set

$$\mathcal{I}_{CovNP} = \{[i, \langle h_1, h_2, \ldots, h_k \rangle] \mid 1 \leq h_1 \leq \ldots \leq h_k \leq i \leq n\}$$

where an item $[i, \langle h_1, h_2, \ldots, h_k \rangle]$ represents the set of forests of the form $F = \{T_1, T_2, \ldots, T_k\}$ such that:

- Every $T_j \in F$ is grounded,
- $head(T_j) = \underline{a}_{h_j}$, for every T_j in F,
- The concatenation of the yields of $T_1, T_2, \ldots, T_k$ forms a permutation of the string $\underline{a}_1 \cdots \underline{a}_i$.

The set of deduction steps is as follows:

$$\text{INITTER:} \quad \frac{}{[1, \langle 1 \rangle]}$$

$$\text{ADVANCE: } \frac{[i, \langle h_1, \dots, h_k \rangle]}{[i+1, \langle h_1, \dots, h_k, i+1 \rangle]}$$

$$\text{L-LINK: } \frac{[i, \langle h_1, \dots, h_k, i \rangle]}{[i, \langle h_1, \dots, h_k \rangle]} \ a_i \to a_j (j < i)$$

$$\text{R-LINK: } \frac{[i, \langle h_1, \dots, h_{j-1}, h_j, h_{j+1}, \dots, h_k \rangle]}{[i, \langle h_1, \dots, h_{j-1}, h_{j+1}, \dots, h_k \rangle]} \ a_{h_j} \to a_i (h_j < i)$$

The set of final items is $\{[n, \langle h \rangle] \mid 1 \le h \le n\}$, the set of items containing a forest with a single dependency tree T headed at an arbitrary word of the string $\underline{a}_h$, and whose yield is a permutation of the whole input string. The time complexity of the algorithm is exponential in the input length n.

Note that, just like in the case of the MST parser, this parsing schema is not correct, but in this case the reason is that Covington's algorithm itself does not prevent the generation of cycles in the dependency graphs it produces. As stated by Covington (2001):

> "Because the parser operates one word at a time, unity can only be checked at the end of the whole process: did it produce a tree with a single root that comprises all of the words?"

Therefore, Covington's LSU algorithm can produce incorrect dependency structures, and a postprocessing mechanism is needed to determine which of the generated structures are, in fact, valid trees. In the parsing schema, this is reflected by the fact that the schema is complete but not sound, since it can produce incorrect items, and we would also need postprocessing to determine which items are correct. Nivre (2007) uses a variant of this algorithm in which cycle detection is used to avoid generating incorrect structures.

7.7 Parsing schemata for Link Grammar parsers

Link Grammar (LG), introduced by Sleator and Temperley (1991, 1993), is a theory of syntax whose structural representation of sentences is closely related to projective dependency representations, but with some important differences, of which we highlight the following:[9]

- Undirected links: like dependency formalisms, LG represents the structure of sentences as a set of links between their words. However, while dependency links are directed, the links used in LG are undirected: there is no distinction between head and dependent.
- Cycles: the sets of links representing the structure of sentences in LG may contain cycles, contrary to dependency structures.

In particular, LG is a grammar-based formalism in which a grammar G consists of a set of words, each of which is associated with a set of linking requirements.

Given an LG G, a set of labelled links between the words of a sentence $a_1 \ldots a_n$ is said to be a *linkage* for that sentence if it satisfies the following conditions:

- Planarity: the links do not cross when drawn above the words.
- Connectivity: the undirected graph defined by links is connected.
- Satisfaction: the links satisfy the linking requirements of all the words in the input.

An input sentence is considered grammatical with respect to an LG G if it is possible to build a linkage for the sentence with the grammar G.

The linking requirements of a word are a set of rules that specify the labels of the links that can be established between that given word and other words in the sentence located to its left or to its right. Linking requirements can include constraints on the order of the links. For example, a requirement can specify that a word w can be linked to two words located to its left in such a way that the link to the farthest (leftmost) word has a particular label L_2 and the link to the closest word has a label L_1.

In our description of LG parsers, we will use the *disjunctive form* notation described by Sleator and Temperley (1991) to denote linking requirements. In this notation, the requirements of each word are expressed by a

---

[9]We only provide a brief outline of LG and its relation to dependency formalisms, in order to illustrate how LG parsers can be described with parsing schemata, and how some dependency parsers can be adapted for LG parsing. A complete treatment of LG is beyond the scope of this book: for further details, refer to Sleator and Temperley (1991, 1993). A detailed comparison between LG and dependency formalisms can be found in Schneider (1998).

set of *disjuncts* associated with it. Each disjunct corresponds to one particular way of satisfying the requirements of the word, so to satisfy the requirements of a word, it is sufficient to satisfy one of its associated disjuncts. We will represent a disjunct for a word w as a pair of strings of the form:

$$\Delta = (R_1 R_2 \ldots R_q, L_1 L_2 \ldots L_p)$$

where $L_1, L_2, \ldots L_p$ are the labels of the links that must connect w to words located to the left of w, which must be monotonically increasing in distance from w (for example, L_p links to the leftmost word that is directly linked to w), and $R_1, R_2, \ldots R_p$ are the labels of the links that must connect w to words to its right, which also must be monotonically increasing in distance from w (for example, R_q links to the rightmost word that is directly connected to w).

Parsing schemata for LG parsers can be defined by following the same general principles used to define them for constituency and dependency formalisms. As in constituency and dependency parsing schemata, item sets for LG parsing schemata can be defined as sets of partial syntactic structures, which in this case are partial linkages:

Definition 7.6. Given an LG G and a string $a_1 \ldots a_n$, a *partial linkage* is any edge-labelled undirected graph G such that:

- The graph G has n vertices $\{v_1, \ldots, v_n\}$, where each vertex v_i is a pair $(\underline{a}_i, \Delta_i)$ such that Δ_i is a disjunct for a_i in the grammar G,
- The graph G is connected and satisfies the planarity requirement with respect to the order $v_1, \ldots, v_n$ of the vertices (i.e., if we draw the vertices in that order, we can draw the links above them in a way that they do not cross).
- Given a vertex $v_i = (\underline{a}_i, \Delta_i)$ such that $\Delta_i = (R_1 R_2 \ldots R_q, L_1 L_2 \ldots L_p)$, the following conditions are satisfied:
  - Every edge $\{v_i, v_j\}$ with $j < i$ must be labelled L_s for some $1 \leq s \leq p$,
  - For every pair of edges $\{v_i, v_j\}, \{v_i, v_k\}$ such that $k < j < i$, we have that $\{v_i, v_j\}$ is labelled L_{s_1}, $\{v_i, v_k\}$ is labelled L_{s_2}, and $s_1 < s_2$.
  - Every edge $\{v_i, v_j\}$ with $j > i$ must be labelled R_t for some $1 \leq t \leq q$,
  - For every pair of edges $\{v_i, v_j\}, \{v_i, v_k\}$ such that $k > j > i$, we have that $\{v_i, v_j\}$ is labelled R_{t_1}, $\{v_i, v_k\}$ is labelled R_{t_2}, and $t_1 < t_2$.

Informally speaking, a partial linkage is the result of choosing a particular disjunct from those available for each word in the input string, and then adding any number of labelled links between words in such a way that they are compatible with the requirements of the disjunct. By *compatible* we mean that, for each word a_i associated with a disjunct $\Delta_i = (R_1 R_2 \ldots R_q, L_1 L_2 \ldots L_p)$, the list of labels of links connecting a_i to words to its right, ordered from the leftmost to the rightmost such word, is of the form $R_{i_1}, R_{i_2}, \ldots R_{i_r}$, with $0 < i_1 < i_2 < \ldots < i_r \le q$ and, symmetrically, the list of labels of links connecting a_i to words to its left, ordered from the rightmost to the leftmost, is of the form $L_{j_1}, L_{j_2}, \ldots L_{j_l}$, with $0 < j_1 < j_2 < \ldots < j_l \le p$. Given such a linkage, we say that the right linking requirements $R_{i_1}, R_{i_2}, \ldots R_{i_r}$ of the word a_i are *satisfied*, and the same for the left linking requirements $L_{j_1}, L_{j_2}, \ldots L_{j_l}$ of a_i. Linking requirements that are not satisfied (for example, the requirement of a link R_k in the disjunct associated with word a_i, with $0 < k \le q$, such that $k \notin \{i_1, \ldots, i_r\}$) are said to be *unsatisfied*.

With the definition of partial linkage, we can define item sets for LG in an analogous way to those defined for dependency parsers (Definition 7.5), where items come from a partition of the set of partial linkages for a given LG G. With these item sets, we define LG parsing schemata analogously to the dependency and constituency cases.

As an example of an LG parsing schema, we will describe the original LG parser by Sleator and Temperley (1991), and then we will show how some of the projective dependency parsers seen in Section 7.3 can be adapted to obtain new parsers for this formalism.

7.7.1   Sleator and Temperley's LG parser

The LG parser by Sleator and Temperley (1991) is a dynamic programming algorithm that builds linkages in a top-down fashion: a link between a_i and a_k is always added before links between a_i and a_j or between a_j and a_k, if $i < j < k$. This contrasts with many of the dependency parsers seen in previous sections (Eisner, 1996; Eisner and Satta, 1999; Yamada and Matsumoto, 2003), which build dependency graphs from the bottom up.

The item set for Sleator and Temperley's parser is:

$$\mathcal{I}_{SlT} = \{[i, j, \alpha \bullet \beta, \gamma \bullet \delta, b, c] \mid 0 \le i \le j \le n+1$$

$$\wedge \; b, c \in \{\textit{True}, \textit{False}\} \text{ and } \alpha, \beta, \gamma, \delta \text{ are strings of link labels}\},$$

where an item $[i, j, \alpha \bullet \beta, \gamma \bullet \delta, b, c]$ represents the set of partial linkages over the substring $a_i \ldots a_j$ of the input, where i is linked to words in that substring by links labelled α and has right linking requirements β unsatisfied,

j is linked to words in the substring by links labelled γ and has left linking requirements δ unsatisfied, b is *True* if and only if there is a direct link between a_i and a_j, and c is *True* if and only if all the inner words in the span are transitively-reflexively linked to one of the end words a_i or a_j, and have all of their linking requirements satisfied.

Note that string positions referenced by the items in $\mathcal{I}_{SlT}$ range from 0 to $n + 1$. The terminal a_0 corresponds to an artificial word (called *wall*) that the LG formalism requires to be inserted at the beginning of every input sentence, so as to be able to represent some linguistic phenomena (see Sleator and Temperley (1991)). Therefore, we will suppose that our strings are extended with this symbol in all our LG parsers. On the other hand, the terminal a_{n+1} is a dummy word that must not be linkable to any other, used by the parser for convenience in the same way as in the schema for Yamada and Matsumoto's dependency parser (Section 7.3.4).

We will use the notation $[i, \alpha, \beta]$ as shorthand for the item $[i, i, \bullet\alpha, \bullet\beta, False, True]$, which is an item used to select a particular disjunct for a word a_i.

The set of deduction steps is the following:

$$\text{SELECTDISJUNCT: } \frac{}{[i, R_q R_{q-1} \ldots R_1, L_p L_{p-1} \ldots L_1]}$$

such that a_i has a disjunct $\Delta = (R_1 R_2 \ldots R_q, L_1 L_2 \ldots L_p)$,

$$\text{INITTER: } \frac{[0, \alpha, \gamma] \qquad [n + 1, \epsilon, \epsilon]}{[0, n + 1, \bullet\alpha, \epsilon, False, False]}$$

$$\text{LEFTPREDICT: } \frac{[i, j, \alpha \bullet \beta, \gamma \bullet \delta, b_1, False] \qquad [w, \sigma, \phi]}{[i, w, \bullet\beta, \bullet\phi, False, (w - i = 1)]} \; i < w < j$$

$$\text{LEFTLINKPREDICT } (a_i \overset{b}{\leftrightarrow} a_w):$$
$$\frac{[i, j, \alpha \bullet b\beta, \gamma \bullet \delta, b_1, False] \qquad [w, \sigma, b\phi]}{[i, w, b \bullet \beta, b \bullet \phi, True, (w - i = 1)]} \; i < w < j$$

$$\text{RIGHTPREDICT: } \frac{[i, j, \alpha \bullet \beta, \gamma \bullet \delta, b_1, False] \qquad [w, \sigma, \phi]}{[w, j, \bullet\sigma, \bullet\delta, False, (j - w = 1)]} \; i < w < j$$

$$\text{RIGHTLINKPREDICT } (a_w \overset{b}{\leftrightarrow} a_j):$$
$$\frac{[i, j, \alpha \bullet \beta, \gamma \bullet b\delta, b_1, False] \qquad [w, b\sigma, \phi]}{[w, j, b \bullet \sigma, b \bullet \delta, True, (j - w = 1)]} \; i < w < j$$

COMPLETER:
$$\frac{[i,j,\alpha \bullet \beta, \gamma \bullet \delta, b_1, \text{False}] \quad [i,w,\beta\bullet, \phi\bullet, b_2, \text{True}]}{[i,j,\alpha\beta\bullet, \gamma\delta\bullet, b_1, \text{True}]} \quad b_2 \vee b_3$$
$$[w,j,\sigma\bullet, \delta\bullet, b_3, \text{True}] \quad [w,\sigma,\phi]$$

An annotation of the form $(a_i \overset{b}{\leftrightarrow} a_j)$ near the name of a step in this and subsequent LG schemata indicates that the corresponding step adds a link labelled b between words a_i and a_j, and can be used to recover a set of complete linkages contained in a final item from each sequence of deduction steps that generates it.

The SELECTDISJUNCT step chooses one of the available disjuncts for a given word a_i. The INITTER step starts the top-down process by constructing a linkage that spans the whole string $a_1 \ldots a_n$, but where no links have been constructed yet. Then, the PREDICT and LINKPREDICT steps proceed by repeatedly dividing the problem of finding a linkage for a substring $a_i \ldots a_j$ into the smaller subproblems of finding linkages for $a_i \ldots a_w$ and $a_w \ldots a_j$, with $i < w < j$. After these smaller linkages have been found, they are combined by a COMPLETER step into a larger linkage. The flags b and c in items are used by the COMPLETER step to ensure that its resulting item will contain a valid linkage satisfying the connectivity constraint. The algorithm runs in time $O(n^3)$ with respect to the length of the input, since none of its deduction steps uses more than three independent string position indexes.

The set of final items is $\{[0, n+1, \alpha\bullet, \beta\bullet, b, \text{True}]\}$. Items of this form contain full valid linkages for the string $a_0 \ldots a_n$, since having the second boolean flag set to *True* implies that their linkage for $a_0 \ldots a_{n+1}$ has at most two connected components, and we have assumed that the word a_{n+1} cannot be linked to any other, so one of the components must link $a_0 \ldots a_n$.

7.7.2 *Adapting projective dependency parsers to LG*

In this section, we take advantage of the similarities between LG linkages and projective dependency structures to adapt some of the projective dependency parsers seen in Section 7.3 to the LG formalism. In particular, we present LG versions of the parsers by Eisner (1996), Eisner and Satta (1999) and Yamada and Matsumoto (2003), which are obtained as follows:

- To adapt item sets from dependency parsers to LG parsers, we consider the set of dependency graphs associated to the forests contained in each dependency item. The corresponding LG items will contain linkages with the same structure as these graphs. For example, if the graphs associated to the forests in an item of the form $[i, j]$ in Yamada and Matsumoto's dependency parsing schema are dependency graphs with two distinct connected components headed at the words a_i and a_j, an item $[i, j]$ in the corresponding LG parsing schema will contain linkages with two connected components, one containing the word a_i and the other containing a_j. Note that the notion of a head is lost in the conversion since, being undirected, LG linkages do not make distinctions between heads and dependents. This will allow us to simplify the notation used to denote items in some cases. For example, we do not need to make a distinction between Eisner items of the form $[i, j, True, False]$ and those of the form $[i, j, False, True]$, since their structure is the same modulo the direction of the links. Therefore, items in the LG version of Eisner's parser will use a single flag, indicating whether linkages contained in them have one or two connected components.

- The combining and linking steps of the dependency parsers can be directly translated to LG. If the original dependency steps always produced items containing projective dependency trees, the resulting LG steps will produce items with planar linkages. When the original dependency steps have constraints related to the position of the head in items (like combiner steps in Eisner and Satta's parser, where we can combine $[i, j, j]$ with $[j, k, k]$ but not with $[j, k, j]$, for example), we ignore these constraints, considering that any word in a linkage can be considered its "head" for the purpose of linking it to other linkages.

- With this, we obtain a parsing schema that can find any *acyclic* linkage for a given input string, since projective dependency parsers do not allow cyclic structures. To allow cycles, we add steps or remove constraints from existing steps so that the parsers are able to link two words that are already in the same connected component of a linkage. In the schema obtained from Eisner's parser, this is done by allowing LINK steps to be applied on items representing fully connected linkages. In the one corresponding to Eisner and Satta's parser we allow COMBINER steps to create a link in addition to joining two linkages and in the one for Yamada and Matsumoto's parser we add a step that creates two links at the same time, combining the functionality of the L-LINK and R-LINK steps.

- Finally, since LG is a grammar-based formalism where the set of valid linkages is constrained by disjuncts associated with words, we must include disjunct information in items in order to enforce that only grammatical linkages are constructed. This is done in a similar way as in the schema for Sleator and Temperley's parser, but in this case items need to specify both left and right linking requirements for each of their end words, since these bottom-up parsers establish links from end words of an item to words outside the item's span (which can be to the left or to the right of the span) rather than to words inside the span (which are always to the right of the left end word, and to the left of the right end word).

7.7.3   Eisner (1996) for LG

By applying the principles in Section 7.7.2, we obtain an LG variant of the projective dependency parser by Eisner (1996), with an item set:

$$\mathcal{I}_{EisLG} = \{[i, j, \alpha_1 \bullet \beta_1, \alpha_2 \bullet \beta_2, \alpha_3, \alpha_4, B] \mid 0 \le i \le j \le n,$$

$$B \in \{\textit{True}, \textit{False}\} \text{ and } \alpha_1, \beta_1, \alpha_2, \beta_2, \alpha_3, \alpha_4 \text{ are strings of link labels}\},$$

where an item of the form $[i, j, \alpha_1 \bullet \beta_1, \alpha_2 \bullet \beta_2, \alpha_3, \alpha_4, B]$ represents the set of partial linkages over the substring $a_i \ldots a_j$ of the input, satisfying the following:

- All words a_k, such that $i < k < j$, have all their linking requirements satisfied,
- The word i has left linking requirements α_3 not satisfied, and right linking requirements $\alpha_1\beta_1$, where the requirements α_1 are satisfied by links to words within the item's span, and the requirements β_1 are not satisfied. Requirements appear in the strings α_3 and $\alpha_1\beta_1$ in increasing order of link distance,
- The word j has right linking requirements α_4 not satisfied, and left linking requirements $\alpha_2\beta_2$, where the requirements α_2 are satisfied by links to words within the item's span, and the requirements β_2 are not satisfied. Requirements appear in the strings α_4 and $\alpha_2\beta_2$ in increasing order of link distance,
- The partial linkage is connected if B equals *True*, or has exactly two connected components (one containing the node a_i and the other containing a_j) if B equals *False*.

The set of deduction steps for this parser is as follows:

INITTER: $\dfrac{}{[i, i+1, \alpha_R, \beta_L, \alpha_L, \beta_R, \mathit{False}]}$ $\quad 0 \le i \le n-1$

such that a_i has a disjunct $\Delta_i = (\alpha_R, \alpha_L)$,

and a_{i+1} has a disjunct $\Delta_{i+1} = (\beta_R, \beta_L)$.

LINK $(a_i \overset{b}{\leftrightarrow} a_j)$: $\dfrac{[i, j, \alpha_1 \bullet b\beta_1, \alpha_2 \bullet b\beta_2, \alpha_3, \alpha_4, B]}{[i, j, \alpha_1 b \bullet \beta_1, \alpha_2 b \bullet \beta_2, \alpha_3, \alpha_4, \mathit{True}]}$

COMBINE: $\dfrac{\begin{array}{c}[i, j, \alpha_1 \bullet \beta_1, \alpha_2\bullet, \alpha_3, \alpha_4, B_1] \\ [j, k, \alpha_4\bullet, \gamma_2 \bullet \delta_2, \alpha_2, \delta_4, B_2]\end{array}}{[i, k, \alpha_1 \bullet \beta_1, \gamma_2 \bullet \delta_2, \alpha_3, \delta_4, B_1 \wedge B_2]}$ $\quad B_1 \vee B_2$

These steps perform actions analogous to those of the steps in the schema for Eisner's dependency parser (Section 7.3.2), with the remarkable exception that the LINK step is able to build links on items that contain fully connected linkages (equivalent to the $[i, j, \mathit{True}, \mathit{False}]$ and $[i, j, \mathit{False}, \mathit{True}]$ items of the dependency parser). A version of the parser restricted to acyclic linkages can be obtained by adding the constraint that B must equal False in the LINK step. The set of final items is $\{[0, n, \alpha\bullet, \beta\bullet, \epsilon, \epsilon, \mathit{True}]\}$, corresponding to the set of items containing fully connected linkages for the whole input string.

7.7.4 *Eisner and Satta (1999) for LG*

The LG parser obtained from adapting the dependency parser by Eisner and Satta (1999) has an item set:

$$\mathcal{I}_{EisSatLG} = \{[i, j, \alpha_1 \bullet \beta_1, \alpha_2 \bullet \beta_2, \alpha_3, \alpha_4] \mid 0 \le i \le j \le n$$
and $\alpha_1, \beta_1, \alpha_2, \beta_2, \alpha_3, \alpha_4$ are strings of link labels$\},$

where each item $[i, j, \alpha_1 \bullet \beta_1, \alpha_2 \bullet \beta_2, \alpha_3, \alpha_4]$ is defined as the item $[i, j, \alpha_1 \bullet \beta_1, \alpha_2 \bullet \beta_2, \alpha_3, \alpha_4, \mathit{True}]$ in $\mathcal{I}_{EisLG}$.

The set of deduction steps in this case is

$$\text{INITTER-L:} \frac{}{[i, i, \alpha_R, \epsilon, \alpha_L, \epsilon]} \quad 0 \le i \le n$$

such that a_i has a disjunct $\Delta_i = (\alpha_R, \alpha_L)$.

$$\text{INITTER-R:} \frac{}{[i, i, \epsilon, \alpha_L, \epsilon, \alpha_R]} \quad 0 \le i \le n$$

such that a_i has a disjunct $\Delta_i = (\alpha_R, \alpha_L)$.

$$\text{LINK } (a_i \overset{b}{\leftrightarrow} a_k): \frac{[i, j, \gamma_1 \bullet b\alpha_1, \gamma_2\bullet, \gamma_3, \epsilon]}{[j+1, k, \delta_1\bullet, \delta_2 \bullet b\beta_2, \epsilon, \delta_4]}{[i, k, \gamma_1 b \bullet \alpha_1, \delta_2 b \bullet \beta_2, \gamma_3, \delta_4]}$$

$$\text{COMBINE: } \frac{[i, j, \gamma_1 \bullet \alpha_1, \gamma_2\bullet, \gamma_3, \delta_1] \qquad [j, k, \delta_1\bullet, \delta_2 \bullet \beta_2, \gamma_2, \delta_4]}{[i, k, \gamma_1 \bullet \alpha_1, \delta_2 \bullet \beta_2, \gamma_3, \delta_4]}$$

$$\text{LINKANDCOMBINE } (a_i \overset{b}{\leftrightarrow} a_k): \frac{[i, j, \gamma_1 \bullet b\alpha_1, \gamma_2\bullet, \gamma_3, \delta_1]}{[j, k, \delta_1\bullet, \delta_2 \bullet b\beta_2, \gamma_2, \delta_4]}{[i, k, \gamma_1 b \bullet \alpha_1, \delta_2 b \bullet \beta_2, \gamma_3, \delta_4]}$$

The INITTER-L and INITTER-R steps are used to initialise the parser with items corresponding to linkages for a single word: two steps are used because it may be needed to consider that single word as the leftmost word of its span (INITTER-L) or as the rightmost (INITTER-R), depending on the words to which it is linked. Note that a single INITTER step generating a consequent $[i, i, \alpha_R, \alpha_L, \alpha_L, \alpha_R]$ would not produce a correct parser, as these items would require each of the linking requirements of the word a_i to be satisfied twice. The LINK and COMBINE steps are analogous to those in the schema for Eisner and Satta's dependency parser (Section 7.3.3). The LINKANDCOMBINE step performs an union of linkages while adding a new dependency link. This step is added in order to support cyclic linkages, so an acyclic version of the parser can be obtained from removing it.

The set of final items for this schema is $\{[0, n, \alpha\bullet, \beta\bullet, \epsilon, \epsilon]\}$, equivalent to the set of final items of the LG version of Eisner's parser.

7.7.5 Yamada and Matsumoto (2003) for LG

Finally, if we adapt to LG the dependency parser by Yamada and Matsumoto (2003), we obtain a schema which uses the same item set $\mathcal{I}_{EisLG}$ as the LG variant of Eisner's parser, and the following deduction steps:

$$\text{INITTER: } \frac{}{[i, i+1, \alpha_R, \beta_L, \alpha_L, \beta_R, \mathit{False}]} \; 0 \leq i \leq n$$

such that a_i has a disjunct $\Delta_i = (\alpha_R, \alpha_L)$,

and a_{i+1} has a disjunct $\Delta_{i+1} = (\beta_R, \beta_L)$.

$$\text{R-LINK } (a_j \overset{b}{\leftrightarrow} a_k): \frac{[i, j, \alpha_1 \bullet \beta_1, \alpha_2 \bullet, \alpha_3, \alpha_4 b, B_1] \quad [j, k, \alpha_4 \bullet b, \gamma_2 \bullet b\delta_2, \alpha_2, \delta_4, B_2]}{[i, k, \alpha_1 \bullet \beta_1, \gamma_2 b \bullet \delta_2, \alpha_3, \delta_4, B_1]}$$

$$\text{L-LINK } (a_i \overset{b}{\leftrightarrow} a_j): \frac{[i, j, \alpha_1 \bullet b\beta_1, \alpha_2 \bullet b, \alpha_3, \alpha_4, B_1] \quad [j, k, \alpha_4 \bullet, \gamma_2 \bullet \delta_2, \alpha_2 b, \delta_4, B_2]}{[i, k, \alpha_1 b \bullet \beta_1, \gamma_2 \bullet \delta_2, \alpha_3, \delta_4, B_2]}$$

$$\text{TWO-LINKS } (a_i \overset{b}{\leftrightarrow} a_j \overset{c}{\leftrightarrow} a_k): \frac{[i, j, \alpha_1 \bullet b\beta_1, \alpha_2 \bullet b, \alpha_3, \alpha_4 c, B_1] \quad [j, k, \alpha_4 \bullet c, \gamma_2 \bullet c\delta_2, \alpha_2 b, \delta_4, B_2]}{[i, k, \alpha_1 b \bullet \beta_1, \gamma_2 c \bullet \delta_2, \alpha_3, \delta_4, \mathit{True}]}$$

The logic of all the steps except for TWO-LINKS is analogous to that of the corresponding steps in the schema for Yamada and Matsumoto's dependency parser. The TWO-LINKS step, that combines the functionality of the other two LINK steps, is added so as to support linkages containing cycles. An acyclic version of the parser can be obtained by removing this step. Note that, in this case, no items with their flag set to *True* can be inferred by the schema, so we can consider that the item set contains only linkages with two connected components, like the item set of the dependency version of the schema. The set of final items is $\{[0, n+1, \alpha\bullet, \beta\bullet, \epsilon, \mathit{False}]\}$, which are guaranteed to contain a full linkage for $a_1 \ldots a_n$ if the dummy symbol a_{n+1} inserted at the end of the string is not allowed to link to any other.

It can be shown that the formal relations between these three LG parsing schemata are the same as between their corresponding dependency parsing schemata, i.e., the LG variants of Eisner and Satta's and Yamada and Matsumoto's dependency parsers are step contractions of the LG variant of Eisner's parser. These relations are proven analogously to the dependency case. The three bottom-up LG parsers run in cubic time with respect to input length, like the algorithm by Sleator and Temperley.

7.8 Discussion

The parsing schemata formalism by Sikkel (1997) has proved very useful for describing, analysing and prototyping parsing algorithms, but it is limited to constituency-based parsers. In this chapter, we have defined a variant of the formalism that can be used to describe dependency parsers.[10] These *dependency parsing schemata* are general enough to describe both grammar-driven and data-driven dependency parsers, be them projective or non-projective. Like constituency parsing schemata, they can be used to prove the correctness of parsers, find relations between them or generate implementations of them with a system like the one described in Chapter 3. Thus, this variant of the formalism makes all the advantages of parsing schemata applicable to the family of dependency parsers, which have been extensively used for practical parsing in recent years.

To demonstrate the theoretical uses of dependency parsing schemata, we have used them to describe a wide range of projective and non-projective dependency parsers from the literature. Additionally, we have clarified relations between parsers which were originally described very differently. For example, while Eisner (1996) presented his algorithm as a dynamic programming algorithm which combines spans into larger spans, the algorithm by Yamada and Matsumoto (2003) works by sequentially executing parsing actions that move a focus point in the input one position to the left or right, (possibly) creating a dependency link. However, in the parsing schemata for these algorithms we can see (and formally prove) that they are related: one is a refinement of the other.

Parsing schemata are also a formal tool that can be used to prove the correctness of parsing algorithms. The relationships between dependency parsers can be exploited to derive properties of a parser from those of others, as we have seen in several examples.

Finally, we have seen how the same general principles used to extend parsing schemata to the realm of dependency parsing can also be applied

---

[10]An alternative framework that formally describes some dependency parsers is that of transition systems (McDonald and Nivre, 2007). This model is based on parser configurations and transitions, and has no clear relationship with the approach described here.

to the related formalism of LG, and how new LG parsers can be obtained as variants of parsing schemata for existing dependency parsers.

However, dependency parsing schemata are not only useful to describe and extend existing parsing algorithms, they can also be used as a theoretical framework to define new parsers. This will be shown in the next chapter, where we use dependency parsing schemata to define novel algorithms for several sets of mildly non-projective dependency structures.

Chapter 8

Mildly non-projective dependency parsing

In this chapter, we use the dependency parsing schemata formalism presented in the previous chapter to present novel parsing algorithms for several sets of mildly non-projective dependency structures, and formally prove their correctness.

First, we define a parser for well-nested structures of gap degree at most 1. Then, we extend this algorithm to handle all well-nested structures with gap degree bounded by a constant k. These algorithms have the same computational complexity as the best existing parsers for constituency formalisms of equivalent generative power.

Finally, we define another extension of the algorithm which is able to analyse a new class of structures with gap degree up to a constant k, which includes some ill-nested structures. This set of structures, which we call mildly ill-nested, includes all the gap degree k structures in a number of dependency treebanks.

The parsing algorithms described in this chapter were first presented in Gómez-Rodríguez *et al.* (2009d), and are described with more detail in Gómez-Rodríguez *et al.* (2010b).

8.1 Motivation

In the previous chapter we saw that, for reasons of computational efficiency, many practical implementations of dependency parsing are restricted to *projective* structures. In these structures, the subtree rooted at each word is required to cover a contiguous substring of the sentence. However, some natural language sentences do not verify this constraint, and therefore cannot be analysed correctly by projective parsers. These *non-projective* sentences appear in many languages (Havelka, 2007), being particularly frequent in free word order languages such as Czech. Unfortunately, parsing without the projectivity constraint is computationally complex. Although it is possible to parse non-projective structures in quadratic time with respect to the input length under a model in which each dependency decision is independent of all the others (as in the parser by McDonald *et al.* (2005b), whose schema has been shown in Section 7.6.3), the problem is intractable in the absence of this assumption (McDonald and Satta, 2007).

Nivre and Nilsson (2005) observe that most non-projective dependency structures appearing in natural language treebanks are "close" to being projective, since they contain only a small proportion of non-projective arcs. This has led to the study of classes of dependency structures that lie between projective and unrestricted non-projective structures (Kuhlmann and Nivre, 2006; Havelka, 2007). Kuhlmann (2007) investigates several such classes, based on well-nestedness and gap degree constraints (Bodirsky *et al.*, 2005), relating them to a number of lexicalised constituency grammar formalisms. Specifically, he shows that: linear context-free rewriting systems (LCFRS) with fan-out k (Vijay-Shanker *et al.*, 1987; Satta, 1992) induce the set of dependency structures with gap degree at most $k-1$; coupled context-free grammars in which the maximal rank of a nonterminal is k (Hotz and Pitsch, 1996) induce the set of well-nested dependency structures with gap degree at most $k-1$; and finally, LTAGs (Joshi and Schabes, 1997) induce the set of well-nested dependency structures with gap degree at most 1.

These results establish that there must be polynomial-time dependency parsing algorithms for well-nested structures with bounded gap degree, since such parsers exist for their corresponding lexicalised constituency-based formalisms. However, as it has been observed by Kuhlmann and Nivre (2006) that most of the non-projective structures in treebanks are well-nested and have a small gap degree, developing efficient dependency parsing strategies for these sets of structures has considerable practical interest, since we would be able to parse these sentences directly with dependencies in a data-driven manner, rather than indirectly by constructing intermediate constituency grammars and extracting dependencies from constituency parses.

We address this problem with the following contributions:

- We define a parsing algorithm for well-nested dependency structures of gap degree 1, and prove its correctness. The parser runs in time $O(n^7)$, the same complexity as the best existing algorithms for LTAG (Eisner and Satta, 2000), and can be optimised to run in time $O(n^6)$ in the non-lexicalised case.

- We generalise the previous algorithm to any well-nested dependency structure with gap degree at most k in time $O(n^{5+2k})$.
- We generalise the previous parsers to be able to analyse not only well-nested structures, but also ill-nested structures with gap degree at most k satisfying certain constraints,[1] in time $O(n^{4+3k})$.
- We characterise the set of structures covered by this parser, which we call *mildly ill-nested* structures, and show that it includes all the trees present in a number of dependency treebanks.

8.2 Preliminaries

To simplify the notation and proofs, since the parsers defined in this chapter only use grounded dependency trees and they do not work with forests containing more than one tree, items in their schemata will be given as sets of partial dependency trees defined only on terminal nodes, rather than the forests of trees with marked and unmarked terminals used in Chapter 7.

In this context, a *dependency graph* for a string $a_1 \ldots a_n$ is a graph $G = (V, E)$, where $V = \{a_1, \ldots, a_n\}$ and $E \subseteq V \times V$. We write the edge (a_i, a_j) as $a_i \to a_j$, meaning that the word a_i is a syntactic *dependent* (or a *child*) of a_j or, conversely, that a_j is the *governor* (*parent*) of a_i. We write $a_i \to^* a_j$ to denote that there exists a (possibly empty) path from a_i to a_j. The *projection* of a node a_i, denoted $\lfloor a_i \rfloor$, is the set of reflexive-transitive dependents of a_i, i.e.: $\lfloor a_i \rfloor = \{a_j \in V \mid a_j \to^* a_i\}$. In contexts where we refer to different graphs that may share nodes, we will use the notation $\lfloor a_i \rfloor_G$ to denote the projection of a node a_i in the graph G. An *interval* (with endpoints i and j) is a set of the form $[i, j] = \{a_k \mid i \le k \le j\}$. We will denote the cardinality of a set S as $\#(S)$, and the difference of two sets S_1, S_2 as $S_1 \smallsetminus S_2$.

A dependency graph is said to be a *tree* if it is:

(1) acyclic: $a_j \in \lfloor a_i \rfloor$ implies $a_i \to a_j \notin E$; and
(2) each node has exactly one parent, except for one node which we call the *root* or *head*.

---

[1] Parsing unrestricted ill-nested structures, even when the gap degree is bounded, is NP-complete: these structures are equivalent to LCFRS for which the recognition problem is NP-complete (Satta, 1992)

A graph satisfying these conditions and having a vertex set $V \subseteq \{a_1, \ldots, a_n\}$ is a *partial dependency tree* for the string $a_1 \ldots a_n$. Given a dependency tree $T = (V, E)$ and a node $u \in V$, the *subtree* induced by the node u is the graph $T_u = (\lfloor u \rfloor, E_u)$ where $E_u = \{a_i \rightarrow a_j \in E \mid a_j \in \lfloor u \rfloor\}$.

Note that items that use this definition of partial dependency trees can easily be converted to sets of forests of dependency trees with marked and unmarked terminals, obtaining schemata compatible with the definitions in Chapter 7, as follows: given an input string $a_1 \ldots a_n$, each dependency tree U with its head in a_h is converted to the unique forest containing a single tree T such that:

- the root node of T is a_h,
- if the dependents of a node a_i in U are $a_{l_1} a_{l_2} \ldots a_{l_p}, a_{r_1} a_{r_2} \ldots a_{r_q}$, with $l_1 < l_2 < \ldots < l_p < i < r_1 < r_2 < \ldots < r_q$; then the children of a_i in T are $a_{l_1} a_{l_2} \ldots a_{l_p} \underline{a_i} a_{r_1} a_{r_2} \ldots a_{r_q}$.

By construction, the tree obtained from this conversion is in the set *D-trees* defined in the previous chapter (Definition 7.1).

We now define the concepts of gap degree and well-nestedness (Bodirsky *et al.*, 2005; Kuhlmann and Nivre, 2006), which will be used to characterise the sets of mildly non-projective dependency structures used by the parsers in this chapter. Let T be a partial dependency tree for the string $a_1 \ldots a_n$:

Definition 8.1. We say that T is *projective* if $\lfloor a_i \rfloor$ is an interval for every word a_i.

Thus, the dependency tree T is projective if every node in the structure dominates a contiguous substring of the sentence.

Definition 8.2. The *gap degree* of a particular node a_k in T is the minimum $g \in (\mathbb{N} \cup \{0\})$ such that $\lfloor a_k \rfloor$ can be written as the union of $g + 1$ intervals, i.e., the number of discontinuities in $\lfloor a_k \rfloor$. The gap degree of the dependency tree T is the maximum among the gap degrees of its nodes.

Note that T has gap degree 0 if and only if T is projective.

Definition 8.3. The subtrees induced by nodes a_p and a_q are *interleaved* if $\lfloor a_p \rfloor \cap \lfloor a_q \rfloor = \varnothing$ and there are nodes $a_i, a_j \in \lfloor a_p \rfloor$ and $a_k, a_l \in \lfloor a_q \rfloor$ such that $i < k < j < l$. A dependency tree T is *well-nested* if it does not contain two interleaved subtrees, and a tree that is not well-nested is said to be *ill-nested*.

Note that projective trees are always well-nested, but well-nested trees are not always projective.

8.3 The WG_1 parser

We now define WG_1, a polynomial-time parser for well-nested dependency structures of gap degree at most 1.

8.3.1 WG_1 parsing schema

The schema for the WG_1 parser is defined as follows:

The item set is $\mathcal{I}_{WG1} = \mathcal{I}_1 \cup \mathcal{I}_2$, with:

$$\mathcal{I}_1 = \{[i,j,h,\diamond,\diamond] \mid i,j,h \in \mathbb{N}, 1 \le h \le n, 1 \le i \le j \le n, h \ne j, h \ne i-1\},$$

where each item of the form $[i,j,h,\diamond,\diamond]$ represents the set of all well-nested partial dependency trees[2] with gap degree at most 1, rooted at a_h, and such that $\lfloor a_h \rfloor = \{a_h\} \cup [i,j]$, and:

$$\mathcal{I}_2 = \{[i,j,h,l,r] \mid i,j,h,l,r \in \mathbb{N}, 1 \le h \le n, 1 \le i < l \le r < j \le n,$$
$$h \ne j, h \ne i-1, h \ne l-1, h \ne r\}$$

where each item of the form $[i,j,h,l,r]$ represents the set of all well-nested partial dependency trees rooted at a_h such that $\lfloor a_h \rfloor = \{a_h\} \cup ([i,j] \setminus [l,r])$, and all the nodes (except possibly h) have gap degree at most 1. We call items of this form *gapped items*, and the interval $[l,r]$ the *gap* of the item. Note that the constraints $h \ne j, h \ne i+1, h \ne l-1, h \ne r$ are added to items to avoid redundancy in the item set. Since the result of the expression $\{a_h\} \cup ([i,j] \setminus [l,r])$ for a given head can be the same for different sets of values of i,j,l,r, we restrict these values so that we cannot get two different items representing the same dependency structures. Items ι violating these constraints always have an alternative representation that does not violate them, that we can express with a normalising function $nm(\iota)$ as follows:

$nm([i,j,j,l,r]) = [i,j-1,j,l,r]$ (if $r \le j-1$ or $r = \diamond$),
   or $[i,l-1,j,\diamond,\diamond]$ (if $r = j-1$).

$nm([i,j,l-1,l,r]) = [i,j,l-1,l-1,r]$(if $l > i+1$),
   or $[r+1,j,l-1,\diamond,\diamond]$ (if $l = i+1$).

---

[2]In this and subsequent schemata, we use D-rules to express parsing decisions, so partial dependency trees are assumed to be taken from the set of trees licensed by a set of D-rules.

$nm([i,j,i-1,l,r]) = [i-1,j,i-1,l,r].$

$nm([i,j,r,l,r]) = [i,j,r,l,r-1]$ (if $l < r$),
    or $[i,j,r,\diamond,\diamond]$ (if $l = r$).

$nm([i,j,h,l,r]) = [i,j,h,l,r]$ for all other items.

When defining the deduction steps for this and other parsers, we assume that they always produce normalised items. For clarity, we do not explicitly write this in the deduction steps, writing ι instead of $nm(\iota)$ as antecedents and consequents of steps.

The set of initial items (hypotheses) is defined as the set:

$$\mathcal{H} = \{[h,h,h,\diamond,\diamond] \mid h \in \mathbb{N}, 1 \le h \le n\},$$

where each item $[h,h,h,\diamond,\diamond]$ represents the set containing the trivial partial dependency tree consisting of a single node a_h and no links. This same set of hypotheses can be used for all the parsers, so we do not make it explicit for subsequent schemata. Note that initial items are separate from the item set $\mathcal{I}_{WG1}$ and not subject to its constraints, so they do not require normalisation.

The set of final items for strings of length n in WG_1 is defined as the set:

$$\mathcal{F} = \{[1,n,h,\diamond,\diamond] \mid h \in \mathbb{N}, 1 \le h \le n\},$$

which is the set of the items in $\mathcal{I}_{WG1}$ containing dependency trees for the complete input string (from position 1 to n), with their head at any word a_h.

Finally, the deduction steps of the WG_1 parser are the following:

$$\text{Link Ungapped:} \quad \frac{[h_1,h_1,h_1,\diamond,\diamond] \quad [i_2,j_2,h_2,\diamond,\diamond]}{[i_2,j_2,h_1,\diamond,\diamond]} \quad a_{h_2} \to a_{h_1}$$

such that $a_{h_2} \in [i_2,j_2] \wedge a_{h_1} \notin [i_2,j_2]$,

$$\text{Link Gapped:} \quad \frac{[h_1,h_1,h_1,\diamond,\diamond] \quad [i_2,j_2,h_2,l_2,r_2]}{[i_2,j_2,h_1,l_2,r_2]} \quad a_{h_2} \to a_{h_1}$$

such that $a_{h_2} \in [i_2,j_2] \setminus [l_2,r_2] \wedge a_{h_1} \notin [i_2,j_2] \setminus [l_2,r_2]$,

$$\text{Combine Ungapped:} \quad \frac{[i,j,h,\diamond,\diamond] \quad [j+1,k,h,\diamond,\diamond]}{[i,k,h,\diamond,\diamond]}$$

COMBINE OPENING GAP:
$$\frac{[i,j,h,\diamond,\diamond] \qquad [k,l,h,\diamond,\diamond]}{[i,l,h,j+1,k-1]}$$

such that $j < k-1$,

COMBINE KEEPING GAP LEFT:
$$\frac{[i,j,h,l,r] \qquad [j+1,k,h,\diamond,\diamond]}{[i,k,h,l,r]}$$

COMBINE KEEPING GAP RIGHT:
$$\frac{[i,j,h,\diamond,\diamond] \qquad [j+1,k,h,l,r]}{[i,k,h,l,r]}$$

COMBINE CLOSING GAP:
$$\frac{[i,j,h,l,r] \qquad [l,r,h,\diamond,\diamond]}{[i,j,h,\diamond,\diamond]}$$

COMBINE SHRINKING GAP CENTRE:
$$\frac{[i,j,h,l,r] \qquad [l,r,h,l_2,r_2]}{[i,j,h,l_2,r_2]}$$

COMBINE SHRINKING GAP LEFT:
$$\frac{[i,j,h,l,r] \qquad [l,k,h,\diamond,\diamond]}{[i,j,h,k+1,r]}$$

COMBINE SHRINKING GAP RIGHT:
$$\frac{[i,j,h,l,r] \qquad [k,r,h,\diamond,\diamond]}{[i,j,h,l,k-1]}$$

The WG_1 parser proceeds bottom-up, by building dependency subtrees and joining them to form larger subtrees, until it finds a complete dependency tree for the input sentence. The logic of the parser can be understood by considering how it infers the item corresponding to the subtree induced by a particular node, given the items for the subtrees induced by the direct dependents of that node. Suppose that, in a complete dependency analysis for a sentence $a_1 \ldots a_n$, the word a_h has $a_{d_1} \ldots a_{d_p}$ as direct dependents (i.e. we have dependency links $a_{d_1} \to a_h, \ldots, a_{d_p} \to a_h$), then, the item corresponding to the subtree induced by a_h is obtained from the ones corresponding to the subtrees induced by $a_{d_1} \ldots a_{d_p}$ by:

(1) applying the LINK UNGAPPED or LINK GAPPED step to each of the items corresponding to the subtrees induced by the direct dependents, and to the hypothesis $[h, h, h, \diamond, \diamond]$. This allows us to infer p items representing the result of linking each of the dependent subtrees to the new head a_h;

(2) applying the various COMBINE steps to join all of the items obtained in the previous step into a single item. The COMBINE steps perform a union operation between subtrees. Therefore, the result is a dependency tree containing all the dependent subtrees, and with all of them linked to h: this is the subtree induced by a_h.

This process is applied repeatedly to build larger subtrees, until, if the parsing process is successful, a final item is found containing a dependency tree for the complete sentence.

8.3.2 *Proof of correctness for* WG_1

To prove that the WG_1 parsing schema is correct, we need to prove its soundness (all valid final items are correct) and completeness (all correct final items are valid). This will be done by the usual method explained in Section 2.3.3 of defining a set of *correct* items for the schema, in such a way that final items in this set satisfy the general definition of correct final items (Section 7.2), and then proving the stronger claims that all valid items are correct and all correct items are valid.

To define the set of correct items for WG_1, we will first provide a definition of the trees that these items must contain: let T be a well-nested partial dependency tree headed at a node a_h. We will call such a tree a *valid tree* for the algorithm WG_1 if it satisfies the following conditions:

(1) $\lfloor a_h \rfloor$ is either of the form $\{a_h\} \cup [i, j]$ or $\{a_h\} \cup ([i, j] \smallsetminus [l, r])$.

(2) All the nodes in T have gap degree at most 1 except for a_h, which can have gap degree up to 2.

Given an input string $a_1 \ldots a_n$ and a set of D-rules G, we say that an item of the form $[i, j, h, \diamond, \diamond] \in \mathcal{I}_{WG1}$ is *correct* if it contains a valid tree T rooted at a_h, such that $\lfloor a_h \rfloor = \{a_h\} \cup [i, j]$, and all the edges in T are licensed by G.

We say that an item of the form $[i, j, h, l, r] \in \mathcal{I}_{WG1}$ is *correct* if it contains a valid tree T headed at a_h, such that $\lfloor a_h \rfloor = \{a_h\} \cup ([i, j] \smallsetminus [l, r])$, and all the edges in T are licensed by G.

Throughout the proof we will suppose that all items are normalised, i.e., $[i,j,h,l,r]$ should always be read as $nm([i,j,h,l,r])$, although we will omit the nm function most of the time for clarity.

Since a final item in WG_1 has the form $[1,n,h,\diamond,\diamond]$, a *correct final item* for this algorithm will contain at least one valid tree rooted at a head a_h and with $\lfloor a_h \rfloor = [1,n]$. This tree must be well-nested because it is valid, and must have gap degree ≤ 1 because the definition of a valid tree implies that every node except for a_h has gap degree ≤ 1, and the fact that $\lfloor a_h \rfloor = [1,n]$ implies that a_h has gap degree 0. Therefore, a correct final item for an input string contains at least one well-nested parse of gap degree ≤ 1 for that string.

Proving the correctness of the WG_1 parser amounts to proving its soundness and completeness.

8.3.2.1 *Soundness*

Proving the soundness of the WG_1 parser is showing that all valid final items (i.e., final items that can be obtained from the hypotheses by applying some sequence of deduction steps) are correct.

We will do this by proving the stronger claim that all valid items are correct. Since all valid items are either hypotheses or obtained by applying a deduction step to other valid items, it suffices to show that:

(i) hypotheses are correct, and

(ii) if the antecedents of a deduction step in WG_1 are correct, then the consequent is also correct.

The proof of (i) is trivial, since any hypothesis $[h,h,h,\diamond,\diamond]$ contains the valid dependency tree consisting of a single node (a_h) and no links.

In order to prove (ii), given a set of D-rules G, we must prove that if the antecedents of a deduction step are items containing a valid tree for WG_1 licensed by the D-rules in G, then the consequent must also contain a valid tree for WG_1 licensed by G. In order for a tree to be valid, it must be well-nested, with $\lfloor a_h \rfloor$ of the form $\{a_h\} \cup [i,j]$ or $\{a_h\} \cup ([i,j] \smallsetminus [l,r])$, and with all the nodes having gap degree at most 1 except for the head, which may have gap degree up to 2.

By definition of items in WG_1, all trees contained in items must satisfy the conditions of a valid tree. Therefore, proving soundness in this case amounts to proving that if the antecedents of a step are nonempty, then the consequent is nonempty.

This can be seen step by step: in the case of a LINK GAPPED step creating a dependency $a_{h_2} \to a_{h_1}$, a tree T_c for the consequent item can be obtained from a tree T_a taken from the second antecedent ($[i_2, j_2, h_2, l_2, r_2]$) by linking its head (which is a_{h_2} by construction of the antecedent) to a_{h_1}. Condition (1) of a valid tree is satisfied by construction, since the projection of the head of T_c is the result of adding a_{h_1} to the projection of a_{h_2} in T_a, and this projection is of the form $[i_2, j_2] \setminus [l_2, r_2]$ by construction of the antecedent and by the constraint imposed by the step on a_{h_2}. Besides, since by this same constraint we know that T_a must have gap degree 1, the tree T_c that we obtain for the consequent satisfies the condition that all of its nodes have gap degree 1 (since their projections are the same as in the antecedent tree) except for its head, that may have gap degree 2 (since its projection is that of the head node of T_a, plus a new node a_{h_1} that may increase the gap degree at most by one). The new link appearing in the consequent item must be licensed by our set of D-rules G, by the side condition of the step. Finally, the well-nestedness constraint is also preserved, since the subtrees induced by nodes in T_c are the same as those in T_a except for the one induced by a_{h_1}, which cannot interleave with any other as it contains them all. Therefore, if the antecedents of a LINK GAPPED step are nonempty, we conclude that the consequent is also nonempty, since it contains the valid tree T_c. The same reasoning can be applied to the LINK UNGAPPED step.

In the case of COMBINE steps, a tree T_c for the consequent item can be obtained from the union of two trees T_a and T_b, each taken from one of the antecedent items, and having a common head a_h. In this case, no new links are created, so the consequent tree is obviously permitted by the D-rules G if the antecedent trees are. Condition (1) of a valid tree is satisfied by construction, since the required projection of the head for a valid tree in the consequent of a COMBINE is the union of those for the antecedents, and by checking the steps one by one we can see that their constraints guarantee that this union satisfies the condition. The gap degree of the head in T_c is guaranteed to be at most 2 by this condition (1), and the gap degree of the rest of the nodes in T_c is guaranteed to be less than or equal 1 because their induced subtrees are the same as in the antecedent tree T_a or T_b in which they appeared (note that, by construction of the antecedents of COMBINE steps, the only node that appears both in T_a and T_b is a_h, so the rest of the nodes in T_c can only come from one of the antecedent trees). Therefore, (2) also holds.

Regarding well-nestedness, we note that the subtree induced by the head of the consequent tree cannot interleave with any other, and the rest of the subtrees are the same as in the antecedent trees. Thus, since the subtrees in each antecedent tree did not interleave among themselves (T_a and T_b are well-nested), the only way in which the consequent tree could be ill-nested would be having a subtree of one antecedent tree interleaving with a subtree of the other antecedent tree. This can be checked step by step, and in every single COMBINER step we can see that two subtrees coming from each of the antecedent trees cannot interleave. As an example, in a COMBINE CLOSING GAP step:

$$\text{COMBINE CLOSING GAP: } \frac{[i,j,h,l,r] \quad [l,r,h,\diamond,\diamond]}{[i,j,h,\diamond,\diamond]}$$

In order for a subtree in the second antecedent to be able to interleave with a subtree in the first antecedent, it would need to have nodes in the interval $[l,r]$ and nodes in the set $[1,i-1] \cup [j+1,n]$, but this is impossible by construction, since the projection of a tree in the second antecedent is of the form $\{a_h\} \cup [l,r]$.

Analogous reasoning can be applied for the rest of the *Combiner* steps, concluding that all of them preserve well-nestedness. With this we have proven (ii), and therefore the soundness of the WG_1 parser.

8.3.2.2 *Order annotations*

In the completeness proof for WG_1, we will use the concept of *order annotations* (Kuhlmann, 2007; Kuhlmann and Möhl, 2007). Here we will outline the concept and some properties relevant to the proof. A more detailed discussion can be found in Kuhlmann (2007).

Order annotations are strings that encode the precedence relation between the nodes of a dependency tree: if we take a dependency tree with its words unordered and decorate each node with an order annotation, we will obtain a particular ordering for the words. Order annotations are related to projectivity, gap degree and well-nestedness. A set of order annotations exist that, when applied to nodes in any structure, will result in an ordering of the nodes that satisfies projectivity, and the same can be said about the properties of well-nestedness and having gap degree bounded by a given constant k. In addition to this, order annotations are closely related to the way in which the parsers defined in this chapter construct subtrees with their COMBINE steps, and this will make them useful for proving their correctness.

Let T be a dependency structure for a string $a_1 \ldots a_n$, and a_k a node in T. Let $a_{d_1} \ldots a_{d_p}$ be the direct dependents of a_k in T, ordered by the position of the leftmost element in their projection, i.e. $min\{i \mid a_i \in \lfloor a_{d_u} \rfloor\} < min\{j \mid a_j \in \lfloor a_{d_v} \rfloor\}$ if and only if $u < v$.

The order annotation for the node a_k is a string over the alphabet $\{0, 1, \ldots, p\} \cup \{","\}$ obtained from the following process:

- Build a string $x(T, a_k) = x_1 x_2 \ldots x_n$, where $x_k = 0$, $x_i = u$ if $a_i \in \lfloor a_{d_u} \rfloor$, and $x_i = ","$ (comma) otherwise (i.e. if $a_i \notin \lfloor a_k \rfloor$).
- The order annotation for a_k, $\hat{o}(T, a_k)$, is the string obtained by collapsing all adjacent occurences of the same symbol in $x(T, a_k)$ into a single occurence, and removing all leading and trailing commas.[3]

By construction, order annotations have the following property:

Property 1. If the order annotation for a node a_k is a string $\hat{o}(T, a_k) = o_1 \ldots o_q$, then there exist unique natural numbers $i_1 < i_2, \ldots < i_{q+1}$ such that:

- If the symbol 0 appears in position v in $\hat{o}(T, a_k)$, then $i_v = k$ and $i_{v+1} = k + 1$.
- If a symbol $s \in (\mathbb{N} \setminus \{0\})$ appears in positions $v_1, \ldots, v_r$ in $\hat{o}(T, a_k)$, then the projection of the sth dependent of a_k in T is $\{[i_{v_1}, i_{v_1+1} - 1]\} \cup \{[i_{v_2}, i_{v_2+1} - 1]\} \cup \ldots \cup \{[i_{v_r}, i_{v_r+1} - 1]\}$.

In particular, it can be checked that i_1 is always the index associated to the leftmost node in $\lfloor a_k \rfloor$, i_{q+1} the index associated to the rightmost node in $\lfloor a_k \rfloor$ plus 1, and for each i_v such that $1 < v \leq q$, the differences $d_v = (i_v - i_1)$ correspond to the positions in the intermediate string $x(T, a_k)$ such that the d_vth symbol in $x(T, a_k)$ differs from the $(d_v + 1)$th.

By using this property to reason about the projections of a dependency tree's nodes, we can show the following, more particular properties:

Property 2. A node a_k has gap degree g in a dependency structure T if, and only if, the comma symbol (,) appears g times in $\hat{o}(T, a_k)$.

(Corollary 1) The gap degree of a dependency structure T is the maximum value among the number of commas in the order annotations of each of its nodes.

(Corollary 2) A dependency structure is projective if, and only if, none of the order annotations associated to its nodes contain a comma.

---

[3]Note that we use a slightly different notation from Kuhlmann (2007). For simplicity in the proofs, we say that each node has a single annotation of the form $\alpha_1, \alpha_2, \ldots, \alpha_n$ instead of saying that it has a list of annotations $\alpha_1, \alpha_2, \ldots \alpha_n$. Of course, the difference is merely notational.

Property 3. If a natural number $s > 0$ appears $g + 1$ times in an order annotation $\hat{o}(T, a_k)$, then the sth direct child of a_k (in the ordering mentioned earlier) has gap degree g, and therefore the dependency structure T has gap degree at least g.

Property 4. A dependency structure T is ill-nested if, and only if, it contains at least one order annotation of the form $\dots a \dots b \dots a \dots b \dots$, for some $a, b \in \mathbb{N}$. Otherwise, T is well-nested.

These properties allow us to define the sets of structures verifying well-nestedness and/or bounded gap degree only in terms of their order annotations. Sets that can be characterised in this way are said to be *algebraically transparent* (Kuhlmann, 2007).

8.3.2.3 *Completeness*

Proving completeness of the WG_1 parser is proving that all correct final items in WG_1 are valid. We will show this by proving the following, stronger claim:

Lemma 8.1. *Let T be a partial dependency tree headed at a node a_h, which is a valid tree for WG_1. Then:*

(1) If $\lfloor a_h \rfloor = \{a_h\} \cup [i, j]$, then the item $[i, j, h, \diamond, \diamond]$ containing T is a valid item in the WG_1 parser.

(2) If $\lfloor a_h \rfloor = \{a_h\} \cup ([i, j] \smallsetminus [l, r])$, then the item $[i, j, h, l, r]$ containing T is a valid item in the WG_1 parser.

It is clear that this lemma implies the completeness of the parser: a final item $[1, n, h, \diamond, \diamond]$ is correct only if it contains a tree rooted at a_h with gap degree at most 1 and projection $[1, n]$. Such a tree is in case (1) of Lemma 8.1, implying that the correct final item $[1, n, h, \diamond, \diamond]$ is valid. Therefore, this lemma implies that all correct final items are valid, and thus that WG_1 is complete.

8.3.2.4 *Proof of Lemma 8.1*

We will prove Lemma 8.1 by strong induction on $\#(\lfloor a_h \rfloor)$. In order to do this, we will show that Lemma 8.1 holds for valid trees T rooted at a_h such that $\#(\lfloor a_h \rfloor) = 1$, and then we will prove that if Lemma 8.1 holds for every valid tree T' such that $\#(\lfloor a_h \rfloor) < N$, then it also holds for all trees T such that $\#(\lfloor a_h \rfloor) = N$.

Base case Let T be a valid tree rooted at a node a_h, such that $\#(\lfloor a_h \rfloor) = 1$. Since T has only one node, it must be the trivial dependency tree consisting of the single node a_h. In this case, Lemma 8.1 trivially holds because the initial item $[h, h, h, \diamond, \diamond]$ contains this tree, and initial items are valid by definition.

Induction step Let T be a valid partial dependency tree rooted at a node a_h, such that $\#(\lfloor a_h \rfloor) = N$ (for some $N > 1$).

We will prove that, if Lemma 8.1 holds for every valid partial dependency tree T' rooted at a'_h such that $\#(\lfloor a'_h \rfloor) < N$, then it also holds for T.

Let $a_{d_1} \ldots a_{d_p}$ be the direct children of a_h in T, ordered by the index of their leftmost transitive dependent, i.e., for every i and j such that $1 \leq i < j \leq p$, then $min\{k \mid a_k \in \lfloor a_{d_i} \rfloor\} < min\{k \mid a_k \in \lfloor a_{d_j} \rfloor\}$.

We know that $p \geq 1$ because if $\#(\lfloor a_h \rfloor) > 1$, then a_h must have at least one dependent. We now consider two cases: $p = 1$ and $p > 1$. In the case where $p = 1$, consider the subtree of T induced by a_{d_1}. Since $\#(\lfloor a_{d_1} \rfloor) = N - 1$, we know by induction hypothesis that the item corresponding to this tree is valid. This item is:

- $[i, j, d_1, \diamond, \diamond]$, if $\lfloor a_{d_1} \rfloor$ is of the form $\{a_{d_1}\} \cup [i, j]$, with $d_1 \in [i, j]$.[4] In this case, applying a LINK step to this item and the initial item $[h, h, h, \diamond, \diamond]$ (which is valid by definition), with the D-rule $a_{d_1} \to a_h$ (which must exist in order for T to be valid), we obtain $[i, j, h, \diamond, \diamond]$, which is the item corresponding to a_h by Lemma 8.1.

- $[i, j, d_1, h, h]$, if $\lfloor a_{d_1} \rfloor$ is of the form $\{a_{d_1}\} \cup ([i, j] \setminus \{a_h\})$. In this case, applying a LINK step to this item and the initial item $[h, h, h, \diamond, \diamond]$ (which is valid by definition), with the D-rule $a_{d_1} \to a_h$ (which must exist, as in the previous case), we obtain $[i, j, h, \diamond, \diamond]$,[5] which is the item corresponding to a_h by Lemma 8.1.

- $[i, j, d_1, l, r]$, if $\lfloor a_{d_1} \rfloor$ is of the form $\{a_{d_1}\} \cup ([i, j] \setminus [l, r])$. In this case, applying a LINK step to this item and the initial item $[h, h, h, \diamond, \diamond]$ (which is valid by definition), with the D-rule $a_{d_1} \to a_h$, we obtain $[i, j, h, l, r]$, which is the item corresponding to a_h by Lemma 8.1.

---

[4]Note that the situation where the projection is of this form but with $d_1 \notin [i, j]$ is covered by the third case in this list if $d_1 < i - 1$ or $d_1 > j + 1$, or by this same case if $d_1 = i - 1$ or $d_1 = j + 1$, by rewriting the projection in the equivalent form $\{a_{d_1}\} \cup [i - 1, j]$ or $\{a_{d_1}\} \cup [i, j + 1]$, respectively.

[5]Note that this item is the normalisation of $[i, j, h, h, h]$.

With this, we have proven the induction step for the case where $p = 1$ (the head node of our partial dependency tree has a single direct child). It now remains to prove it for the case where $p > 1$ (the head node has more than one direct dependent).

In order to show this, let $\hat{o}(T, a_h)$ be the order annotation associated with the head node a_h in the tree T. By construction, $\hat{o}(T, a_h)$ must be a string of symbols in the alphabet $\{0\} \cup \{1\} \cup \ldots \cup \{p\} \cup \{,\}$, containing a single appearance of the symbol 0. Additionally, by the definition of a valid tree and Property 3 of order annotations, $\hat{o}(T, a_h)$ must contain either 1 or 2 appearances of each symbol 1 through p (since more than 2 appearances of a symbol q could only occur if a_{d_q} had gap degree ≥ 2). And, from the possible forms of $\lfloor a_h \rfloor$ in a valid tree, we know that $\hat{o}(T, a_h)$ must have one of the following forms, where α and β are (possibly empty) strings that only contain symbols in $\{1\} \cup \ldots \cup \{p\}$ (not zeros or commas):

(i) $\alpha 0 \beta$
(ii) $\alpha, \beta 0 \gamma$
(iii) $\alpha 0 \beta, \gamma$
(iv) $0, \alpha, \beta$
(v) $\alpha, \beta, 0$
(vi) $\alpha, 0, \beta$

Note that, by Property 2 of order annotations, the first case corresponds to a tree where the head has gap degree 0, in the next two cases the head has gap degree 1 and the last three are the cases where the gap degree of the head is 2. In these three latter cases, the constraint that $\lfloor a_h \rfloor$ must be of the form $\{a_h\} \cup ([i, j] \smallsetminus [l, r])$ for the tree T to be valid implies that the symbol 0 representing the head in the annotation must be surrounded by commas. If we have a gap degree 2 annotation of any other form (for example $\alpha 0, \beta, \gamma$, for nonempty α), the projection of a_h does not meet this constraint. This can be seen by using Property 1 of order annotations to obtain this projection.

Taking these considerations into account, we will now divide the proof into different cases and subcases based on $\hat{o}(T, a_h)$, starting with its first symbol:

(1) If $\hat{o}(T, a_h)$ begins with the symbol 1:

    (a) If there are no more appearances of the symbol 1 in $\hat{o}(T, a_h)$:
        Then we consider the following trees:

- T_1: The tree obtained by taking the subtree induced by a_{d_1} (which by Property 1 must have a yield of the form $[i, j]$, as the symbol 1 appears only once in $\hat{o}(T, a_h)$), and adding the node a_h and dependency $a_{d_1} \to a_h$ to it.
- T_2: The tree obtained by taking the union of subtrees induced by $a_{d_2} \ldots a_{d_p}$, and adding the node a_h and dependencies $a_{d_2} \to a_h, \ldots, a_{d_p} \to a_h$ to it.

And we divide this case into three further cases:

i. If $\hat{o}(T, a_h)$ does not contain any comma: then, by Property 1,[6] the projection of a_h in T_2 will be of the form $[j+1, k] \cup \{a_h\}$. By applying the induction hypothesis to T_1 and T_2, we know that the items $[i, j, h, \diamond, \diamond]$ and $[j+1, k, h, \diamond, \diamond]$ are valid. Therefore, the item $[i, k, h, \diamond, \diamond]$ is also valid because it can be obtained from these two items by applying a COMBINE UNGAPPED step. As in this case the projection of a_h in T is $[i, k] \cup [h]$, this item $[i, k, h, \diamond, \diamond]$ is the item containing the tree T, and its validity proves Lemma 8.1 in this particular subcase.

ii. If $\hat{o}(T, a_h)$ contains at least one comma, and the second symbol in $\hat{o}(T, a_h)$ is a comma: then $\hat{o}(T, a_h)$ must be of the form ii, v or vi and the projection of a_h in T_2 will be of the form $[i_2, k] \cup \{a_h\}$, for $i_2 > j + 1$. Therefore, we know by the induction hypothesis that the items $[i, j, h, \diamond, \diamond]$ (for T_1) and $[i_2, k, h, \diamond, \diamond]$ (for T_2) are valid, and by applying COMBINE OPENING GAP to these items, we obtain $[i, k, h, j+1, i_2 - 1]$, which is the item containing the tree T.

iii. If $\hat{o}(T, a_h)$ contains at least one comma, but the second symbol in $\hat{o}(T, a_h)$ is not a comma:

A. First, in the case that $\hat{o}(T, a_h)$ contains exactly one comma, then it is of the form $1\beta_1, \beta_2$, where either β_1 or β_2 contains the symbol 0 and neither of them is empty. In this case, we can see that the projection of a_h in T_2 is of the form $\{a_h\} \cup [j+1, l-1] \cup [r+1, k]$, so by induction hypothesis the item $[j+1, k, h, l, r]$ is valid. We apply COMBINE KEEPING GAP RIGHT to $[i, j, h, \diamond, \diamond]$ (which is valid by T_1 as in the previous cases) and $[j+1, k, h, l, r]$ to obtain $[i, k, h, l, r]$, which is the item containing T.

---

[6]In the remainder of the proof, we will always use Property 1 of order annotations to relate them to projections, so we will not mention it explicitly in subsequent cases.

B. Second, in the case where $\hat{o}(T, a_h)$ contains two commas, then it is of the form $1\beta_1, 0, \beta_2$ or $1\beta_1, \beta_2, 0$. Then the projection of a_h in T_2 will again be of the form $\{a_h\} \cup [j+1, l-1] \cup [r+1, k]$, so we can follow the same reasoning as in the previous case to show that the item $[i, k, h, l, r]$ containing T is valid.

(b) If there is a second appearance of the symbol 1 in $\hat{o}(T, a_h)$: then $\hat{o}(T, a_h)$ is of the form $1\beta_1 1\beta_2$. Due to the well-nestedness constraint, we know that there is no symbol $s \in \{1\} \cup \{2\} \cup \ldots \cup \{p\}$ that appears both in β_1 and in β_2. This allows us to consider the following trees:

- T_1: The tree obtained by taking the subtree induced by a_{d_1} (which must have a yield of the form $[i, l-1] \cup [r+1, j]$, as the symbol 1 appears twice in $\hat{o}(T, a_h)$), and adding the node a_h and dependency $a_{d_1} \to a_h$ to it.
- T_2: The tree obtained by taking the union of subtrees induced by $a_{d_{b_1}} \ldots a_{d_{b_q}}$, where $b_1 \ldots b_q$ are the non-comma, non-zero symbols appearing in β_1, and adding the node a_h and dependencies $a_{d_{b_1}} \to a_h, \ldots, a_{d_{b_q}} \to a_h$ to it.
- T_3: The tree obtained by taking the union of subtrees induced by $a_{d_{c_1}} \ldots a_{d_{c_q}}$, where $c_1 \ldots c_q$ are the non-comma, non-zero symbols appearing in β_2, and adding the node a_h and dependencies $a_{d_{c_1}} \to a_h, \ldots, a_{d_{c_q}} \to a_h$ to it.

Note that T_2 or T_3 may be empty trees, since it is possible that the strings β_1 or β_2 do not contain any symbol except for zeros and commas. However, both trees cannot be empty at the same time, since in that case we would have $p = 1$.

With this, we divide this case into further cases:

i. If β_1 does not contain any comma: then, by construction and by the well-nestedness constraint, we know that the projection of a_h in T_2 is of the form $\{a_h\} \cup [l, r]$. Applying the induction hypothesis to T_1, we know that the item $[i, j, h, l, r]$ is valid, and applying it to T_2, we know that $[l, r, h, \diamond, \diamond]$ is also valid. By applying a COMBINE CLOSING GAP step to these items, we obtain that $\iota = [i, j, h, \diamond, \diamond]$ is valid. Now, we divide into further cases according to the form of β_2:

A. If T_3 is empty (β_2 is empty except for a possible 0 symbol), then we are done, as $[i, j, h, \diamond, \diamond]$ is already the item containing the tree T.

B. If β_2 does not contain a comma, then the projection of a_h in T_3 is of the form $\{a_h\} \cup [j+1, k]$, so by induction hypothesis the item $[j+1, k, h, \diamond, \diamond]$ is valid. By applying COMBINE UNGAPPED to this item and ι, we obtain $[i, k, h, \diamond, \diamond]$, the item containing the tree T.

C. If β_2 contains one or two commas, then the projection of a_h in T_3 is of the form $\{a_h\} \cup [j+1, l'-1] \cup [r'+1, m]$, and by induction hypothesis, $[j+1, k, h, l', r']$ is valid. By applying COMBINE KEEPING GAP RIGHT to this item and ι, we get that $[i, k, h, l', r']$ is valid, and this is the item containing the tree T in this case.

ii. If β_1 contains a single symbol, and it is a comma: in this case, T_2 is empty, but we know that T_3 must be nonempty (since $p > 1$) and it must either have no commas, or be of the form $\beta_3, 0$, corresponding to the expression v. In any of these cases, we know that the projection of a_h in T_3 will be of the form $\{a_h\} \cup [j+1, k]$. Therefore, applying the induction hypothesis to T_1 we know that the item $[i, j, h, l, r]$ is valid, and with T_3 we know that $[j+1, k, h, \diamond, \diamond]$ is also valid. By applying the COMBINE KEEPING GAP LEFT step to these two items, we obtain $[i, k, h, l, r]$, the item containing the tree T.

iii. If β_1 is of the form ",β_3", where β_3 is not empty and does not contain commas: then, by construction and by the well-nestedness constraint, we know that the projection of a_h in T_2 is of the form $\{a_h\} \cup [l', r]$, with $l < l' \leq r$; so the items $[i, j, h, l, r]$ (for T_1) and $[l', r, h, \diamond, \diamond]$ (for T_2) are valid. By applying COMBINE SHRINKING GAP RIGHT to these two items, we obtain that $\iota = [i, j, h, l, l'-1]$ is a valid item. Now, if β_2 is empty, we are done: ι is the item containing the tree T. And if β_2 is nonempty, then it must either contain no commas, or be of the form $\beta_4, 0$ (corresponding to the expression v). In any of these cases, we know that the projection of a_h in T_3 will be of the form $\{a_h\} \cup [j+1, k]$. So, by induction hypothesis, the item $[j+1, k, h, \diamond, \diamond]$ is valid and by applying COMBINE KEEPING GAP LEFT to ι and this item we obtain that $[i, k, h, l, l'-1]$ is valid: this is the item containing the tree T in this case.

iv. If β_1 is of the form "β_3,", where β_3 is not empty and does not contain commas, this case is symmetric with respect to the last one: in this case, the projection of a_h in T_2 is of the form $\{a_h\} \cup [l, r']$, with $l \le r' < r$; and the step COMBINE SHRINKING GAP LEFT is applied to the item $[l, r', h, \diamond, \diamond]$ (for T_2) and the item $[i, j, h, l, r]$ (for T_1), obtaining $\iota = [i, j, h, r' + 1, r]$. As in the previous case, if β_2 is empty we do not need to do anything else, and if it is nonempty we apply COMBINE KEEPING GAP LEFT to obtain $[i, k, h, r' + 1, r]$, the item containing T.

v. If β_1 is of the form "β_3, β_4", where β_3 and β_4 are not empty and do not contain commas: in this case, by construction and by the well-nestedness constraint, we know that the projection of a_h in T_2 is of the form $\{a_h\} \cup [l, l' - 1] \cup [r' + 1, r]$, with $l < l' \le r' < r$. With this, this case is analogous to the previous two cases: from T_1 we know that the item $[i, j, h, l, r]$ is valid, and we combine it with the item $[l, r, h, l', r']$ (from T_2), in this case using COMBINE SHRINKING GAP CENTRE. With this, we obtain that the item $\iota = [i, j, h, l', r']$ is valid. If β_2 is empty, this is the item containing the tree T. If not, we make the same reasoning as in the two previous cases to conclude that the item $[j + 1, k, h, \diamond, \diamond]$ is valid, and we combine it with ι by the COMBINE KEEPING GAP LEFT step to obtain $[i, k, h, l', r']$, the item containing T.

vi. If β_1 contains two commas: in this case, by construction of the valid tree T, β_1 must be of the form $\beta_3, 0, \beta_4$, where β_3 and β_4 may or may not be empty. So we divide into subcases:

A. If β_3 and β_4 are both empty, we apply the same reasoning as in case 1-b-ii, except that in this case we know that β_2 cannot contain any commas.

B. If β_3 is empty and β_4 is nonempty, we apply the same reasoning as in case 1-b-iii, except that in this case we know that β_2 cannot contain any commas.

C. If β_3 is nonempty and β_4 is empty, we apply the same reasoning as in case 1-b-iv, except that in this case we know that β_2 cannot contain any commas.

D. If neither β_3 nor β_4 are empty, we apply the same reasoning as in case 1-b-v, except that in this case we know that β_2 cannot contain any commas.

(2) If $\hat{o}(T, a_h)$ begins with the symbol 0:

(a) If $\hat{o}(T, a_h)$ begins with 01, we can apply the same reasonings as in case 1, because the expressions for the projections do not change.

(b) If $\hat{o}(T, a_h)$ begins with 0 followed immediately by a comma, then we have an annotation of the form iv: $0, \alpha, \beta$. In this case, we can apply symmetric reasoning considering the last symbol of $\hat{o}(T, a_h)$ instead of the first (note that the case $\alpha, \beta, 0$ has already been proven as part of case 1, and all the steps in the schema are symmetric).

As this covers all the possible cases of the order annotation $\hat{o}(T, a_h)$, we have completed the proof of the induction step for Lemma 8.1, and this concludes the proof of completeness for the WG_1 parsing schema.

8.3.3 *Computational complexity of WG_1*

The time complexity of WG_1 is $O(n^7)$, as the step COMBINE SHRINKING GAP CENTRE works with 7 free string positions. This complexity with respect to the length of the input is as expected for this set of structures, since Kuhlmann (2007) shows that their generative power is equivalent to that of LTAG, and the best existing parsers for this formalism also perform in $O(n^7)$ (Eisner and Satta, 2000).[7] Note that the COMBINE step which is the bottleneck only uses the 7 indexes, and not any other entities like D-rules, so its $O(n^7)$ complexity does not have any additional factors due to grammar size or other variables.

It is possible to build a variant of this parser with time complexity $O(n^6)$, as with parsers for unlexicalised TAG, if we work with unlexicalised D-rules specifying the possibility of dependencies between pairs of categories instead of pairs of words. In order to do this, we expand the item set with unlexicalised items of the form $[i, j, C, l, r]$, where C is a category, apart from the existing items $[i, j, h, l, r]$. Steps in the parser are duplicated, to work both with lexicalised and unlexicalised items, except for the LINK steps, which always work with a lexicalised item and an unlexicalised hypothesis to produce an unlexicalised item, and the COMBINE SHRINKING GAP steps, which can work only with unlexicalised items. Steps are added to obtain lexicalised items from their unlexicalised equivalents by binding the head to particular string positions. Finally, we need certain variants of

---

[7]Although standard TAG parsing algorithms run in time $O(n^6)$ with respect to the input length, they also have a complexity factor related to grammar size. Eisner and Satta (2000) show that, in the case of lexicalised TAG, this factor is a function of the input length n, hence the additional complexity.

the COMBINE SHRINKING GAP steps that take 2 unlexicalised antecedents and produce a lexicalised consequent. An example is the following:

$$\text{COMBINE SHRINKING GAP CENTRE L:} \quad \frac{\begin{array}{c}[i,j,C,l,r]\\ [l+1,r,C,l_2,r_2]\end{array}}{[i,j,l,l_2,r_2]} \quad cat(a_l)=C$$

Although this version of the algorithm reduces time complexity with respect to the length of the input to $O(n^6)$, it also adds a factor related to the number of categories, as well as constant factors due to using more kinds of items and steps than the original WG_1 algorithm. This, together with the advantages of lexicalised dependency parsing, may mean that the original WG_1 algorithm is more practical than this version.

8.4 The WG_k parser

The WG_1 parsing schema can be generalised to obtain a parser for all well-nested dependency structures with gap degree bounded by a constant $k(k \geq 1)$, which we call WG_k parser. In order to do this, we extend the item set so that it can contain items with up to k gaps, and modify the deduction steps to work with these multi-gapped items.

8.4.1 WG_k parsing schema

The item set for the WG_k parsing schema is:

$$\mathcal{I}_{WGk} = \{[i,j,h,\langle(l_1,r_1),\ldots,(l_g,r_g)\rangle]\}$$

where $i,j,h \in (\mathbb{N} \cup \{0\})$, $0 \leq g \leq k$, $1 \leq h \leq n$, $1 \leq i \leq j \leq n$, $h \neq j$, $h \neq i - 1$; and for each $p \in \{1,2,\ldots,g\}$: $l_p, r_p \in \mathbb{N}$, $i < l_p \leq r_p < j$, $r_p < l_{p+1} - 1$, $h \neq l_p - 1$, $h \neq r_p$.

An item $[i,j,h,\langle(l_1,r_1),\ldots,(l_g,r_g)\rangle]$ represents the set of all well-nested partial dependency trees rooted at a_h such that $\lfloor a_h \rfloor = \{a_h\} \cup ([i,j] \smallsetminus \bigcup_{p=1}^{g}[l_p,r_p])$, where each interval $[l_p,r_p]$ is called a gap. The constraints $h \neq j, h \neq i + 1, h \neq l_p - 1, h \neq r_p$ are added to avoid redundancy, and normalisation is defined as in WG_1. The set of final items is defined as the set $\mathcal{F} = \{[1,n,h,\langle\rangle] \mid h \in \mathbb{N}, 1 \leq h \leq n\}$. Note that this set is the same as in WG_1, as these are the items that we denoted $[1,n,h,\diamond,\diamond]$ in the previous parser.

The parser has the following deduction steps:

$$\text{LINK:} \quad \frac{[h_1, h_1, h_1, \langle\rangle] \qquad [i_2, j_2, h_2, \langle(l_1, r_1), \ldots, (l_g, r_g)\rangle]}{[i_2, j_2, h_1, \langle(l_1, r_1), \ldots, (l_g, r_g)\rangle]} \; a_{h_2} \to a_{h_1}$$

such that $a_{h_2} \in [i_2, j_2] \smallsetminus \bigcup_{p=1}^{g} [l_p, r_p] \wedge a_{h_1} \notin [i_2, j_2] \smallsetminus \bigcup_{p=1}^{g} [l_p, r_p]$.

COMBINE OPENING GAP :

$$\frac{\begin{array}{c}[i, l_q - 1, h, \langle(l_1, r_1), \ldots, (l_{q-1}, r_{q-1})\rangle] \\ [r_q + 1, m, h, \langle(l_{q+1}, r_{q+1}), \ldots, (l_g, r_g)\rangle]\end{array}}{[i, m, h, \langle(l_1, r_1), \ldots, (l_g, r_g)\rangle]} \; g \le k \wedge l_q \le r_q$$

COMBINE KEEPING GAPS :

$$\frac{\begin{array}{c}[i, j, h, \langle(l_1, r_1), \ldots, (l_q, r_q)\rangle] \\ [j + 1, m, h, \langle(l_{q+1}, r_{q+1}), \ldots, (l_g, r_g)\rangle]\end{array}}{[i, m, h, \langle(l_1, r_1), \ldots, (l_g, r_g)\rangle]} \; g \le k$$

COMBINE SHRINKING GAP LEFT :

$$\frac{\begin{array}{c}[i, j, h, \langle(l_1, r_1), \ldots, (l_q, r_q), (l', r_s), (l_{s+1}, r_{s+1}), \ldots, (l_g, r_g)\rangle] \\ [l', l_s - 1, h, \langle(l_{q+1}, r_{q+1}), \ldots, (l_{s-1}, r_{s-1})\rangle]\end{array}}{[i, j, h, \langle(l_1, r_1), \ldots, (l_g, r_g)\rangle]} \; g \le k$$

COMBINE SHRINKING GAP RIGHT:

$$\frac{\begin{array}{c}[i, j, h, \langle(l_1, r_1), \ldots, (l_{q-1}, r_{q-1}), (l_q, r'), (l_s, r_s), \ldots, (l_g, r_g)\rangle] \\ [r_q + 1, r', h, \langle(l_{q+1}, r_{q+1}), \ldots, (l_{s-1}, r_{s-1})\rangle]\end{array}}{[i, j, h, \langle(l_1, r_1), \ldots, (l_g, r_g)\rangle]} \; g \le k$$

COMBINE SHRINKING GAP CENTRE :

$$\frac{\begin{array}{c}[i, j, h, \langle(l_1, r_1), \ldots, (l_q, r_q), (l', r'), (l_s, r_s), \ldots, (l_g, r_g)\rangle] \\ [l', r', h, \langle(l_{q+1}, r_{q+1}), \ldots, (l_{s-1}, r_{s-1})\rangle]\end{array}}{[i, j, h, \langle(l_1, r_1), \ldots, (l_g, r_g)\rangle]} \; g \le k$$

As expected, the WG_1 parser corresponds to WG_k when we make $k = 1$. WG_k works in the same way as WG_1, except for the fact that COMBINE steps can create items with more than one gap.[8]

8.4.2 *Proof of correctness for WG_k*

The proof of correctness for WG_k is analogous to that of WG_1, but generalising the definition of valid trees to a higher gap degree. A valid tree in WG_k can be defined as a partial dependency tree T, headed at a word a_h of the input sentence, such that:

(1) $\lfloor a_h \rfloor$ is of the form $\{a_h\} \cup ([i,j] \setminus \bigcup_{p=1}^{g}[l_p, r_p])$, with $0 \le g \le k$,
(2) All the nodes in T have gap degree at most k except for a_h, which can have gap degree up to $k + 1$.

With this, we can define correct items and correct final items analogously to their definition in WG_1.

Soundness is proven as in WG_1. Changing the constraints for nodes so that any node can have gap degree up to k and the head of a correct tree can have gap degree $k + 1$, the same reasonings can be applied to this case.

Completeness is proven by induction on $\#(\lfloor a_h \rfloor)$, just as in WG_1. The base case is the same as in WG_1, and for the induction step, we also consider the direct children $a_{d_1} \ldots a_{d_p}$ of a_h. The case where p equals 1 is proven by using LINKER steps just as in WG_1. In the case for $p \ge 1$, we also base our proof on the order annotation $\hat{o}(T, a_h)$, but we have to take into account that the set of possible annotations is larger when we allow the gap degree to be greater than 1, so we must take into account more cases in this part of the proof.

In particular, an order annotation $\hat{o}(T, a_h)$ for a valid tree for WG_k can contain up to $k + 1$ commas and up to $k + 1$ appearances of each symbol in $\{1\} \cup \ldots \cup \{p\}$, since the head of such a tree can have gap degree at most $k + 1$ and the rest of its nodes are limited to gap degree k. If the head has gap degree exactly $k + 1$ (i.e., if $\hat{o}(T, a_h)$ contains $k + 1$ commas), then the constraint on the form of $\lfloor a_h \rfloor$ in valid trees implies that the symbol 0 cannot be contiguous to any non-comma symbol in $\hat{o}(T, a_h)$.

---

[8]In all the parsers described in this chapter, COMBINE steps may be applied in different orders to produce the same result, causing spurious ambiguity. In WG_1 and WG_k, this can be avoided when implementing the schemata, by adding flags to items so as to impose a particular order on the execution of these steps.

With this, the cases 1a) of the completeness proof for WG_1 can be directly used for WG_k, only taking into account that $\hat{o}(T, a_h)$ can contain up to $k+1$ commas. As a consequence of this, instead of COMBINE KEEPING GAP RIGHT we employ a general COMBINE KEEPING GAPS step with more than one gap allowed in its rightmost antecedent item. In the cases 1b), we need to take into account that the symbol 1 can appear up to $k+1$ times in the order annotation $\hat{o}(T, a_h)$. We write $\hat{o}(T, a_h)$ as $1\beta_1 1\beta_2 \ldots 1\beta_{g+1}(g \leq k)$ and then do with each β_i (for $i < g + 1$) the same case analysis as we do with β_1 in the WG_1 case, and with β_{g+1} the same case analysis as with β_2 in the WG_1 case. Each of these cases is proven in the same way as in the WG_1 parser, with the difference that each string β_i can contain more than one comma, so that instead of the COMBINE SHRINKING GAP steps in WG_1 we now need to use the general COMBINE SHRINKING GAP steps in WG_k, which allow their inner items to have more than one gap. In the same way, the cases in which we used COMBINE KEEPING GAP steps in the proof for WG_1 are solved by using the general COMBINE KEEPING GAP step in WG_k.

8.4.3   Computational complexity of WG_k

The WG_k parser runs in time $O(n^{5+2k})$. As in the case of WG_1, the deduction step with most free variables is COMBINE SHRINKING GAP CENTRE, and in this case it has $5 + 2k$ free indexes.

Again, this complexity result is in line with what could be expected from previous research in constituency parsing. Kuhlmann (2007) shows that the set of well-nested dependency structures with gap degree at most k is closely related to coupled context-free grammars in which the maximal rank of a nonterminal is $k + 1$, and the constituency parser defined by Hotz and Pitsch (1996) for these grammars also adds an n^2 factor for each unit increment of k.

Note that a small value of k should be enough to cover the vast majority of the non-projective sentences found in natural language treebanks. For example, the Prague Dependency Treebank (Hajič *et al.*, 2006) contains no structures with gap degree greater than 4. Therefore, a WG_4 parser would be able to analyse all the well-nested structures in this treebank, which represent 99.89% of the total. Increasing k beyond 4 would not produce further improvements in coverage.

8.5 Parsing ill-nested structures

The WG_k parser analyses dependency structures with bounded gap degree as long as they are well-nested. This covers the vast majority of the structures that occur in natural-language treebanks (Kuhlmann and Nivre, 2006), but there is still a significant minority of sentences that contain ill-nested structures.[9]

Unfortunately, the general problem of parsing ill-nested structures is NP-complete, even when the gap degree is bounded: this set of structures is closely related to LCFRS with bounded fan-out and unbounded production length, and parsing in this formalism has been proven to be NP-complete (Satta, 1992). The reason for this high complexity is the problem of *unrestricted crossing configurations*, appearing when dependency subtrees are allowed to interleave in every possible way. However, just as it has been noted that most non-projective structures appearing in practice are only "slightly" non-projective (Nivre and Nilsson, 2005), we characterise a sense in which the structures appearing in treebanks can be viewed as being only "slightly" ill-nested.

In this section, we generalise the algorithms WG_1 and WG_k to parse a proper superset of the set of well-nested structures in polynomial time, and give a characterisation of this new set of structures, which includes all the structures in several dependency treebanks.

8.5.1 *The MG_1 and MG_k parsers*

The WG_k parser for well-nested structures presented previously is based on a bottom-up process, where LINK steps are used to link completed subtrees to a head, and COMBINE steps are used to join subtrees governed by a common head to obtain a larger structure. As WG_k is a parser for well-nested structures of gap degree up to k, its COMBINER steps correspond to all the ways in which we can join two sets of sibling subtrees meeting these constraints, and having a common head, into another. Therefore, this parser does not use COMBINER steps that produce interleaved subtrees, since these would generate items corresponding to ill-nested structures.

We obtain a polynomial parser for a wider set of structures of gap degree at most k, including some ill-nested ones, by having COMBINER steps representing every way in which two sets of sibling subtrees of gap degree

---

[9]Maier and Lichte (2009) provide examples of some linguistic phenomena that cause ill-nestedness in German sentences.

at most k with a common head can be joined into another, including those producing interleaved subtrees, like the steps for gap degree 1 shown in Figure 8.1. Note that this does not mean that we can build every possible ill-nested structure as some structures with complex crossed configurations have gap degree k, but cannot be built by combining two structures of that gap degree. More specifically, our algorithm will be able to parse a dependency structure (well-nested or not) if there exists a *binarisation* of that structure that has gap degree at most k. The parser implicitly works by finding such a binarisation, since COMBINE steps are always applied to two items and no intermediate item generated by them can exceed gap degree k (not counting the position of the head in the projection).

Definition 8.4. Let $a_1 \ldots a_n$ be a string, and T a partial dependency tree headed at a node a_h. A *binarisation* of T is a tree B in which each node has at most two children, and such that:

(a) Each node in B can be either unlabelled, or labelled with a word a_i. Note that several nodes may have the same label (in contrast with the definition of a dependency graph, where the set of nodes is the set of word occurrences itself, so a word a_i cannot appear twice in the graph).

(b) A node labelled a_i is a descendant of a_j in B if and only if $a_i \to^* a_j$ in T.

The projection of a node in a binarisation is the set of reflexive-transitive children of that node. With this, we can define the gap degree of a binarisation in the same way as that of a dependency structure. If we denote by $\lfloor n \rfloor_T$ the projection of a node n in a tree T, the condition (b) of a binarisation can be rewritten as follows: $a_i \in \lfloor a_j \rfloor_B \Leftrightarrow a_i \in \lfloor a_j \rfloor_T$.

Definition 8.5. A dependency structure is *mildly ill-nested* for gap degree k if it has at least one binarisation of gap degree $\leq k$. Otherwise, we say that it is *strongly ill-nested* for gap degree k.

It can be shown that the set of mildly ill-nested structures for gap degree k includes all well-nested structures with gap degree up to k.

We define MG_1, a parser for mildly ill-nested structures for gap degree 1, as follows:

- the item set is the same as that of WG_1, except that items can now contain any mildly ill-nested structures for gap degree 1, instead of being restricted to well-nested structures; and

$$\text{COMBINE INTERLEAVING: } \frac{[i,j,h,l,r] \qquad [l,k,h,r+1,j]}{[i,k,h,\diamond,\diamond]}$$

$$\text{COMBINE INTERLEAVING GAP C: } \frac{[i,j,h,l,r] \qquad [l,k,h,m,j]}{[i,k,h,m,r]}\ m < r+1$$

$$\text{COMBINE INTERLEAVING GAP L: } \frac{[i,j,h,l,r] \qquad [l,k,h,r+1,u]}{[i,k,h,j+1,u]}\ u > j$$

$$\text{COMBINE INTERLEAVING GAP R: } \frac{[i,j,h,l,r] \qquad [k,m,h,r+1,j]}{[i,m,h,l,k-1]}\ k > l$$

Fig. 8.1 Additional steps to turn the WG_1 parser into the MG_1 parser.

$$\frac{\begin{array}{c}[i_{a_1}, i_{a_p+1}-1, h, \langle (i_{a_1+1}, i_{a_2}-1), \ldots, (i_{a_{p-1}+1}, i_{a_p}-1)\rangle] \\ [i_{b_1}, i_{b_q+1}-1, h, \langle (i_{b_1+1}, i_{b_2}-1), \ldots, (i_{b_{q-1}+1}, i_{b_q}-1)\rangle]\end{array}}{[i_{min(a_1,b_1)}, i_{max(a_p+1,b_q+1)}-1, h, \langle (i_{g_1}, i_{g_1+1}-1), \ldots, (i_{g_r}, i_{g_r+1}-1)\rangle]}$$

for each string of length n with a's located at positions $a_1 \ldots a_p (1 \le a_1 < \ldots < a_p \le n)$, b's at positions $b_1 \ldots b_q (1 \le b_1 < \ldots < b_q \le n)$, and g's at positions $g_1 \ldots g_r (2 \le g_1 < \ldots < g_r \le n-1)$, such that $1 \le p \le k$, $1 \le q \le k$, $0 \le r \le k-1$, $p+q+r = n$, and the string does not contain more than one consecutive appearance of the same symbol.

Fig. 8.2 General form of the MG_k COMBINE step.

- deduction steps are the same as in WG_1, plus the additional steps shown in Figure 8.1. These extra COMBINE steps allow the parser to combine interleaved subtrees with simple crossing configurations. The MG_1 parser still runs in $O(n^7)$, as these new steps do not use more than 7 string positions.

In order to generalise this algorithm to mildly ill-nested structures for gap degree k, we need to add a COMBINE step for every possible way of joining two structures of gap degree at most k into another. This can be done in a systematic way by considering a set of strings over an alphabet of three symbols: a and b to represent intervals of words in the projection of each of the structures, and g to represent intervals that are not in the projection of either of the structures, and will correspond to gaps in the joined structure. The legal combinations of structures for gap degree k will correspond to strings where symbols a and b each appear at most $k+1$ times, g appears at most k times and is not the first or last symbol, and there is no more than one consecutive appearance of any symbol. Given a string of this form, the corresponding COMBINE step is given by the expression in Figure 8.2. As a particular example, the COMBINE INTERLEAVING GAP C step in Figure 8.1 can be obtained from this expression by using the string *abgab*.

Therefore, we define the parsing schema for MG_k, a parser for mildly ill-nested structures for gap degree k, as the schema where:

- the item set is the same as that of WG_k, except that items can now contain any mildly ill-nested structures for gap degree k, instead of being restricted to well-nested structures; and
- the set of deduction steps consists of a LINK step as the one in WG_k, plus a set of COMBINE steps obtained as expressed in Figure 8.2.

8.5.2   *Complexity of MG_k*

As the string used to generate a COMBINER step can have length at most $3k+2$, and the resulting step contains an index for each symbol of the string plus two extra indexes, it is easy to see that the MG_k parser has complexity $O(n^{3k+4})$ with respect to the length of the input.[10]

The item and deduction step sets of an MG_k parser are always supersets of those of WG_k. In particular, the steps for WG_k are those obtained from strings that do not contain *abab* or *baba* as a scattered substring.

8.5.3   *Proof of correctness for MG_k*

In order to prove the correctness of the MG_k parser, we will first introduce some properties of binarisations that arise as corollaries of their definition (8.4). If a tree B is a binarisation of a (partial) dependency tree T headed at a_h, then we have that:

---

[10]Note that this expression denotes the complexity of the particular MG_k parser obtained for a given value of k. If we consider k as a variable, we have to add an additional $O(3^{3k})$ complexity factor, since the number of different COMBINER steps that can be applied to a given item grows exponentially with k.

(i) A node a_i appears in T if and only if a node labelled a_i appears in B,

(ii) $\lfloor a_i \rfloor_B = \lfloor a_i \rfloor_T$,

(iii) If the root of B is labelled, then its label is a_h.

Properties (i) and (ii) are direct consequences of condition (b) of the definition of a binarisation. Property (iii) is obtained from (b) and property (i): the label of the root node of B cannot be an $a_d \neq a_h$ because this would require a_h to be a transitive dependent of a_d in T. These properties of binarisations will be used throughout the proof.

As for the previous algorithms, we will start the proof by defining the sets of valid trees and correct items for this algorithm, which we will use to prove soundness and completeness.

Let T be a partial dependency tree headed at a node a_h. We will call such a tree a *valid tree* for the algorithm MG_k if it satisfies the following conditions:

(1) $\lfloor a_h \rfloor$ is of the form $\{a_h\} \cup ([i,j] \smallsetminus \bigcup_{p=1}^{g}[l_p, r_p])$, with $0 \leq g \leq k$,

(2) There exists a binarisation of T such that all the nodes in it have gap degree at most k except for its root node, which can have gap degree up to $k+1$.

Note that, since by property (ii) a binarisation cannot decrease the gap degree of a tree, condition (2) implies that all the nodes in T must have gap degree at most k except for a_h, which can have gap degree at most $k+1$.

That is, the definition of a valid tree in this case is as in WG_k, but changing the well-nestedness constraint to the weaker requirement of having a binarisation of gap degree k (except for the particular case of the root node, which can have gap degree $k+1$). As in WG_1 and WG_k, we will say that an item is *correct* if it contains some valid tree T licensed by a set of D-rules G, and throughout the proof we will suppose that all items are normalised.

Given an input string $a_1 \ldots a_n$, a correct final item for MG_k will have the form $[1, n, h, \langle \rangle]$, and contain at least one valid tree T rooted at a head a_h and with $\lfloor a_h \rfloor = [1, n]$, which is a complete parse for the input. Since in a tree contained in an item of this form the projection of the head cannot have any gaps and thus the head has gap degree 0, we have that there exists a binarisation of T such that every one of its nodes, including the head, has gap degree at most k. Therefore, T is mildly ill-nested for gap degree k and, more generally, final items in MG_k only contain mildly ill-nested trees for gap degree k, as expected.

To prove correctness of the MG_k parser, we need to prove its soundness and completeness.

8.5.3.1 *Soundness*

As in the proofs for the previous algorithms, we prove soundness of the MG_k parser by showing that (i) hypotheses are correct, and (ii) if the antecedents of a deduction step in WG_1 are correct, then the consequent is also correct. (i) is trivial, since each hypothesis in the MG_k parser contains a tree consisting of a single node a_h, which is trivially a valid tree.

To show (ii), given a set of D-rules G, we must prove that if the antecedents of a deduction step are items containing a valid tree for MG_k licensed by the D-rules in G, then the consequent must also contain a valid tree for MG_k licensed by G. In order to do this, we obtain a valid tree for the consequent item of each step from a valid tree for each of its antecedents exactly in the same way as in WG_k: by adding a new head node and linking the head of the antecedent tree to it, for LINK steps, and by considering the union of the trees corresponding to the antecedents, for COMBINE steps.

We can show that the resulting tree is licensed by G and that it satisfies the condition (1) of a valid tree in the same way as we did in WG_1 and WG_k. So, to prove soundness, it only remains to show that the resulting tree has a binarisation verifying the gap degree constraint (2).

To prove this, we show that a binarisation satisfying (2) of the tree corresponding to the consequent item can be constructed from the corresponding binarisations of the antecedent items. We will prove the stronger claim that such a binarisation can be constructed, with the additional constraints that:

(3) its root node must be labelled (therefore, by one of the properties of binarisations, its label corresponds to the head node of the original tree) and can have at most one direct child, and that:

(4) the binarisation can only contain more than one node labelled a_h if the item is of the form $[i, j, h, \langle (l_1, r_1) \dots (l_g, r_g) \rangle]$ such that $a_h \in ([i, j] \smallsetminus \bigcup_{p=1}^{g} [l_p, r_p])$.

In the case of each LINK step adding a link $a_d \to a_h$, such a binarisation can be constructed by taking the binarisation B_a corresponding to the non-initial antecedent item, and linking its head to a new node labelled a_h. The resulting tree is a binarisation of the consequent tree, and it satisfies (2) because the head can have gap degree at most $k+1$ (by construction of the antecedents of LINK steps, the antecedent item must have a binarisation whose head does not have gap degree greater than k, and linking it to a new head adds at most one gap), and the rest of the nodes have gap degree at most k because their projections do not change with respect to the binarisation of the antecedent tree. This binarisation trivially verifies (3), because its root node is labelled a_h and has the head of the B_a as its only child, and (4) because it can only contain one node labelled a_h, which is the root, as a_h cannot appear in B_a.

In the case of COMBINER steps, if B_1 and B_2 are the binarisations corresponding to the antecedent items, we can construct a binarisation for the consequent B_c from B_1 and B_2 as follows:

- If the consequent item is of the form $[i,j,h,\langle(l_1,r_1)\dots(l_g,r_g)\rangle]$ such that $a_h \notin ([i,j] \smallsetminus \bigcup_{p=1}^{g}[l_p,r_p])$, then we take the binarisations B_1 and B_2, we remove their head nodes labelled a_h from them, we link the direct children of that head in each of the two binarisations (which must be two, d_1 and d_2, since B_1 and B_2 verify condition (3)) to a fresh unlabelled node, and finally we link this unlabelled node to a_h. This tree B_c is a binarisation for the tree in the consequent item obtained by performing the union of two trees in the antecedent items. It can be shown that the projection of a_h in B_c satisfies condition (1) by construction, following the same reasoning as in the proof for WG_1. And we can see that B_c also meets the constraints of (2) because:

  - The projection of a_h in B_c is the union of the projections of a_h in B_1 and B_2, which by construction of the consequent of COMBINER steps, and property (ii) of binarisations, must be of the form $\lfloor a_h \rfloor_{B_c} = \{a_h\} \cup ([i,j] \smallsetminus \bigcup_{p=1}^{g}[l_p,r_p])$ with $g \le k$. Since the gap degree of $([i,j] \smallsetminus \bigcup_{p=1}^{g}[l_p,r_p])$ cannot exceed k, the gap degree of $\lfloor a_h \rfloor_{B_c}$ cannot exceed $k+1$.
  - The fresh unlabelled node that we have added does not dominate any node labelled a_h. We know this because no antecedent item can be of the form described in (4), since if one of the antecedent items were of that form, then the consequent item would be of that form too, by construction of consequent items. Therefore, for the binarisations corresponding to antecedent items, we know that they contain a single node labelled a_h, and thus our unlabelled node does not dominate any node labelled a_h. Therefore, the projection of this node must be $\lfloor a_h \rfloor_{B_c} \smallsetminus \{a_h\}$, which in this case equals $([i,j] \smallsetminus \bigcup_{p=1}^{g}[l_p,r_p])$ with $g \le k$, and therefore the node has gap degree $\le k$.

– The rest of the nodes in B_c have the same projection as they had in B_1 or B_2, so they have gap degree $\leq k$.

It can be seen that this binarisation also satisfies (3) and (4) because, by construction, it has a single node labelled a_h which is its root, and this node has a single child.

• If the consequent item is of the form $[i, j, h, \langle (l_1, r_1) \ldots (l_g, r_g) \rangle]$ such that $a_h \in ([i, j] \smallsetminus \bigcup_{p=1}^g [l_p, r_p])$, then we take the binarisations B_1 and B_2, we remove their head nodes labelled a_h from them, we link the direct children of that head in each of the two binarisations (which must be two nodes, d_1 and d_2, as B_1 and B_2 satisfy (3)) to a fresh node labelled a_h and finally we link this node to another node also labelled a_h. The obtained tree B_c is a binarisation for the valid tree in the consequent item obtained by performing the union of two trees in the antecedent items. It satisfies condition (1) by construction, as in the previous case, and meets the constraints of (2) because:

– By construction, the projection of both fresh nodes labelled a_h in this case is $\lfloor a_h \rfloor_{B_1} \cup \lfloor a_h \rfloor_{B_2}$, and by the hypothesis of this case we know that that projection is of the form $\lfloor a_h \rfloor_{B_c} = ([i, j] \smallsetminus \bigcup_{p=1}^g [l_p, r_p])$, and therefore has gap degree at most k.

– The rest of the nodes in B_c have the same projection as they had in B_1 or B_2, so they have gap degree $\leq k$.

This binarisation trivially verifies (3), and it also meets (4) because the item associated to the consequent is of the form that allows several nodes to be labelled a_h.

With this, we have proven that if an MG_k step is applied to correct antecedents, it produces correct consequents, and we conclude the soundness proof for MG_k.

8.5.3.2 Completeness

Proving completeness for the MG_k parser consists of proving that all correct final items are valid. We will show this by proving the following, stronger claim:

Proposition 8.1. *Let T be a partial dependency tree headed at node a_h, and valid for MG_k. Then, if $\lfloor a_h \rfloor = \{a_h\} \cup ([i, j] \smallsetminus \bigcup_{p=1}^g [l_p, r_p])$, for $g \leq k$, the item $[i, j, h, \langle (l_1, r_1), \ldots, (l_g, r_g) \rangle]$ containing T is valid under this parser.*

It is clear that this proposition implies the completeness of the parser: a final item $[1, n, h, \langle\rangle]$ is correct only if it contains a tree rooted at a_h, valid for MG_k and with projection $\lfloor a_h \rfloor = [1, n]$. By Proposition 8.1, having such a tree implies that the correct final item $[1, n, h, \langle\rangle]$ is valid. Therefore, this proposition implies that all correct final items are valid, and thus that MG_k is complete.

Since valid trees for the MG_k parser must be mildly ill-nested for gap degree k, every valid tree must have at least one binarisation where every node has gap degree $\leq k$ except possibly the head, that can have gap degree $k + 1$. We will call a binarisation satisfying this property a well-formed binarisation for MG_k.

Using this, we can prove Proposition 8.1 if we prove the following lemma:

Lemma 8.2. *Let B be a well-formed binarisation of a partial dependency tree T, headed at a node a_h and valid for MG_k. If the projection of a_h in T is $\lfloor a_h \rfloor_T = \lfloor a_h \rfloor_B = \{a_h\} \cup ([i, j] \smallsetminus \bigcup_{p=1}^{g}[l_p, r_p])$, for $g \leq k$, the item $[i, j, h, \langle(l_1, r_1), \ldots, (l_g, r_g)\rangle]$ containing T is valid under this parser.*

8.5.3.3 *Proof of Lemma 8.2*

We will prove this lemma by induction on the number of nodes of B (denoted $\#B$). In order to do this, we will show that Lemma 8.2 holds for well-formed binarisations B of trees T rooted at a_h such that $\#B = 1$, and then we will prove that if Lemma 8.2 holds for every well-formed binarisation B' such that $\#B' < N$, then it also holds for binarisations B such that $\#B = N$.

Base case Let B be a well-formed binarisation of a partial dependency tree T, rooted at a node a_h and valid for MG_k, and such that $\#B = 1$. In this case, since B has only one node, it must be a binarisation of the trivial dependency tree consisting of the single node a_h. Thus, Lemma 8.2 trivially holds because the initial item $[h, h, h, \langle\rangle]$ contains this tree, and initial items are valid by definition.

Induction step Let B be a well-formed binarisation of some partial dependency tree T, headed at node a_h and valid for MG_k, such that $\lfloor a_h \rfloor_T = \{a_h\} \cup ([i, j] \smallsetminus \bigcup_{p=1}^{g}[l_p, r_p]))$, and $\#B = N$; and suppose that Lemma 8.2 holds for every well-formed binarisation B' of a tree T' such that $\#B' < N$. We will prove that Lemma 8.2 holds for B.

In order to do this, we consider different cases depending on the number and type of children of the head node labelled a_h in B:

- If a_h has a single child in B, and it is a node labelled a_d $(a_d \neq a_h)$, then, the subtree B' induced by a_d in B is a binarisation of some tree T', such that $\lfloor a_d \rfloor_{T'} = \lfloor a_h \rfloor_T \smallsetminus \{a_h\}$ (note that no nodes labelled a_h can appear in B', since a_h cannot be a dependent of a_d). As $\#B' < N$ and B' is well-formed because all its nodes are non-head nodes of B, by applying the induction hypothesis, we obtain that the item $\iota = [i, j, d, \langle (l_1, r_1), \ldots, (l_g, r_g) \rangle]$ (which contains T' by construction) is valid. The item $[i, j, h, \langle (l_1, r_1), \ldots, (l_g, r_g) \rangle]$ containing T can be obtained from ι and the initial item $[h, h, h, \langle \rangle]$ by a LINK step, and therefore it is valid, so we have proven Lemma 8.2 in this case.

- If a_h has a single child in B, and it is an unlabelled node, call this unlabelled node n. Then, the tree B' obtained from removing n from B and linking its children directly to a_h is a binarisation of the same tree as B. We know that B' is well-formed because its non-head nodes have the same projections as in B and therefore must have gap degree $\leq k$ and, as B is well-formed, n has gap degree $\leq k$, so the tree created by linking the children of n to a_h can have gap degree at most $k + 1$, and it only will have degree $k + 1$ if $\lfloor a_h \rfloor_{B'} \smallsetminus \{a_h\}$ has k gaps. As B and B' are well-formed binarisations of the same tree, if Lemma 8.2 holds for B', it also must hold for B. As we know that $\#B' < N$ (since it contains one less node than B), Lemma 8.2 holds for B' by the induction hypothesis, so this case is proven.

- If a_h has a single child in B, and it is a node labelled a_h, then, the subtree B' induced by this single child node is a binarisation of the same tree as B. We know that B' is well-formed because its nodes have the same projections as they had in B, and therefore they must all have gap degree $\leq k$ by the well-formedness of B. Reasoning as in the previous case, since B and B' are binarisations of the same tree and we know that Lemma 8.2 holds for B' by the induction hypothesis, this implies that it holds for B as well.

- If a_h has two children in B. In this case, regardless of whether the direct children of a_h are labelled or unlabelled nodes, we call them c_1 and c_2 and consider two partial dependency trees B'_1 and B'_2:

  - B'_1 is the tree obtained by taking the subtree induced by c_1 and linking its head c_1 to a_h,

– B_2' is the tree obtained by taking the subtree induced by c_2 and linking its head c_2 to a_h.

We know that all the nodes in B_1' and B_2', except for the head, must have gap degree $\leq k$ because their projection in B_1' and B_2' is the same as their projection in B, which is a well-formed binarisation. We know that a_h must have degree $\leq k+1$ in B_1' and B_2' because, by construction, $\lfloor a_h \rfloor_{B_1'} = \lfloor c_1 \rfloor_B \cup \{a_h\}$, and $\lfloor c_1 \rfloor_B$ has gap degree $\leq k$, and a similar reasoning can be made in B_2'. Thus, we have that B_1' and B_2' are well-formed binarisations.

By applying the induction hypothesis to B_1' and B_2', we obtain that the items containing their associated dependency trees T_1' and T_2' are valid. By construction, since c_1 has gap degree $\leq k$ in B_1' and c_2 has gap degree $\leq k$ in B_2', the projection of a_h in the trees T_1' and T_2' obtained by unbinarising B_1' and B_2' by removing the unlabelled and redundant nodes will be the union of g_1 and g_2 intervals respectively, for $g_1, g_2 \leq k + 1$. We also know that the union of the projections of a_h in T_1' and T_2' is the union of $g_c \leq k + 1$ intervals, and is the same as the projection of a_h in T. Therefore, as the indexes of the COMBINER steps in MG_k correspond to all the ways in which two unions of up to $k + 1$ intervals each can be combined into another by performing their union, we know that the item that contains T can be obtained from the items containing T_1' and T_2' by a COMBINER step, and thus this item is valid, concluding the completeness proof.

8.5.4 *Mildly ill-nested dependency structures*

The MG_k algorithm defined in the previous section allows us to parse any mildly ill-nested structure for a given gap degree k in polynomial time. We have characterised the set of mildly ill-nested structures for gap degree k as those that have a binarisation of gap degree $\leq k$. Since a binarisation of a dependency structure cannot have lower gap degree than the original structure, the set of mildly ill-nested structures for gap degree k only contains structures with gap degree at most k. Furthermore, by the relation between MG_k and WG_k, we know that it contains all the well-nested structures with gap degree up to k.

Figure 8.3 shows an example of a structure that has gap degree 1, but is strongly ill-nested for gap degree 1. This is one of the smallest possible such structures. By generating all the possible trees up to 10 nodes (without

Table 8.1 Counts of dependency trees classified by gap degree, and mild and strong ill-nestedness (for their gap degree), appearing in treebanks for Arabic (Hajič *et al.*, 2004), Czech (Hajič *et al.*, 2006), Danish (Kromann, 2003), Dutch (van der Beek *et al.*, 2002), Latin (Bamman and Crane, 2006), Portuguese (Afonso *et al.*, 2002), Slovene (Džeroski *et al.*, 2006), Swedish (Nilsson *et al.*, 2005) and Turkish (Oflazer *et al.*, 2003; Atalay *et al.*, 2003).

Language		Structures							
		Non-projective							
			By gap degree				By nestedness		
	Total	Total Non-p.	Gap deg. 1	Gap d. 2	Gap d. 3	Gap d. > 3	Well-Nested	Mildly Ill-Nest.	Strongly Ill-Nest.
Arabic	2,995	205	189	13	2	1	204	1	0
Czech	87,889	20,353	19,989	359	4	1	20,257	96	0
Danish	5,430	864	854	10	0	0	856	8	0
Dutch	13,349	4,865	4,425	427	13	0	4,850	15	0
Latin	3,473	1,743	1,543	188	10	2	1,552	191	0
Portuguese	9,071	1,718	1,302	351	51	14	1,711	7	0
Slovene	1,998	555	443	81	21	10	550	5	0
Swedish	11,042	1,079	1,048	19	7	5	1,008	71	0
Turkish	5,583	685	656	29	0	0	665	20	0

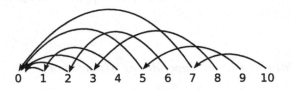

Fig. 8.3 One of the smallest strongly ill-nested dependency structures. This structure has gap degree 1, but is only mildly ill-nested for gap degree ≥ 2.

counting a dummy root node located at position 0), it can be shown that all the structures of any gap degree k with length smaller than 10 are well-nested or only mildly ill-nested for that gap degree k.

Even if a structure T is strongly ill-nested for a given gap degree, there is always some $m \in \mathbb{N}$ such that T is mildly ill-nested for m (since every dependency structure can be binarised, and binarisations have finite gap degree). For example, the structure in Figure 8.3 is mildly ill-nested for gap degree 2. Therefore, MG_k parsers have the property of being able to parse any possible dependency structure as long as we make k large enough.

In practice, structures like the one in Figure 8.3 do not seem to appear in dependency treebanks. We have analysed treebanks for nine different languages, obtaining the data presented in Table 8.1. None of these treebanks contain structures that are strongly ill-nested for their gap degree. Therefore, in any of these treebanks, the MG_k parser can parse every sentence with gap degree at most k.

8.6   Discussion

Using the dependency parsing schemata framework described in Chapter 7, we have defined a parsing algorithm for well-nested dependency structures with bounded gap degree. In terms of computational complexity, this algorithm is comparable to the best parsers for related constituency-based formalisms: when the gap degree is at most 1, it runs in $O(n^7)$, like the fastest known parsers for LTAG, and can be made $O(n^6)$ if we use unlexicalised dependencies. When the gap degree is greater than 1, the time complexity goes up by a factor of n^2 for each extra unit of gap degree, as in parsers for coupled context-free grammars. Most of the non-projective sentences appearing in treebanks are well-nested and have a small gap degree, so this algorithm directly parses the vast majority of the non-projective constructions present in natural languages, without requiring the construction of a constituency grammar as an intermediate step.

Additionally, we have defined a set of structures for any gap degree k which we call mildly ill-nested. This set includes ill-nested structures verifying certain conditions, and can be parsed in $O(n^{3k+4})$ with a variant of the parser for well-nested structures. The practical interest of mildly ill-nested structures can be seen in the data obtained from several dependency treebanks, showing that all of the ill-nested structures in them are mildly ill-nested for their corresponding gap degree. Therefore, our $O(n^{3k+4})$ parser can analyse all the gap degree k structures in these treebanks. Note that the strategy used by this algorithm for parsing mildly ill-nested structures has also been adapted to solve the problem of finding binarisations of LCFRS that improve parsing efficiency (see Gómez-Rodríguez *et al.* (2009b)).

The set of mildly ill-nested structures for gap degree k is defined as the set of structures that have a binarisation of gap degree at most k. This definition is directly related to the way the MG_k parser works, since it implicitly finds such a binarisation. An interesting line of future work would be to find an equivalent characterisation of the set of mildly ill-nested structures which is more grammar-oriented and would provide a more linguistic insight into these structures.[11] Another possible research direction is to provide implementations of the mildly non-projective dependency parsers presented here, using probabilistic models to guide their linking decisions, and compare their practical performance and accuracy to those of other non-projective dependency parsers.

---

[11] An alternative generalisation of the concept of well-nestedness has recently been introduced by Maier and Lichte (2009). The definition of this property of structures, called *k-ill-nestedness*, is more declarative than that of mildly ill-nestedness. However, it is based on properties that are not local to projections or subtrees, and there is no evidence that k-ill-nested structures are parsable in polynomial time.

PART 5

Conclusion

Chapter 9

Conclusions

The main goal of the research presented in this book was to provide theoretical and practical extensions to the parsing schemata framework by Sikkel (1997), broadening its applicability to practical parsing and using it to solve problems in research areas currently being addressed by the computational linguistics community. A variety of approaches and methods were used to achieve this goal, including software engineering (Chapter 3), empirical analyses (Chapters 4, 5) and formal approaches (Chapters 5, 6, 7, 8).

In Part 2, we addressed a limitation arising when using the formal framework of parsing schemata to design parsing algorithms for practical settings. Although their high level of abstraction makes schemata useful to reason about formal properties of parsers, they do not suffice when it is necessary to evaluate parsers in practice. In this case, a working implementation of the parsers must be obtained, and the efficiency of such an implementation depends on decisions about data and control structures that are not represented in the schema. Our approach to this problem was to design and implement a compiler able to make these decisions automatically, by performing a static analysis of parsing schemata in order to determine a set of suitable indexes on items that, when combined with a generic control structure, ensures that the resulting implementation will achieve a computational complexity comparable to that of ad-hoc implementations. The interest of this system is that it allows a parser developer to automatically obtain working prototypes of parsing algorithms, efficient enough to be used with real-sized natural language grammars, from formal specifications of the parsers in the form of schemata. The system works with schemata for several grammar formalisms, and more can be supported through an extensibility mechanism that allows the user to define custom notational elements.

After presenting this parsing schema compiler, we demostrated its use by applying it to schemata describing several well-known constituency parsers, both for context-free grammars (CFG) and tree-adjoining grammars (TAG), and performing empirical studies to compare their performance. In a first study, we used the system to generate implementations of three popular parsers for CFG and used them to analyse sentences with three natural language grammars taken from real-life corpora. We then did an experiment with TAG, in which we compiled schemata describing four different well-known TAG parsers from the literature, and compared their implementations by parsing sentences with the XTAG English Grammar. To the best of our knowledge, this was the first comparison of TAG parsing algorithms performed with real-sized grammars rather than "toy" grammars. From the performance results obtained from the experiments, we observed that the best choice of a parsing algorithm for a particular application strongly depends on the nature of the sentences to be parsed and the grammar to be used, so it is useful to use a tool like this compiler to quickly prototype and test several parsers in order to find the best one for a particular application.

Apart from these studies with real natural language grammars, we also performed a comparison of TAG and CFG algorithms on artificially-generated grammars. This study provided further insight into the influence of factors such as string length and grammar size in performance, since using artificial grammars allowed us to vary them freely. Among our conclusions, we observed that both factors can be influential on final parsing performance, and grammar size becomes particularly important when using real-sized TAG.

In Part 3 of the book, we presented error-repair parsing schemata, an extension of the parsing schemata formalism which can be used to define error-repair parsers that can provide analyses for ungrammatical sentences. Since the original formulation of parsing schemata was based on the assumption that all the intermediate results generated by parsers must conform to the rules of a given grammar, it was necessary to redefine the underlying concepts behind schemata in order to obtain a variant to support these robust parsers. The obtained formalism extends to error-repair parsers all the advantages that regular parsing schemata provide for regular parsers. Not only can we describe, analyse and compare error-repair parsers and study their formal properties, but we can also obtain implementations of them with the compiler presented in Part 2. These implementations can be configured to use global, regional or local error-repair strategies by changing the control structures used to schedule inferences.

As an example of these applications of the formalism, we used it to describe a well-known error-repair parser from the literature, to prove its correctness, and to generate implementations of it with global and regional error-repair strategies, measuring their performance.

Additionally, we defined a general transformation technique that can be used to add error-repair capabilities to parsing algorithms that do not have them. This method transforms correct parsing schemata meeting certain conditions into correct error-repair parsing schemata. Since the transformation is totally systematic, it can be applied automatically as a preprocessing step before compiling a schema, so that the compiler defined previously can be used to obtain working implementations of error-repair parsers from standard parsing schemata without error-repair functionality.

Part 4 of the book extended parsing schemata in a different direction, by defining a variant of the formalism that can represent dependency-based parsers. This required a redefinition of the core concepts behind the parsing schemata theory, which was originally limited to constituency parsers. This extension, called dependency parsing schemata, is attractive given the increasing interest that dependency-based parsers have received in recent years, since it provides a common formal framework that can be used to describe, relate and prove the correctness of a wide range of such parsers, as well as obtaining working implementations of them with the compiler described earlier.

We demonstrated the use of dependency parsing schemata by using them to describe a wide variety of dependency parsing algorithms from the literature, including projective and non-projective, grammar-driven and data-driven, graph-based and transition-based parsers. We used the formal tools provided by the formalism to prove the correctness of some of the parsers, as well as to establish formal relations between parsers that had been described very differently in their original formulations. We also showed how the same ideas that led to the generalisation of parsing schemata to dependency parsing could be adapted to other formalisms, by defining schemata for Link Grammar (LG) parsers and obtaining LG variants of some well-known dependency parsers.

Finally, we used the dependency parsing schemata formalism to solve the problem of efficiently parsing mildly non-projective dependency structures. This is a relevant problem for practical parsing, since these sets of structures strike a good balance between coverage and efficiency, as they cover a vast majority of the structures observed in treebanks while being polynomially parsable.

We defined an algorithm that can parse any well-nested dependency structure with gap degree bounded by a constant k with time complexity $O(n^{2k+5})$ (with n being the length of the input), the same achieved by the existing parsers for constituency formalisms of similar generative power. Additionally, we defined a wider set of structures that we call mildly ill-nested for a given gap degree k, and a variant of the previous parser that can parse them in time $O(n^{3k+4})$. The practical relevance of this set of structures can be seen in the data obtained from several dependency tree-banks, showing that all the sentences contained in them are in this set, and thus they are parsable with this algorithm.

9.1 Future work

The results presented in this book open up several interesting directions for future work:

- While the parsing schema compiler introduced in Chapter 3 generates efficient implementations of parsers in terms of computational complexity, it should be possible to optimise it more in order to obtain faster absolute runtimes. For instance, a possible aspect that allows for further optimisation is the order in which indexes are considered when the generated implementations check for items conforming to a given specification. Slight improvements in runtime are obtained if the most often used indexes are considered first, since this minimises the amount of false "if" conditions that have to be checked. Thus, it should be possible to improve performance by gathering data in runtime and changing this order dynamically, prioritising the indexes that get used most frequently.
- Although the error-repair parsing schemata formalism described in Chapter 5 is defined for any class of constituency grammars, the practical examples that we explored were all context-free grammar parsers. An interesting line of work would be to apply this formalism to tree-adjoining grammars, obtaining and implementing TAG parsers able to behave robustly in the presence of ungrammatical sentences. The transformation presented in Chapter 6 could be used to systematically obtain schemata for these parsers from existing TAG parsing schemata,

after extending the definition of yield union step sets to support the discontinuous yields that can appear in TAG items. Due to the overhead of TAG parsing over CFG parsing, the parsers so obtained would probably be too inefficient to be used with real-sized grammars under a global error-repair strategy, but they could be used in realistic conditions by applying a local or regional repair strategy.

- It would be interesting to add probabilistic models or machine learning techniques to make linking decisions to the parsers for mildly non-projective dependency structures defined in Chapter 8, and test their performance and accuracy on real examples, comparing them to other projective and non-projective dependency parsers.

- The definition of mildly ill-nested dependency structures given in Chapter 8 is closely related with the way the MG_k parser works. It would be interesting to find a more grammar-oriented definition of these structures that would provide linguistic insight into them, and to study whether it is possible or not to find strongly ill-nested structures in natural languages.

- An interesting research direction which has already produced results is to apply variants of the MG_k parser's strategy to the related problem of binarising linear context-free rewriting systems, reducing the number of nonterminals in their productions to improve parsing efficiency. In Gómez-Rodríguez *et al.* (2009b), an algorithm is presented to solve this problem, whose strategy to merge nonterminal symbols is directly related to the way in which the MG_k COMBINER steps join dependency subtrees.

- As we have seen throughout this book, the parsing schemata formalism can be used to describe any parser as long as it is constructive, based on the principle of combining structures into larger structures so as to find a full parse. While we have used schemata to describe constituency, dependency and link grammar parsers, it could also be applied to other syntactic formalisms allowing the definition of constructive parsers. Furthermore, while the framework of parsing schemata was defined with parsing in mind, the background idea of combining partial structures that can be represented as items is shared by other problems, such as natural language generation (Reiter and Dale, 2000). Thus, it should be possible to reformulate parsing schemata for generation and other problems that fall into this constructive template.

Parsing Schemata for Practical Text Analysis

In a broader sense, the results presented in this book can facilitate the use of linguistic resources (and, in particular, syntactic information) in applications that work with written natural language text, such as information retrieval, information extraction and question answering systems.

List of Acronyms

BOS   Beginning Of Sentence
CFG   Context-Free Grammar
CNF   Chomsky Normal Form
CYK   Cocke-Younger-Kasami parsing algorithm
EBNF   Extended Backus-Naur Form
EOS   End Of Sentence
LCFRS   Linear Context-Free Rewriting Systems
LG   Link Grammar
LTAG   Lexicalised Tree-Adjoining Grammar
MST   Maximum Spanning Tree
NP   Noun Phrase
TAG   Tree-Adjoining Grammar
TAL   Tree-Adjoining Languages
VP   Verb Phrase
VPP   Valid Prefix Property
XTAG   XTAG English Grammar

Bibliography

Afonso, S., Bick, E., Haber, R. and Santos, D. (2002). "Floresta sintá(c)tica": a treebank for Portuguese, in *Proceedings of the 3rd International Conference on Language Resources and Evaluation (LREC 2002)* (ELRA, Paris, France), pp. 1968–1703.

Aho, A. V., Sethi, R. and Ullman, J. D. (1986). *Compilers: principles, techniques, and tools* (Addison-Wesley Longman Publishing Co., Inc., Boston, MA, USA).

Alonso, M. A., Cabrero, D., Éric Villemonte de la Clergerie and Vilares, M. (1999). Tabular algorithms for TAG parsing, in *Proceedings of the Ninth Conference of the European Chapter of the Association for Computational Linguistics (EACL-99)* (Association for Computational Linguistics, Morristown, NJ, USA), pp. 150–157.

Alonso, M. A., Éric Villemonte de la Clergerie, Díaz, V. J. and Vilares, M. (2004). Relating tabular parsing algorithms for LIG and TAG, in Harry Bunt, John Carroll, Giorgio Satta (eds.), *New developments in parsing technology* (Kluwer Academic Publishers, Norwell, MA, USA), ISBN 1-4020-2293-X, pp. 157–184.

Alonso, M. A. and Díaz, V. J. (2003a). Parsing tree adjoining grammars and tree insertion grammars with simultaneous adjunctions, in *Proceedings of 8th International Workshop on Parsing Technologies (IWPT 2003)* (ACL/SIGPARSE), pp. 19–30.

Alonso, M. A. and Díaz, V. J. (2003b). Variants of mixed parsing of TAG and TIG, *Traitement Automatique des Langues* **44**, 3, pp. 41–65.

Amaral, C., Cassan, A., Figueira, H., Martins, A., Mendes, A., Mendes, P., Pinto, C. and Vidal, D. (2008). Priberam's question answering system in QA@CLEF 2007, in *Advances in Multilingual and Multimodal Information Retrieval: 8th Workshop of the Cross-Language Evaluation Forum (CLEF 2007)* , volume 5152 of *Lecture Notes in Computer Science* (Springer-Verlag, Berlin-Heidelberg-New York), ISBN 978-3-540-85759-4, pp. 364–371.

Atalay, N. B., Oflazer, K. and Say, B. (2003). The annotation process in the Turkish treebank, in *Proceedings of EACL Workshop on Linguistically In-*

terpreted Corpora (LINC-03) (Association for Computational Linguistics, Morristown, NJ, USA), pp. 243–246.

Attardi, G. (2006). Experiments with a multilanguage non-projective dependency parser, in *Proceedings of the 10th Conference on Computational Natural Language Learning (CoNLL-X)* (Association for Computational Linguistics, Morristown, NJ, USA), pp. 166–170.

Bamman, D. and Crane, G. (2006). The design and use of a Latin dependency treebank, in *Proceedings of the Fifth Workshop on Treebanks and Linguistic Theories (TLT 2006)* (Institute of Formal and Applied Linguistics, Prague, Czech Republic), pp. 67–78.

Barbero, C., Lesmo, L., Lombardo, V. and Merlo, P. (1998). Integration of syntactic and lexical information in a hierarchical dependency grammar, in *Proceedings of COLING-ACL '98 Workshop on Processing of Dependency-Based Grammars* (Association for Computational Linguistics, Morristown, NJ, USA), pp. 58–67.

Bertsch, E. and Nederhof, M.-J. (1999). On failure of the pruning technique in "Error repair in shift-reduce parsers", *ACM Transactions on Programming Languages and Systems* **21**, 1, pp. 1–10.

Billot, S. and Lang, B. (1989). The structure of shared forest in ambiguous parsing, in *Proceedings of the 27th Annual Meeting of the Association for Computational Linguistics (ACL'89)* (Association for Computational Linguistics, Morristown, NJ, USA), pp. 143–151.

Bodirsky, M., Kuhlmann, M. and Möhl, M. (2005). Well-nested drawings as models of syntactic structure (extended version), Tech. rep., Saarland University.

Bonhomme, P. and Lopez, P. (2000). Resources for lexicalized tree adjoining grammars and XML encoding: TagML, in *Proceedings of the 2nd International Conference on Language Resources and Evaluation (LREC 2000)* (ELRA, Paris, France).

Bouma, G., Mur, J., van Noord, G., van der Plas, L. and Tiedemann, J. (2005). Question answering for Dutch using dependency relations, in *Accessing Multilingual Information Repositories: 6th Workshop of the Cross-Language Evaluation Forum (CLEF 2005), Lecture Notes in Computer Science*, Vol. 4022 (Springer-Verlag, Berlin-Heidelberg-New York), ISBN 3-540-45697-X, pp. 370–379.

Carpenter, B. (1992). *The logic of typed feature structures* (Cambridge University Press, New York, NY, USA), ISBN 0-521-41932-8.

Carroll, J. A. (1993). Practical unification-based parsing of natural language, Technical report No. 314, University of Cambridge, Computer Laboratory, England. PhD Thesis.

Cerecke, C. (2002). Repairing syntax errors in LR-based parsers, *Australian Computer Science Communications* **24**, 1, pp. 17–22.

Che, W., Li, Z., Hu, Y., Li, Y., Qin, B., Liu, T. and Li, S. (2008). A cascaded syntactic and semantic dependency parsing system, in *Proceedings of the 12th Conference on Computational Natural Language Learning (CoNLL 2008)* (Association for Computational Linguistics, Morristown, NJ, USA), pp.

238–242.

Chen, J. and Vijay-Shanker, K. (2000). Automated extraction of TAGs from the Penn treebank, in *Proceedings of the Sixth International Workshop on Parsing Technologies (IWPT 2000)* (ACL/SIGPARSE), pp. 65–76.

Chiang, D. (2005). A hierarchical phrase-based model for statistical machine translation, in *ACL '05: Proceedings of the 43rd Annual Meeting of the Association for Computational Linguistics* (Association for Computational Linguistics, Morristown, NJ, USA), pp. 263–270.

Chomsky, N. (1956). Three models for the description of language, *IRI Transactions on Information Theory* **2**, 3, pp. 113–124.

Chomsky, N. (1959). On certain formal properties of grammars, *Information and Control* **2**, 2, pp. 137–167.

Collins, M. J. (1996). A new statistical parser based on bigram lexical dependencies, in *Proceedings of the 34th Annual Meeting of the Association for Computational Linguistics (ACL'96)* (Association for Computational Linguistics, Morristown, NJ, USA), pp. 184–191.

Corchuelo, R., Pérez, J. A., Ruiz, A. and Toro, M. (2002). Repairing syntax errors in LR parsers, *ACM Transactions on Programming Languages and Systems* **24**, 6, pp. 698–710.

Corston-Oliver, S., Aue, A., Duh, K. and Ringger, E. (2006). Multilingual dependency parsing using Bayes Point Machines, in *Proceedings of the Human Language Technology Conference of the North American Chapter of the Association for Computational Linguistics (NAACL HLT 2006)* (Association for Computational Linguistics, Morristown, NJ, USA), pp. 160–167.

Courtin, J. and Genthial, D. (1998). Parsing with dependency relations and robust parsing, in *Proceedings of COLING-ACL '98 Workshop on Processing of Dependency-Based Grammars* (Association for Computational Linguistics, Morristown, NJ, USA), pp. 88–94.

Covington, M. A. (1990). A dependency parser for variable-word-order languages, Tech. Rep. AI-1990-01, University of Georgia, Athens, GA.

Covington, M. A. (2001). A fundamental algorithm for dependency parsing, in *Proceedings of the 39th Annual ACM Southeast Conference* (ACM, New York, NY, USA), pp. 95–102.

Cui, H., Sun, R., Li, K., Kan, M.-Y. and Chua, T.-S. (2005). Question answering passage retrieval using dependency relations, in *SIGIR '05: Proceedings of the 28th Annual International ACM SIGIR Conference on Research and Development in Information Retrieval* (ACM, New York, NY, USA), ISBN 1-59593-034-5, pp. 400–407.

Culotta, A. and Sorensen, J. (2004). Dependency tree kernels for relation extraction, in *ACL '04: Proceedings of the 42nd Annual Meeting of the Association for Computational Linguistics* (Association for Computational Linguistics, Morristown, NJ, USA), pp. 423–429.

de la Clergerie, E. V. (2005). DyALog: a tabular logic programming based environment for NLP, in *Proceedings of 2nd International Workshop on Constraint Solving and Language Processing (CSLP'05)* (Barcelona, Spain).

de Vreught, J. and Honig, H. (1989). A tabular bottom-up recognizer, Report 89-78, Delft University of Technology, Delft, the Netherlands.

Díaz, V. and Alonso, M. (2000). Comparing tabular parsers for tree adjoining grammars, in D. S. Warren, M. Vilares, L. Rodríguez Liñares and M. A. Alonso (eds.), *Proceedings of the 2nd Workshop on Tabulation in Parsing and Deduction (TAPD 2000)* (University of Vigo, Spain), pp. 91–100.

Díaz, V. J., Carrillo, V. and Toro, M. (1998). Elementary tree representation, in *Proceedings of the 1st Workshop on Tabulation in Parsing and Deduction (TAPD 98)* (INRIA Rocquencourt, France), pp. 10–15.

Ding, Y. and Palmer, M. (2005). Machine translation using probabilistic synchronous dependency insertion grammars, in *ACL '05: Proceedings of the 43rd Annual Meeting of the Association for Computational Linguistics* (Association for Computational Linguistics, Morristown, NJ, USA), pp. 541–548.

Džeroski, S., Erjavec, T., Ledinek, N., Pajas, P., Žabokrtský, Z. and Žele, A. (2006). Towards a Slovene dependency treebank, in *Proceedings of the 5th International Conference on Language Resources and Evaluation (LREC 2006)* (ELRA, Paris, France), ISBN 2-9517408-2-4, pp. 1388–1391.

Earley, J. (1970). An efficient context-free parsing algorithm, *Communications of the ACM* **13**, 2, pp. 94–102.

Eisner, J. (1996). Three new probabilistic models for dependency parsing: An exploration, in *Proceedings of the 16th International Conference on Computational Linguistics (COLING-96)* (ACL / Morgan Kaufmann, San Francisco, CA, USA), pp. 340–345.

Eisner, J. (2000). Bilexical grammars and their cubic-time parsing algorithms, in H. Bunt and A. Nijholt (eds.), *Advances in Probabilistic and Other Parsing Technologies* (Kluwer Academic Publishers, Dordrecht, the Netherlands), pp. 29–62.

Eisner, J., Goldlust, E. and Smith, N. A. (2004). Dyna: A declarative language for implementing dynamic programs, in *Proceedings of the 42nd Annual Meeting of the Association for Computational Linguistics (ACL 2004) (Companion Volume)* (Association for Computational Linguistics, Morristown, NJ, USA), pp. 218–221.

Eisner, J. and Satta, G. (1999). Efficient parsing for bilexical context-free grammars and head automaton grammars, in *Proceedings of the 37th Annual Meeting of the Association for Computational Linguistics (ACL'99)* (Association for Computational Linguistics, Morristown, NJ, USA), ISBN 1-55860-609-3, pp. 457–464.

Eisner, J. and Satta, G. (2000). A faster parsing algorithm for lexicalized tree-adjoining grammars, in *Proceedings of the 5th Workshop on Tree-Adjoining Grammars and Related Formalisms (TAG+5)* (Université Paris 7, Paris, France), pp. 14–19.

Fundel, K., Küffner, R. and Zimmer, R. (2006). RelEx—Relation extraction using dependency parse trees, *Bioinformatics* **23**, 3, pp. 365–371.

Gaifman, H. (1965). Dependency systems and phrase-structure systems, *Information and Control* **8**, 3, pp. 304–337.

Gamma, E., Helm, R., Johnson, R. and Vlissides, J. (1995). *Design Patterns – Elements of Reusable Object-Oriented Software* (Addison-Wesley, Reading, MA, USA).

Gómez-Rodríguez, C. (2009). *Parsing Schemata for Practical Text Analysis*, Ph.D. thesis, Universidade da Coruña.

Gómez-Rodríguez, C., Alonso, M. A. and Vilares, M. (2006a). Estudio comparativo del rendimiento de analizadores sintácticos para gramáticas de adjunción de árboles, *Procesamiento del Lenguaje Natural* **37**, pp. 179–186.

Gómez-Rodríguez, C., Alonso, M. A. and Vilares, M. (2006b). Generating XTAG parsers from algebraic specifications, in *Proceedings of TAG+8, the Eighth International Workshop on Tree Adjoining Grammar and Related Formalisms* (Association for Computational Linguistics, Morristown, NJ, USA), pp. 103–108.

Gómez-Rodríguez, C., Alonso, M. A. and Vilares, M. (2006c). On theoretical and practical complexity of TAG parsers, in Shuly Wintner (ed.), *Proceedings of FG 2006: The 11th conference on Formal Grammar,* volume of *FG Online Proceedings* (CSLI publications, Stanford, CA, USA), pp. 87–101.

Gómez-Rodríguez, C., Alonso, M. A. and Vilares, M. (2007a). Generation of indexes for compiling efficient parsers from formal specifications, in R. Moreno-Díaz, F. Pichler and A. Quesada-Arencibia (eds.), *Computer Aided Systems Theory,* volume 4739 of *Lecture Notes in Computer Science* (Springer-Verlag, Berlin-Heidelberg-New York), pp. 257–264.

Gómez-Rodríguez, C., Alonso, M. A. and Vilares, M. (2007b). Técnicas deductivas para el análisis sintáctico con corrección de errores, *Procesamiento del Lenguaje Natural* **39**, pp. 13–20.

Gómez-Rodríguez, C., Alonso, M. A. and Vilares, M. (2009a). A general method for transforming standard parsers into error-repair parsers, in A. Gelbukh (ed.), *Computational Linguistics and Intelligent Text Processing,* volume 5449 of *Lecture Notes in Computer Science* (Springer-Verlag, Berlin-Heidelberg-New York), pp. 207–219.

Gómez-Rodríguez, C., Alonso, M. A. and Vilares, M. (2010a). Error-repair parsing schemata, *Theoretical Computer Science* **411**, 7-9, pp. 1121–1139.

Gómez-Rodríguez, C., Carroll, J. and Weir, D. (2008). A deductive approach to dependency parsing, in *Proceedings of the 46th Annual Meeting of the Association for Computational Linguistics: Human Language Technologies (ACL'08:HLT)* (Association for Computational Linguistics, Morristown, NJ, USA), pp. 968–976.

Gómez-Rodríguez, C., Carroll, J. and Weir, D. (2010b). Dependency parsing schemata and mildly non-projective dependency parsing, submitted to *Computational Linguistics* (pending reviews) .

Gómez-Rodríguez, C., Kuhlmann, M., Satta, G. and Weir, D. (2009b). Optimal reduction of rule length in linear context-free rewriting systems, in *Proceedings of NAACL HLT 2009: the Conference of the North American Chapter of the Association for Computational Linguistics* (Association for Computational Linguistics, Morristown, NJ, USA), pp. 539–547.

Gómez-Rodríguez, C., Vilares, J. and Alonso, M. A. (2006d). Automatic generation of natural language parsers from declarative specifications, in *Proceedings of the Third Starting AI Researchers' Symposium (STAIRS 2006)* (IOS Press, Amsterdam, the Netherlands), pp. 159–160, long version available at http://www.grupocole.org/GomVilAlo2006a_long.pdf.

Gómez-Rodríguez, C., Vilares, J. and Alonso, M. A. (2007c). Compiling declarative specifications of parsing algorithms, in R. Wagner, N. Revell and G. Pernul (eds.), *Database and Expert Systems Applications,* volume 4653 of *Lecture Notes in Computer Science* (Springer-Verlag, Berlin-Heidelberg-New York), pp. 529–538.

Gómez-Rodríguez, C., Vilares, J. and Alonso, M. A. (2007d). Prototyping efficient natural language parsers, in *Proceedings of Recent Advances in Natural Language Processing (International Conference RANLP 2007)*, ISBN 978-954-91743-7-3, pp. 246–250.

Gómez-Rodríguez, C., Vilares, J. and Alonso, M. A. (2009c). A compiler for parsing schemata, *Software: Practice and Experience* **39**, 5, pp. 441–470.

Gómez-Rodríguez, C., Weir, D. and Carroll, J. (2009d). Parsing mildly non-projective dependency structures, in *Proceedings of the 12th Conference of the European Chapter of the Association for Computational Linguistics (EACL-09)* (Association for Computational Linguistics, Morristown, NJ, USA), ISBN 978-1-932432-16-9, pp. 291–299.

Grune, D. and Jacobs, C. J. (2008). *Parsing Techniques. A Practical Guide — Second edition* (Springer Science+Business Media, Berlin).

Hajič, J., Panevová, J., Hajičová, E., Panevová, J., Sgall, P., Pajas, P., Štěpánek, J., Havelka, J. and Mikulová, M. (2006). Prague Dependency Treebank 2.0, CDROM CAT: LDC2006T01, ISBN 1-58563-370-4. Linguistic Data Consortium.

Hajič, J., Smrž, O., Zemánek, P., Šnaidauf, J. and Beška, E. (2004). Prague Arabic dependency treebank: Development in data and tools, in *Proceedings of the NEMLAR International Conference on Arabic Language Resources and Tools*, pp. 110–117.

Havelka, J. (2007). Beyond projectivity: Multilingual evaluation of constraints and measures on non-projective structures, in *ACL 2007: Proceedings of the 45th Annual Meeting of the Association for Computational Linguistics* (Association for Computational Linguistics, Morristown, NJ, USA), pp. 608–615.

Hays, D. (1964). Dependency theory: a formalism and some observations, *Language* **40**, 4, pp. 511–525.

Herrera, J., Peñas, A. and Verdejo, F. (2005). Textual entailment recognition based on dependency analysis and WordNet, in *Machine Learning Challenges,* volume 3944 of *Lecture Notes in Computer Science* (Springer-Verlag, Berlin-Heidelberg-New York), pp. 231–239.

Hopcroft, J. E., Motwani, R. and Ullman, J. D. (2006). *Introduction to Automata Theory, Languages, and Computation*, 3rd edn. (Addison-Wesley Longman Publishing Co., Inc., Boston, MA, USA), ISBN 0321455363.

Hotz, G. and Pitsch, G. (1996). On parsing coupled-context-free languages, *Theoretical Computer Science* **161**, 1-2, pp. 205–233.

Huybregts, R. (1984). The weak inadequacy of context-free phrase structure grammars, in G. de Haan, M. Trommelen and W. Zonneveld (eds.), *Van periferie naar kern* (Foris, Dordrecht, the Netherlands), pp. 81–99.

Johnson, S. C. (1975). YACC: Yet another compiler compiler, Computer Science Technical Report 32, AT&T Bell Laboratories, Murray Hill, New Jersey, USA.

Joshi, A. K. (1985). Tree Adjoining Grammars: How much context-sensitivity is required to provide reasonable structural descriptions? in D. R. Dowty, L. Karttunen and A. M. Zwicky (eds.), *Natural Language Parsing* (Cambridge University Press), pp. 206–250.

Joshi, A. K. (1987). An introduction to tree adjoining grammars, in A. Manaster-Ramer (ed.), *Mathematics of Language* (John Benjamins Publishing Co., Amsterdam/Philadelphia), ISBN 90-272-2049-2 (Eur.)/1-55619-032-8 (USA), pp. 87–115.

Joshi, A. K., Levy, L. S. and Takahashi, M. (1975). Tree Adjunct Grammars, *Journal of Computer and System Sciences* **10**, 2, pp. 136–163.

Joshi, A. K. and Schabes, Y. (1997). Tree-Adjoining Grammars, in G. Rozenberg and A. Salomaa (eds.), *Handbook of Formal Languages*, Vol. 3 (Springer, Berlin-Heidelberg-New York), ISBN 3-540-60649-1, pp. 69–123.

Joshi, A. K., Vijay-Shanker, K. and Weir, D. J. (1991). The convergence of mildly context-sensitive grammar formalisms, in P. Sells, S. M. Shieber and T. Wasow (eds.), *Foundational Issues in Natural Language Processing* (MIT Press, Cambridge, MA, USA), pp. 31–81.

Kahane, S., Nasr, A. and Rambow, O. (1998). Pseudo-projectivity: A polynomially parsable non-projective dependency grammar, in *Proceedings of the 36th Annual Meeting of the Association for Computational Linguistics and the 17th International Conference on Computational Linguistics (COLING-ACL'98)* (ACL / Morgan Kaufmann, San Francisco, CA, USA), pp. 646–652.

Kasami, T. (1965). An efficient recognition and syntax algorithm for context-free languages, Scientific Report AFCRL-65-758, Air Force Cambridge Research Lab., Bedford, Massachussetts.

Kasper, W., Kiefer, B., Krieger, H. U., Rupp, C. J. and Worm, K. L. (1999). Charting the depths of robust speech parsing, in *Proceedings of the 37th Annual Meeting of the Association for Computational Linguistics (ACL'99)* (Association for Computational Linguistics, Morristown, NJ, USA), ISBN 1-55860-609-3, pp. 405–412.

Kay, M. (1980). Algorithm schemata and data structures in syntactic processing, Technical Report CSL-80-12, Xerox PARC, Palo Alto, CA, USA.

Kim, I.-S. and Choe, K.-M. (2001). Error repair with validation in LR-based parsing, *ACM Transactions on Programming Languages and Systems* **23**, 4, pp. 451–471.

Kromann, M. T. (2003). The Danish dependency treebank and the underlying linguistic theory, in *Proceedings of the 2nd Workshop on Treebanks and*

Linguistic Theories (TLT) (Växjö University Press, Växjö, Sweden), pp. 217–220.

Kuhlmann, M. (2007). *Dependency Structures and Lexicalized Grammars*, Doctoral dissertation, Saarland University, Saarbrücken, Germany.

Kuhlmann, M. and Möhl, M. (2007). Mildly context-sensitive dependency languages, in *Proceedings of the 45th Annual Meeting of the Association for Computational Linguistics (ACL 2007)* (Association for Computational Linguistics, Morristown, NJ, USA), pp. 160–167.

Kuhlmann, M. and Nivre, J. (2006). Mildly non-projective dependency structures, in *Proceedings of the COLING/ACL 2006 Main Conference Poster Sessions* (Association for Computational Linguistics, Morristown, NJ, USA), pp. 507–514.

Levenshtein, V. I. (1966). Binary codes capable of correcting deletions, insertions, and reversals, *Soviet Physics Doklady* **10**, 8, pp. 707–710.

Liu, Y. A. and Stoller, S. D. (2003). From Datalog rules to efficient programs with time and space guarantees, in *Proceedings of the Fifth ACM-SIGPLAN International Conference on Principles and Practice of Declarative Programming (PPDP 2003)* (ACM Press, New York, NY, USA), pp. 172–183.

Lombardo, V. and Lesmo, L. (1996). An Earley-type recognizer for dependency grammar, in *Proceedings of the 16th International Conference on Computational Linguistics (COLING 96)* (ACL / Morgan Kaufmann, San Francisco, CA, USA), pp. 723–728.

Lyon, G. (1974). Syntax-directed least-errors analysis for context-free languages: a practical approach, *Communications of the ACM* **17**, 1, pp. 3–14.

Maier, W. and Lichte, T. (2009). Characterizing discontinuity in constituent treebanks, in *Proceedings of the 14th conference on Formal Grammar,* volume 5591 of *Lecture Notes in Computer Science* (Springer-Verlag, Berlin-Heidelberg-New York).

Manning, C. D. and Schütze, H. (1999). *Foundations of Statistical Natural Language Processing* (MIT Press, Cambridge, MA, USA).

McAllester, D. A. (1999). On the complexity analysis of static analyses, in *SAS '99: Proceedings of the 6th International Symposium on Static Analysis,* volume 1694 of *Lecture Notes in Computer Science* (Springer-Verlag, Berlin-Heidelberg-New York), pp. 312–329.

McDonald, R., Crammer, K. and Pereira, F. (2005a). Online large-margin training of dependency parsers, in *ACL '05: Proceedings of the 43rd Annual Meeting of the Association for Computational Linguistics* (Association for Computational Linguistics, Morristown, NJ, USA), pp. 91–98.

McDonald, R. and Nivre, J. (2007). Characterizing the errors of data-driven dependency parsing models, in *Proceedings of the 2007 Joint Conference on Empirical Methods in Natural Language Processing and Computational Natural Language Learning (EMNLP-CoNLL 2007)* (Association for Computational Linguistics, Morristown, NJ, USA), pp. 122–131.

McDonald, R., Pereira, F., Ribarov, K. and Hajič, J. (2005b). Non-projective dependency parsing using spanning tree algorithms, in *HLT/EMNLP 2005: Proceedings of the conference on Human Language Technology and Empir-*

ical Methods in Natural Language Processing (Association for Computational Linguistics, Morristown, NJ, USA), pp. 523–530.

McDonald, R. and Satta, G. (2007). On the complexity of non-projective data-driven dependency parsing, in *IWPT 2007: Proceedings of the 10th International Conference on Parsing Technologies* (Association for Computational Linguistics, Morristown, NJ, USA), pp. 121–132.

McKenzie, B. J., Yeatman, C. and de Vere, L. (1995). Error repair in shift-reduce parsers, *ACM Transactions on Programming Languages and Systems* **17**, 4, pp. 672–689.

Mellish, C. (1989). Some chart-based techniques for parsing ill-formed input, in *Proceedings of the 27th Annual Meeting of the Association for Computational Linguistics (ACL'89)* (Association for Computational Linguistics, Morristown, NJ, USA), pp. 102–109.

Moore, R. C. (2000). Improved left-corner chart parsing for large context-free grammars, in *Proceedings of the 6th International Workshop on Parsing Technologies (IWPT 2000)* (ACL/SIGPARSE), pp. 171–182.

Nederhof, M.-J. (1997). Solving the correct-prefix property for TAGs, in T. Becker and H.-U. Krieger (eds.), *Proceedings of the Fifth Meeting on Mathematics of Language* (DFKI, Saarbrücken, Germany), pp. 124–130.

Nederhof, M.-J. (1999). The computational complexity of the correct-prefix property for TAGs, *Computational Linguistics* **25**, 3, pp. 345–360.

Neuhaus, P. and Bröker, N. (1997). The complexity of recognition of linguistically adequate dependency grammars, in *Proceedings of the 8th Conference of the European Chapter of the Association for Computational Linguistics* (Association for Computational Linguistics, Morristown, NJ, USA), pp. 337–343.

Nilsson, J., Hall, J. and Nivre, J. (2005). MAMBA meets TIGER: Reconstructing a Swedish treebank from antiquity, in *Proceedings of NODALIDA 2005 Special Session on Treebanks* (Samfundslitteratur, Frederiksberg, Denmark), pp. 119–132.

Nivre, J. (2003). An efficient algorithm for projective dependency parsing, in *Proceedings of the 8th International Workshop on Parsing Technologies (IWPT 03)* (ACL/SIGPARSE), pp. 149–160.

Nivre, J. (2006a). *Inductive Dependency Parsing (Text, Speech and Language Technology)* (Springer-Verlag New York, Inc., Secaucus, NJ, USA), ISBN 1402048882.

Nivre, J. (2006b). Two strategies for text parsing, *Journal of Linguistics* **19**, pp. 440–448.

Nivre, J. (2007). Incremental non-projective dependency parsing, in *Proceedings of NAACL HLT 2007: the Annual Conference of the North American Chapter of the Association for Computational Linguistics* (Association for Computational Linguistics, Morristown, NJ, USA), pp. 396–403.

Nivre, J., Hall, J., Kübler, S., McDonald, R., Nilsson, J., Riedel, S. and Yuret, D. (2007a). The CoNLL 2007 shared task on dependency parsing, in *Proceedings of the CoNLL Shared Task Session of EMNLP-CoNLL 2007*, pp. 915–932.

Nivre, J., Hall, J. and Nilsson, J. (2004). Memory-based dependency parsing, in *Proceedings of the 8th Conference on Computational Natural Language Learning (CoNLL-2004)* (Association for Computational Linguistics, Morristown, NJ, USA), pp. 49–56.

Nivre, J., Hall, J., Nilsson, J., Chanev, A., Eryiğit, G., Kübler, S., Marinov, S. and Marsi, E. (2007b). MaltParser: A language-independent system for data-driven dependency parsing, *Natural Language Engineering Journal* **13**, 2, pp. 99–135.

Nivre, J., Hall, J., Nilsson, J., Eryiğit, G. and Marinov, S. (2006). Labeled pseudo-projective dependency parsing with support vector machines, in *Proceedings of the 10th Conference on Computational Natural Language Learning (CoNLL-X)* (Association for Computational Linguistics, Morristown, NJ, USA), pp. 221–225.

Nivre, J. and McDonald, R. (2008). Integrating graph-based and transition-based dependency parsers, in *Proceedings of the 46th Annual Meeting of the Association for Computational Linguistics: Human Language Technologies (ACL-08: HLT)* (Association for Computational Linguistics, Morristown, NJ, USA), pp. 950–958.

Nivre, J. and Nilsson, J. (2005). Pseudo-projective dependency parsing, in *ACL '05: Proceedings of the 43rd Annual Meeting of the Association for Computational Linguistics* (Association for Computational Linguistics, Morristown, NJ, USA), pp. 99–106.

Oflazer, K., Say, B., Hakkani-Tür, D. Z. and Tür, G. (2003). Building a Turkish treebank, in A. Abeille (ed.), *Building and Exploiting Syntactically-annotated Corpora* (Kluwer, Dordrecht, the Netherlands), pp. 261–277.

Paskin, M. A. (2001). Cubic-time parsing and learning algorithms for grammatical bigram models, Tech. Rep. UCB/CSD-01-1148, University of California at Berkeley, Berkeley, CA, USA.

Perez-Cortes, J. C., Amengual, J. C., Arlandis, J. and Llobet, R. (2000). Stochastic error-correcting parsing for OCR post-processing, in *ICPR '00: Proceedings of the International Conference on Pattern Recognition* (IEEE Computer Society, Los Alamitos, CA, USA), p. 4405.

Reiter, E. and Dale, R. (2000). *Building natural language generation systems* (Cambridge University Press, New York, NY, USA), ISBN 0-521-62036-8.

Rosenkrantz, D. J. and Lewis II, P. M. (1970). Deterministic Left Corner parsing, in *Conference Record of 1970 Eleventh Annual Meeting on Switching and Automata Theory* (IEEE Computer Society, Los Alamitos, CA, USA), pp. 139–152.

Sampson, G. (1994). The Susanne corpus, release 3, School of Cognitive and Computing Sciences, University of Sussex, Falmer, Brighton, England.

Sarkar, A. (2000). Practical experiments in parsing using tree adjoining grammars, in *Proceedings of the 5th International Workshop on Tree Adjoining Grammars and Related Formalisms (TAG+5)* (Université Paris 7, Paris, France), pp. 193–198.

Satta, G. (1992). Recognition of linear context-free rewriting systems, in *Proceedings of the 30th Annual Meeting of the Association for Computational*

Linguistics (ACL'92) (Association for Computational Linguistics, Morristown, NJ, USA), pp. 89–95.

Schabes, Y. (1994). Left to right parsing of lexicalized tree-adjoining grammars, *Computational Intelligence* **10**, 4, pp. 506–515.

Schabes, Y. and Joshi, A. K. (1991). Parsing with lexicalized tree adjoining grammar, in M. Tomita (ed.), *Current Issues in Parsing Technologies*, chap. 3 (Kluwer Academic Publishers, Norwell, MA, USA), ISBN 0-7923-9131-4, pp. 25–47.

Schneider, G. (1998). *A Linguistic Comparison of Constituency, Dependency, and Link Grammar*, M.Sc. thesis, University of Zurich.

Schoorl, J. J. and Belder, S. (1990). Computational linguistics at Delft: A status report, Report WTM/TT 90–09. Delft University of Technology, Applied Linguistics Unit.

Shen, L., Xu, J. and Weischedel, R. (2008). A new string-to-dependency machine translation algorithm with a target dependency language model, in *Proceedings of the 46th Annual Meeting of the Association for Computational Linguistics: Human Language Technologies (ACL-08: HLT)* (Association for Computational Linguistics, Morristown, NJ, USA), pp. 577–585.

Shieber, S. M. (1985). Evidence against the context-freeness of natural language, *Linguistics and Philosophy* **8**, 3, pp. 333–343.

Shieber, S. M., Schabes, Y. and Pereira, F. C. (1995). Principles and implementation of deductive parsing, *Journal of Logic Programming* **24**, pp. 3–36.

Sikkel, K. (1994). How to compare the structure of parsing algorithms, in G. Pighizzini and P. S. Pietro (eds.), *Proceedings of ASMICS Workshop on Parsing Theory. Milano, Italy, Oct 1994* (University of Milan, Italy), pp. 21–39.

Sikkel, K. (1997). *Parsing Schemata — A Framework for Specification and Analysis of Parsing Algorithms*, Texts in Theoretical Computer Science — An EATCS Series (Springer-Verlag, Berlin-Heidelberg-New York), ISBN 3-540-61650-0.

Sikkel, K. (1998). Parsing schemata and correctness of parsing algorithms, *Theoretical Computer Science* **199**, 1–2, pp. 87–103.

Sleator, D. and Temperley, D. (1991). Parsing English with a Link Grammar, Tech. rep., Carnegie Mellon University, Pittsburgh, PA, USA.

Sleator, D. and Temperley, D. (1993). Parsing English with a Link Grammar, in *Proceedings of the Third International Workshop on Parsing Technologies (IWPT'93)* (ACL/SIGPARSE), pp. 277–292.

Surdeanu, M., Harabagiu, S., Williams, J. and Aarseth, P. (2003). Using predicate-argument structures for information extraction, in *ACL '03: Proceedings of the 41st Annual Meeting of the Association for Computational Linguistics* (Association for Computational Linguistics, Morristown, NJ, USA), pp. 8–15.

Surdeanu, M., Johansson, R., Meyers, A., Màrquez, L. and Nivre, J. (2008). The CoNLL-2008 shared task on joint parsing of syntactic and semantic dependencies, in *Proceedings of the 12th Conference on Computational Natural Language Learning (CoNLL-2008)* (Association for Computational Linguistics, Morristown, NJ, USA), pp. 159–177.

van der Beek, L., Bouma, G., Malouf, R. and van Noord, G. (2002). The Alpino dependency treebank, in *Language and Computers, Computational Linguistics in the Netherlands 2001. Selected Papers from the Twelfth CLIN Meeting* (Rodopi, Amsterdam, the Netherlands), pp. 8–22.

van der Spek, P., Plat, N. and Pronk, C. (2005). Syntax error repair for a Java-based parser generator, *ACM SIGPLAN Notices* **40**, 4, pp. 47–50.

van Noord, G. (1997). An efficient implementation of the head-corner parser, *Computational Linguistics* **23**, 3, pp. 425–456.

Vijay-Shanker, K. and Joshi, A. K. (1985). Some computational properties of tree adjoining grammars, in *Proceedings of the 23rd Annual Meeting of the Association for Computational Linguistics (ACL'85)* (Association for Computational Linguistics, Morristown, NJ, USA), pp. 82–93.

Vijay-Shanker, K. and Joshi, A. K. (1988). Feature structures based tree adjoining grammars, in *COLING-88: Proceedings of the 12th International Conference on Computational Linguistics*, Vol. 2 (Association for Computational Linguistics, Morristown, NJ, USA), ISBN 963-8431-56-3, pp. 714–719.

Vijay-Shanker, K., Weir, D. J. and Joshi, A. K. (1987). Characterizing structural descriptions produced by various grammatical formalisms, in *Proceedings of the 25th Annual Meeting of the Association for Computational Linguistics (ACL'87)* (Association for Computational Linguistics, Morristown, NJ, USA), pp. 104–111.

Vilares, J., Alonso, M. A. and Vilares, M. (2008). Extraction of complex index terms in non-English IR: A shallow parsing based approach, *Information Processing and Management* **44**, 4, pp. 1517–1537.

Vilares, M., Darriba, V. M. and Alonso, M. A. (2002). Searching for asymptotic error repair, in J.-M. Champarnaud and D. Maurel (eds.), *Implementation and Application of Automata, Lecture Notes in Computer Science*, Vol. 2608 (Springer, Berlin-Heidelberg), ISBN 3-540-40391-4, pp. 276–281.

Vilares, M., Darriba, V. M. and Ribadas, F. J. (2001). Regional least-cost error repair, in *CIAA '00: Revised Papers from the 5th International Conference on Implementation and Application of Automata*, volume 2088 of *Lecture Notes in Computer Science* (Springer-Verlag, London, UK), ISBN 3-540-42491-1, pp. 293–301.

Vilares, M., Darriba, V. M., Vilares, J. and Ribadas, F. J. (2004). A formal frame for robust parsing, *Theoretical Computer Science* **328**, 1-2, pp. 171–186.

Viswanadha, S. (2006). Java Compiler Compiler (JavaCC): The Java parser generator, URL: https://javacc.dev.java.net/.

Weir, D. J. (1988). *Characterizing Mildly Context-Sensitive Grammar Formalisms*, Ph.D. thesis, University of Pennsylvania, Philadelphia, USA.

Wilcoxon, F. (1945). Individual comparisons by ranking methods, *Biometrics Bulletin* **1**, 6, pp. 80–83.

XTAG Research Group (2001). A lexicalized tree adjoining grammar for English, Tech. Rep. IRCS-01-03, IRCS, University of Pennsylvania.

Yamada, H. and Matsumoto, Y. (2003). Statistical dependency analysis with support vector machines, in *Proceedings of 8th International Workshop on*

Parsing Technologies (IWPT 2003) (ACL/SIGPARSE), pp. 195–206.

Younger, D. H. (1967). Recognition and parsing of context-free languages in time n^3, *Information and Control* **10**, 2, pp. 189–208.

Index